MW01071562

English Alliterative Verse tells the story of the medieval poetic tradition that includes *Beowulf, Piers Plowman,* and *Sir Gawain and the Green Knight*, stretching from the eighth century, when English poetry first appeared in manuscripts, to the sixteenth century, when alliterative poetry ceased to be composed. Eric Weiskott draws on the study of meter to challenge the traditional division of medieval English literary history into 'Old English' and 'Middle English' periods. The two halves of the alliterative tradition, divided by the Norman Conquest of 1066, have been studied separately since the nineteenth century; this book uses the history of metrical form and its cultural meanings to bring the two halves back together. In combining literary history and metrical description into a new kind of history he calls 'verse history,' Weiskott reimagines the historical study of poetics.

ERIC WEISKOTT is Assistant Professor of English at Boston College. In addition to publishing widely on alliterative verse and early English literary history in journals such as *Anglo-Saxon England, ELH, Modern Language Quarterly, Modern Philology, Review of English Studies,* and *Yearbook of Langland Studies,* Weiskott is also a practicing poet. Most recently, his poems have appeared in *burnt-district, Cricket Online Review,* and *paper nautilus*. His first poetry chapbook was *Sharp Fish* (2008). With Irina Dumitrescu, he has co-edited a volume of essays with the working title *Early English Poetics and the History of Style*.

CAMBRIDGE STUDIES IN MEDIEVAL LITERATURE

General Editor
Alastair Minnis, *Yale University*

Editorial Board
Zygmunt G. Barański, *University of Cambridge*
Christopher C. Baswell, *Barnard College and Columbia University*
John Burrow, *University of Bristol*
Mary Carruthers, *New York University*
Rita Copeland, *University of Pennsylvania*
Roberta Frank, *Yale University*
Simon Gaunt, *King's College, London*
Steven Kruger, *City University of New York*
Nigel Palmer, *University of Oxford*
Winthrop Wetherbee, *Cornell University*
Jocelyn Wogan-Browne, *Fordham University*

This series of critical books seeks to cover the whole area of literature written in the major medieval languages – the main European vernaculars, and medieval Latin and Greek – during the period *c.* 1100–1500. Its chief aim is to publish and stimulate fresh scholarship and criticism on medieval literature, special emphasis being placed on understanding major works of poetry, prose, and drama in relation to the contemporary culture and learning which fostered them.

Recent Titles in the Series
Martin Eisner *Boccaccio and the Invention of Italian Literature: Dante, Petrarch, Cavalcanti, and the Authority of the Vernacular*
Emily V. Thornbury *Becoming a Poet in Anglo-Saxon England*
Lawrence Warner *The Myth of "Piers Plowman"*
Lee Manion *Narrating the Crusades: Loss and Recovery in Medieval and Early Modern English Literature*
Daniel Wakelin *Scribal Correction and Literary Craft: English Manuscripts 1375–1510*
Jon Whitman (ed.) *Romance and History: Imagining Time from the Medieval to the Early Modern Period*
Virginie Greene *Logical Fictions in Medieval Literature and Philosophy*
Michael Johnston and Michael Van Dussen (eds.) *The Medieval Manuscript Book: Cultural Approaches*
Tim William Machan (ed.) *Imagining Medieval English: Language Structures and Theories, 500–1500*

A complete list of titles in the series can be found at the end of the volume.

ENGLISH ALLITERATIVE VERSE

Poetic Tradition and Literary History

ERIC WEISKOTT

CAMBRIDGE
UNIVERSITY PRESS

CAMBRIDGE
UNIVERSITY PRESS

University Printing House, Cambridge CB2 8BS, United Kingdom

One Liberty Plaza, 20th Floor, New York, NY 10006, USA

477 Williamstown Road, Port Melbourne, VIC 3207, Australia

314-321, 3rd Floor, Plot 3, Splendor Forum, Jasola District Centre, New Delhi - 110025, India

79 Anson Road, #06-04/06, Singapore 079906

Cambridge University Press is part of the University of Cambridge.

It furthers the University's mission by disseminating knowledge in the pursuit of education, learning and research at the highest international levels of excellence.

www.cambridge.org
Information on this title: www.cambridge.org/9781316620700
10.1017/9781316718674

© Eric Weiskott 2016

This publication is in copyright. Subject to statutory exception and to the provisions of relevant collective licensing agreements, no reproduction of any part may take place without the written permission of Cambridge University Press.

First published 2016
First paperback edition 2018

A catalogue record for this publication is available from the British Library

ISBN 978-1-107-16965-4 Hardback
ISBN 978-1-316-62070-0 Paperback

Cambridge University Press has no responsibility for the persistence or accuracy of URLs for external or third-party internet websites referred to in this publication, and does not guarantee that any content on such websites is, or will remain, accurate or appropriate.

To my parents

Contents

Figures

Acknowledgments

In the course of writing this book I have benefited from the advice and guidance of mentors, colleagues, and friends. My first debt of gratitude is to Roberta Frank, whose erudition and good humor have been abiding resources. Jessica Brantley, Ardis Butterfield, Ian Cornelius, Paul Freedman, Ben Glaser, Alastair Minnis, and Denys Turner helped me conceptualize and revise the 2014 Yale University dissertation that forms the kernel of this book. While at Yale, I shared seminars, ideas, friendships, and in two cases apartments with Anya Adair, Abbey Agresta, Mary Kate Hurley, Andrew Kraebel, Geoff Moseley, Madeleine Saraceni, Anne Schindel, Joe Stadolnik, Arvind Thomas, Emily Ulrich, and Aaron Vanides, among others. Part of the research for Chapter 4 was completed under the auspices of the H. P. Kraus Fellowship in Early Books and Manuscripts at the Beinecke Library in 2013. I am grateful for the focused time in the archives.

Boston College is a wonderful place to work and a wonderful place to finish a book. Robert Stanton, my medievalist colleague in the English Department, is a beacon of collegiality and good advice. I am fortunate to have so many learned and generous colleagues. Those who encouraged me in the final stages of this project include Amy Boesky, Mary Crane, Rhonda Frederick, Dayton Haskin, Beth Kowaleski-Wallace, Adam Lewis, Suzanne Matson, and Andrew Sofer. Part of the research for Chapter 6 was completed through a Boston College Research Expense Grant in 2015, for which I am grateful.

I continue to profit from conversations with a number of other colleagues and friends in the fields of medieval literature and poetics, especially Tom Cable, Irina Dumitrescu, Tony Edwards, Will Eggers (my first teacher in medieval literature), Natalie Gerber, Alex Mueller, Nick Myklebust, Ryan (R. D.) Perry, Carla Thomas, and Elaine Treharne. They have consistently enriched my thinking and sustained my optimism about the academic profession.

I presented modified excerpts from this book at the following confer-
ences, whose organizers and attendees I warmly thank: the 7th
International Layamon Conference in Paris in 2012; the 48th and 50th
International Congress on Medieval Studies in Kalamazoo, MI in 2013 and
2015; the American Comparative Literature Association 2014 Meeting in
New York; the MLA Annual Convention in Vancouver in 2015; Poetry by
the Sea in Madison, CT in 2015; the Sixth International Piers Plowman
Society Conference in Seattle in 2015; and the New England Medieval
Conference in Boston in 2015. I presented a draft of Chapter 6 at the
Harvard English Department Medieval Colloquium in 2014. My gratitude
to Helen Cushman and Erica Weaver for the invitation.

I thank Linda Bree and Alastair Minnis (again) for expertly seeing this
project through all phases of the editorial process at Cambridge.

Finally, I thank my parents, Roberta Garris and Jack Weiskott, for their
love and support, and for a tattered copy of F. N. Robinson's *Works of
Geoffrey Chaucer*, which initiated me into a new literary universe; my
brother Carl, for asking the big questions; and my wife, Sofia Warner,
for all the love and patience. I owe my family more than I am able to say.
This book is small recompense for their kindness.

An earlier version of Chapter 3 appeared as "Lawman, the Last Old
English Poet and the First Middle English Poet," in *Laʒamon's Brut and
other Medieval Chronicles: 14 Essays*, ed. Marie-Françoise Alamichel (Paris:
L'Harmattan, 2013), pp. 11–57. A modified version of the Conclusion will
appear as the conclusion of "Before Prosody: Early English Poetics in
Practice and Theory," in *Modern Language Quarterly* (in press).

EBW

Abbreviations

ASCCE	*The Anglo-Saxon Chronicle: A Collaborative Edition*, ed. Dumville and Keynes
ASE	*Anglo-Saxon England*
ASPR	*Anglo-Saxon Poetic Records*, ed. Krapp and Dobbie
CR	*Chaucer Review*
DOE	*Dictionary of Old English*
EETS	Early English Text Society. Oxford: Oxford University Press
	ES Extra Series
	OS Original Series
	SS Supplementary Series
EME	Early Middle English
ES	*English Studies*
JEGP	*Journal of English and Germanic Philology*
L	Latin
LC	*Literature Compass*
LSE	*Leeds Studies in English*
MÆ	*Medium Ævum*
ME	Middle English
MED	*Middle English Dictionary*
MLQ	*Modern Language Quarterly*
MP	*Modern Philology*
N&Q	*Notes & Queries*
NIMEV	Boffey and Edwards, *A New Index of Middle English Verse*
OE	Old English
OED	*Oxford English Dictionary*
OF	Old French

ON	Old Norse
PMLA	*Publications of the Modern Language Association*
RES	*Review of English Studies*
SIP	*Studies in Philology*
YLS	*Yearbook of Langland Studies*

Evolution of the Alliterative B-Verse, 650–1550

p: verbal prefix or negative particle omitted from meter by the prefix license
S: lift
x: an unstressed syllable in a dip

Old English (*c.* 650–950)		Early Middle English (*c.* 950–1250)		Middle English (*c.* 1250–1550)
pSx(x …)Sx (A)	=	xSx … xSx (1)	=	" ", later xSx … xS(x)
x(x …)SpSx (C)	=	x … xSxSx (2)	=	" ", later x … xSxS(x)
Sx(x …)Sx (A)	=	Sx … xSx (3)	=	" ", later Sx … xS(x)
x(x …)SxS (B)	=	x … xSxS (4)	=	x … xSxSx, later x … xSxS(x)
x(x …)SSx (C)	=	x … xSSx (5)	=	" ", later x … xSS(x)
SSSx (A/D)				
SSxS (D/E)	=	b-verse patterns	=	" "
Sx(x …)SS (A/E)		with more than		
x(x …)SSS (B/C)		two lifts (rare)		
SSSS (A/D/E)				

xiv

Introduction: The Durable Alliterative Tradition

> Grammar is coral
> a gabled light
> against the blue
> a dark museum
> Durable thing
>> Elizabeth Willis, "Sonnet," from *Turneresque*
>> (Providence, RI: Burning Deck, 2003)

The chapters of this book form an essay in a type of history I call 'verse history,' a concept not covered by any of the usual terms applied to the study of literature. Verse history is the history of a tradition of composing poems in a certain meter. It is distinct from literary history, because two works from one genre, place, or time, even two works by one poet, may be in different meters. The inverse is also true, in that verse history can connect poems from very different local contexts. The relationship between Elizabeth Barrett Browning's "How do I love thee? Let me count the ways" and a twenty-first-century sonnet on supercomputers is more general than literary influence, a genre, or a school. What any two sonnets have in common is that they belong to the same verse history, the same centuries-long sweep of metrical practice. The English sonnet tradition is a living tradition, that is, it has enjoyed a continuous formal evolution reaching to the present day. It will be the major preoccupation of this book to demonstrate that there is a particular verse history that corresponds to the notion of 'the alliterative tradition' and that this history extended continuously from *c.* 650–1550 CE. Along the way, the division of medieval English literary history into 'Old' and 'Middle' subperiods will be repeatedly challenged and renegotiated. I seek to make a medievalist contribution to the emerging field of historical poetics as it is understood by Simon Jarvis, for whom verse is "an institution, a series of practices as real as the belief in them and the capacity for them," but with the added difficulty that medieval English poets have left no *ars poetica* and indeed

I

little explicit reflection of any kind on their own metrical practices in the vernacular.[1]

The choice of the words 'living' and 'evolution' is meant to invite an analogy to species and languages as they are understood by biology and linguistics, respectively. Like a species or a language, a poetic tradition is a historical object, whose development constitutes a discrete historical series. Like evolutionary history or linguistic history, verse history unfolds continuously on a large temporal scale. And like genes in biology or grammar in linguistics, poetic meter accounts for the identity of poetic traditions from one developmental phase to the next. By invoking biology and linguistics, I mean to call to mind the present-day, non-teleological manifestations of these disciplines, as opposed to the familiar nineteenth-century conceptions of evolutionary or linguistic history as essentially progressive or regressive. Accordingly, I narrate the millennium-long history of alliterative verse without adverting to origins, renaissances, or decadence.

Verse history does not imply stasis in its object of inquiry any more than cultural history, linguistic history, political history, textual history, or evolutionary history do in theirs. I do not contend that alliterative meter *c.* 650 was identical to alliterative meter *c.* 1550. On the contrary, I seek to elucidate the processes, formal and cultural, that shaped alliterative composition over time.

Poetic form, in this view, is not a disembodied notation, so many *tum*s and *ti*s, waiting to be plucked down from the ether. Meter is the historical object, of which metrical theory is but a convenient representation. More precisely, meter is a historically mediated event that occurs in the minds of poets, scribes, and readers.[2] Pronunciation, spelling, linguistic rhythm, performance, and even metrical notation itself are all posterior to this mental event, which therefore assumes central importance in the kind of historical poetics I am envisioning here. In order to emphasize the mental nature of metrical phenomena, in this book the term 'pattern' is preferred to 'rhythm' to designate historically specific metrical forms. Where this book offers scansions, these must not be understood as representations of some objectively measurable feature of language, but instead as representations of the metrical expectations projected onto language in specific and sometimes contradictory ways by poets and audiences. This book does not posit meter as the transhistorical essence of poetry or the literary. Rather, it seeks to recover meter as a historically durable and culturally significant practice, that is, a *habitus*, in both the medieval and the Bourdieusian sense of the term. I argue throughout that meter was the most centrally important *habitus* in the production, consumption, and historical development of medieval English poetry.

If meter is a phenomenological event rather than an objective attribute, the verse historian's initial task is to recover the formal knowledge that made the event possible. There is something disconcerting about the extent to which students of medieval English literature are prepared to equivocate about poetic meter. The *Digital Index of Middle English Verse* organizes poems by meter and stanzaic form, including the catch-all categories 'irregular' (sixty-nine items) and 'various' (two items). These labels do not name medieval meters but modern uncertainty about them. A recent hand-list of Middle English alliterative poems notes "quatrains and couplets which shift in and out of four-stress and homomorphic meter," elsewhere "sometimes arguably hexameter."[3] On the view put forth in this book, metrical form is not 'arguable,' at least not in the sense that it is a matter of arbitrary post hoc analysis. A poem that appears to skirt the boundaries of two meters may be in a third (in the case of the first quotation, template meter: see below). Poems that mix meters, like *Sir Gawain and the Green Knight* (late fourteenth century; alliterative meter and template meter) and Chaucer's *Anelida and Arcite* (late fourteenth century; pentameter and tetrameter), switch back and forth in perceptibly patterned ways, not imperceptibly or willy-nilly. Meter is not an optional ornament; it is just that set of historically variable practices by which verse comes to be recognized as verse.

The history of alliterative verse is the history of poems composed wholly or partially in the alliterative meter. It is not the history of any other poems. Simply put, there existed a living alliterative tradition to which *Beowulf* (?eighth/tenth centuries), Lawman's (=Laȝamon's) *Brut* (c. 1200), *St. Erkenwald* (late fourteenth/mid fifteenth centuries), William Dunbar's *Tretis of the Tua Mariit Wemen and the Wedo* (c. 1500), etc., being in the alliterative meter, belong in sequence, but to which *Poema Morale* (c. 1180), *Pearl* (late fourteenth century), Chaucer's *Canterbury Tales* (late fourteenth century), the poems in *Tottel's Miscellany* (1557), etc., being in other meters, do not belong. This book is primarily concerned to describe the historical development of the alliterative tradition. However, I will continually note how alliterative verse history inflected and was inflected by the history of adjacent poetic traditions in English and other languages.

This book coordinates verse history with the history of poetic styles. Though I apply the term to a variety of literary phenomena in the course of my historical arguments, 'style' is made more concrete in this book in two complementary ways. First, Chapters 2, 3, 4, and 5 develop a theory of poetic prologues, which I take to be exceptionally dense expressions of style. I identify the use of prologues as an overlooked form of continuity between Old English and Middle English (alliterative) poetry, running parallel to metrical continuity in alliterative verse history. The analysis of prologues also contributes to the study of literary genres. On the basis of a typology of prologues, I posit fundamental distinctions between long and short poems and between historicizing and contemporary narrative compositions. I argue that mapping the field of medieval English literature by form rather than content clarifies questions of genre and literary history. Just as my use of metrical form to define a study corpus challenges form-neutral notions of 'Old English literature' and 'Middle English literature,' so my use of a typology of prologues challenges the thematic distinctions ('*chanson d'aventure*,' 'hagiography,' 'Matter of Britain,' etc.) that have traditionally organized the study of medieval English literary texts.

The second meaning of style comes from an examination of textual activity extrinsic to the practice of alliterative meter. I scour the manuscript contexts, scribal texts, and literary (re)presentations of alliterative poetry for indirect evidence of the preconceptions that medieval practitioners brought to verse craft. Medieval writers sometimes identify meters with styles directly, as when Chaucer has his Parson plead inability to "geeste 'rum, ram, ruf,' by lettre" (*Canterbury Tales* X 43; all quotations of Chaucer are from *Riverside Chaucer*, ed. Benson). Here, the idea of alliterative verse is connected automatically with chivalric romance. Yet for all their historical interest, testimonia fall short of describing the total capacity of a verse form. I interpret Chaucer's Parson's remark and similar moments as evidence of the circulation of cultural stereotypes about meters, while remaining aware that such stereotypes are as much symptoms as causes of the historical pressures bearing on metrical traditions. I will use the term 'alliterative style' to cover all types of style, metrical and non-metrical, available at any given point in the development of the alliterative tradition.

The thematic argument threading through this book is that the alliterative tradition adopts a characteristic attitude toward the distant past, as realized most powerfully in *Beowulf*, the *Brut*, and *St. Erkenwald*, the subjects of Chapters 1, 3, and 5, respectively. This means neither that all alliterative poems adopt such an attitude, nor that non-alliterative poems never do so. I will have occasion to notice both kinds of crossover in poetic practice. Ultimately, I argue that long, historicizing poems like *Beowulf,*

Progress in alliterative metrics brings into sharper focus the priorities of past scholarship. Blake's and Turville-Petre's skepticism about the continuity of the alliterative tradition can now be understood in part as a defense and consolidation of the idea of 'Middle English literature.' Middle English literature has been an immensely influential idea, with many accomplishments to its credit; yet metrical scholarship has begun to suggest how such periodization distorts the history of alliterative form. Indeed, it is unclear on what basis one could detach a corpus of 'Middle English' alliterative poetry from earlier alliterative verse, now that the gap in the written record at the turn of the fourteenth century seems best explained as an accident of manuscript survival (Ch. 4). The question of identifying the Middle English meter closest to Old English meter does not arise in the first place, because the development of 'Old English' meter extends well into the sixteenth century. If recent work on alliterative meter holds a lesson for future scholarship, it is that the study of Old English literature and the study of Middle English literature must be integrated. The habitual reliance on 1066 as a zero-point, uncomfortably reminiscent of some early modernists' reliance on 1534, is counterproductive for alliterative verse. It may be that medieval English literary history as a whole will make more sense when disengaged from the outmoded political history that continues to divide it, for modern scholars, into two glorious epochs (Old English and Middle English) bracketing one forgettable interlude (Early Middle English).

Chapter 1, "*Beowulf* and Verse History," charts the evolution of the alliterative meter, 950–1100, and adduces new evidence of synchronic metrical variety in this misunderstood period. The second section reevaluates certain metrical tests thought to establish a very early date (before *c.* 750) for the composition of *Beowulf*. I argue that previous studies have discovered a metrically old *Beowulf* only by reducing verse history to language history a priori. The dynamism of alliterative meter, demonstrable after 950 and presumable before 950, problematizes the methods by which metrists have sought to locate *Beowulf* in the early eighth century. A third section reviews and challenges four non-metrical arguments for a very early *Beowulf*.

Chapter 2, "Prologues to Old English Poetry," develops a typology of prologues to long Old English poems, modeled on the typology of medieval academic prologues developed by R. W. Hunt and elaborated by Alastair Minnis. As prominent stylistic gestures, poetic prologues offer a rare opportunity to understand how Old English poets perceived poetic style and to discover affiliations between undated, unlocalized, and anonymous texts. Comparison of prologues unsettles the received view of Old English literary landscapes by juxtaposing acknowledged masterpieces like *Beowulf* and the *Dream of the Rood* with ill-appreciated pious and didactic poems. After surveying the types of prologue and their use in individual compositions, this chapter concludes by exploring the implications of the prologue typology for historicizing the style of *Beowulf.*

Chapter 3, "Lawman, the Last Old English Poet and the First Middle English Poet," seeks to rehabilitate a much-maligned but centrally important poet. This chapter clarifies recent scholarship on the meter of the *Brut* and extends it to other Early Middle English alliterative poetry. I show Lawman's meter to be highly organized, directly related to Old English and to Middle English alliterative meter, and distinct from Ælfric of Eynsham's 'rhythmical alliteration.' Through consideration of particular words and passages, the second section demonstrates how Lawman's conservative style resembles that of his Old English predecessors, how the two manuscript versions of the *Brut* represent two different visions for the future of alliterative verse, and how Lawman's treatment of the Arthurian past anticipates Middle English romance.

Chapter 4, "Prologues to Middle English Alliterative Poetry," argues that the lack of firm documentary evidence for the composition of alliterative poetry between the Middle English *Physiologus* and *William of Palerne* (1336–61) is an accident of manuscript survival, not evidence of the death of alliterative verse and a subsequent 'Alliterative Revival.' The first section presents metrical, lexical, and textual evidence for the continuity of the alliterative tradition across the ninety-year gap in the written record. The second section offers metrical, syntactical, and codicological evidence against the conflation of the (unrhymed) alliterative meter with alliterating stanzaic meters. The third section develops a typology of prologues to long Middle English alliterative poems, with reference to similar prologues to non-alliterative Middle English, Anglo-Norman, and French poems and with special emphasis on *Piers Plowman.* The typology has a twofold purpose: first, to measure prologues to Middle English alliterative poetry against the prologues to earlier alliterative poems, discussed in Chapters 2 and 3, and so to extrapolate a stylistic *longue durée* for alliterative verse; second, to measure alliterative poetry against non-alliterative poetry (especially romance), and so to gauge the position of alliterative verse in late medieval English literary culture.

Chapter 5, "The *Erkenwald* Poet's Sense of History," offers a case in point for the arguments of Chapter 4 through a reading of the understudied Middle English alliterative poem *St. Erkenwald.* This chapter reads

St. Erkenwald as a serious meditation on history. The second section contrasts *St. Erkenwald* with some short English alliterative poems embedded in Latin prose and rhyming English verse, in an effort to infer the connotations of the alliterative meter in late medieval English literary culture. I argue that the *Erkenwald* poet's sense of history and use of alliterative style are more robust than the impression of an archaistic alliterative meter shared by some thirteenth- and fourteenth-century writers and some modern critics of *St. Erkenwald*. The third section challenges the traditional attribution of *St. Erkenwald* to the *Gawain* poet.

Chapter 6, "The Alliterative Tradition in the Sixteenth Century," traces the generic, codicological, textual, and cultural contexts for alliterative meter in the century before it disappeared from the active repertoire of verse forms. In doing so, this chapter lays the groundwork for a new literary history of the sixteenth century. After surveying the extant alliterative poems composed after 1450, I describe the systemic changes manifested in alliterative meter in this period. The second section considers mid sixteenth- to mid seventeenth-century print and manuscript evidence for the reception of earlier alliterative meter, focusing on the two manuscript texts of *Scottish Field* (1515–47), Robert Crowley's first edition of *Piers Plowman* (1550), and Crowley's own poetry. The chapter concludes by arguing that the contribution of the alliterative tradition to the so-called invention of modern literature has been underestimated by literary histories that enforce a division between 'medieval' and 'modern' periods of literary activity.

In conclusion, I would like to isolate a general literary-historical problem addressed throughout this study and discuss my proposed solutions to it. Traditionally, the writing of literary history has focused on choices (Gower chooses to compose in French) and events (the Alliterative Revival). This configuration of a research field recalls the methods of a certain kind of political history. An uncritical equation between literary history and political history forms one of the targets of my arguments in Chapters 1, 3, 4, and 6. Even literary scholars who would readily disavow the equation, however, tend to perpetuate its functional effects, the focus on choice and events as the parameters within which literary history becomes intelligible. Yet composition in the alliterative meter was not a choice in any sense before the invention of non-alliterative meters toward the end of the twelfth century: if one composed poetry in English at all before *c.* 1150, one inevitably composed alliterative poetry. Certainly later English poets recognized the metrical choices that lay before them in the vernacular, but they do not appear to have constructed a metadiscourse about those choices. And then, the protagonist of this book, the alliterative tradition, developed precisely by a series of non-events: it did not melt into alliterating prose in the tenth century, nor template meter in the thirteenth and fourteenth, nor alliterating stanzaic meters in the fourteenth and fifteenth; it did not wither away after the Norman Conquest in the face of new French- and Latin-inspired English meters; it did not perish at the end of the thirteenth century and it was not revived in the middle of the fourteenth; it was not completely subsumed in the cosmopolitan romance tradition; and the invention of print and the canonization of Chaucer's pentameter did not immediately cut short its tenure. The alliterative meter underwent profound evolutionary change between 650 and 1550, but the changes were so gradual as to be imperceptible to individual practitioners. None of them was an event in any journalistic sense. This is the particular meaning of 'durable' in the title of this Introduction, but it is also a substantial literary-historical problem that this book seeks to formulate in a new way.

What seems to be needed, and what I have endeavored to provide, is a literary history concerned with poetic traditions as institutions and series of practices. Shifting the focus of inquiry from historical actors and events to traditions will throw into sharper relief the actors and events left over in the analysis. In my account, Lawman's choice of the alliterative meter *c.* 1200 was a non-choice and thus a non-problem, but Langland's identical choice *c.* 1370, a century after the promotion of non-alliterative metrical traditions in English, poses a real problem. Similarly, the Alliterative Revival emerges in my account as a non-event and thus a non-problem, but the death of the alliterative tradition in the sixteenth century requires a historical explanation. Both choices and non-choices, events and non-events, are always, in this line of thinking, structured by the historically specific formal practices that constitute poetic traditions. Which persons adopted or eschewed these practices, and when, and where, and why, can only be determined by attending to the circulation of the practices and the cultural meanings that accrue to them in the aggregate. By 'literary history' in this context I mean the shape that literary practices describe in time.

The overwhelmingly anonymous nature of the extant alliterative corpus likewise directs attention to traditions rather than authors. For most alliterative poems, no information about authorship is available. Even the authors of such poems as *Elene*, the *Brut*, *Piers Plowman*, and the *Destruction of Troy*, who designate themselves within their fictions, exist in modern scholarship as little more than floating names ('Cynewulf,' 'Lawman,' 'William Langland,' and 'John Clerk,' respectively). Nevertheless, this book can be understood as a study of one vector of being a poet in medieval England. From those rare instances in which an extant alliterative poem may be assigned to a wider literary *oeuvre*, it is clear that the alliterative tradition cuts across the authorial self. Thus the *Gawain* poet composed at least three alliterative poems (*Cleanness, Patience*, and *Gawain*) but also at least one non-alliterative one (*Pearl*), and Dunbar composed at least one alliterative poem (the *Tretis*) but also at least eighty-three non-alliterative ones. The metaphor of the institution offers a way to understand why this should be so. Investigating metrical traditions as institutions illuminates the dialectical relationship between meters and authorial selves, in the same way that, e.g., ecclesiastical history intertwines the history of ethics. The authorial self was in no sense prior to the alliterative tradition as institution: no one poet invented or resuscitated this tradition. Yet the alliterative tradition as institution did precede, impinge upon, and shape the authorial self.

I do not venture to predict whether the verse history of traditions-as-institutions will solve more problems than it creates for analysis of the English tetrameter tradition, the pentameter from Chaucer to Frost, or indeed the "rise and fall of meter," 1860–1930, recently narrated from a complementary perspective by Meredith Martin. On the one hand, I would readily agree that authority and tradition meant different things at different times, not least in light of the inauguration of metadiscourses of English meter toward the end of the sixteenth century. Thus the concept of tradition as used in this book may be susceptible to further historicizing from the perspective of post-medieval meter and prosody. On the other hand, verse history should not be understood to entail a denial of the metaliterary acumen of medieval writers in general or alliterative poets in particular. Any periodizing narrative whereby an unconscious repertoire of medieval metrical practices gives way to a self-conscious repertoire of modern ones is bound to falsify the record in the process of erecting an impossible chronological partition. So too, it would be wrong to assume that alliterative poets thought less critically about their positions in literary culture than, say, Chaucer, only because we have so much less information about the former than about the latter. The problem with such assumptions, I believe, lies precisely in defining traditionality, ahistorically, as the opposite of originality. A goal of any historical poetics should be to resist the false dichotomy between traditions and authors – a false dichotomy, it must be said, that has vexed modern minds more often than medieval ones. The solution offered by verse history is not to remove authors and authorial choice from the equation, but, on the contrary, to enrich our sense of historical agents and our appreciation of imaginative compositions by historicizing the forms and styles in which the agents were implicated and the compositions expressed. For this essential task, it will be necessary to attend as closely to non-choices as choices and to non-events as events.

CHAPTER I

Beowulf *and Verse History*

Since the poem first came to scholarly attention in the early nineteenth century, it has been conventional to regard *Beowulf* as the apotheosis of the so-called classical alliterative long line. Every theory of Old English meter has been measured by the measures of *Beowulf*. But the date of *Beowulf* and the contours of alliterative verse history before roughly 950 are interdependent reconstructions. Is *Beowulf* metrically old or metrically conservative? And how old or conservative? The meter of *Beowulf* cannot be contextualized without first inquiring into the development of alliterative meter in the unreliably documented earlier period. Metrists have sidestepped the problem either by assuming an early date for *Beowulf*, which is circular, or by subsuming verse history in language history, which is a category mistake.

This chapter reviews some metrical tests thought to establish a very early date (before *c.* 750) for the composition of *Beowulf*. The first section charts the evolution of the alliterative meter, 950–1100, and adduces new evidence of synchronic metrical variety in this misunderstood period. The second section argues that previous studies have discovered a metrically old *Beowulf* only by reducing verse history to language history a priori. The dynamism of alliterative meter, demonstrable after 950 and presumable before 950, problematizes the methods by which metrists have sought to locate *Beowulf* in the early eighth century. A third section reviews and challenges four non-metrical arguments for a very early *Beowulf*. Together, the three sections demonstrate a key conclusion of the book as a whole: metrical form has a history of its own, which cannot be reduced to cultural, linguistic, political, or textual history. To the extent that verse history registers events in these other historical series – whether the circulation of legends, the loss of inflectional vowels, the conquest of a political territory, or the transcription of an exemplar – it does so through the medium of its own logic.

The Evolution of Alliterative Meter, 950–1100

Before evaluating the methods by which metrists have sought to reconstruct the shape of alliterative verse history before 950, it will be useful to trace the development of the alliterative meter after 950. Here I coordinate two synchronic systems of notation, one designed to describe the *Beowulf* meter and the other to describe the meter of Lawman's *Brut* (*c.* 1200), in order to reveal the metrical regularity and historical dynamism of late Old English poetry. This newly precise description of alliterative verse history, 950–1100, aids in two essential tasks. First, it substantially revises received understandings of metrical form in the period. I show how scholars' impression of a decadent late Old English meter results from an insufficiently diachronic perspective onto the alliterative metrical system. Second, the knowable history of post-950 alliterative verse acts as the best available control on inferences about the texture of verse history before 950. The next section brings both considerations to bear on the question of dating *Beowulf* on metrical grounds.

A richer historical perspective onto late Old English meter has been made newly possible by advances in the study of the *Beowulf* meter and the *Brut* meter. Nicolay Yakovlev, the author of a fundamental study of alliterative meter (still unpublished), discloses a new theoretical paradigm for Old English meter. Yakovlev dispenses with alliteration, secondary stress, feet, word boundaries, and the restriction to two metrical stresses and defines the half-line as a sequence of four metrical positions, either lifts or dips. By definition, no two dips can be adjacent, for in that case they would merge into a single dip. Where most previous commentators described Old English meter as accentual, i.e., based on the stress of individual words, Yakovlev describes it as morphological, i.e., based on the category membership of individual morphemes regardless of their position within the word. Eduard Sievers's Five Types are replaced with eight permutations of lifts and dips in a frame of four positions:

OE (Sievers)		OE (Yakovlev)
A	=	Sx(x . . .)Sx
B	=	x(x . . .)SxS
C	=	x(x . . .)SSx
A/D	=	SSSx
D/E	=	SSxS
A/E	=	Sx(x . . .)SS
B/C	=	x(x . . .)SSS
A/D/E	=	SSSS

To the basic four-position structure Yakovlev adds three more metrical principles: resolution and its suspension; prohibition of long dips in the third and fourth positions; and the 'prefix license,' whereby verbal prefixes and the negative particle *ne* may optionally be omitted from the metrical count. Each of these principles adds a minor complication to the way that Old English meter maps language onto metrical positions. Resolution and the prohibition against third- and fourth-position long dips already appeared in many prior theories of Old English meter; both are discussed in the Introduction. The prefix license represents Yakovlev's original synthesis of diverse conclusions in previous scholarship. Many of these earlier discussions concerned 'anacrusis,' which referred to an extrametrical syllable before the a-verse. By offering the prefix license as a general principle of Old English meter, Yakovlev effectively reduces 'anacrusis' to the status of a special case.

Yakovlev's morphological theory of Old English meter explains many mysteries, including why Type A is the commonest contour (it occurs in the most permutations); why it is impossible to tell whether verses like *wyrd oft nereð* belong to Type A or to Type D (both are SSSx) or whether verses like *flod blode weol* belong to Type D or to Type E (both are SSxS); why metrical resolution occurs indifferently under, and is suspended indifferently after, 'primary,' 'secondary,' and 'tertiary' stress (there is no metrical significance to these varieties of linguistic stress); why curiosities such as resolution, clashing stress, and the optional expansion of dips are permitted in the first place (the meter counts positions, not accentual rhythms); and why prefixes may count or not count in the meter (metrical value – stressed, unstressed, or omitted – is assigned morpheme by morpheme, not word by word or foot by foot). At last, the Five Types can be understood as "the epiphenomenal results of a simpler paradigm."[1] The occurrence of 'secondary stress' in Sievers Types C, D, and E follows from the structure of Old English words, but the metrical principles operate at a deeper level of abstraction. In the prominence it accords to the concept of 'metrical position,' Yakovlev's theory draws on a long tradition of prosodic scholarship, stretching from Sievers to Thomas Cable; but the proposition that Old English meter was morphological, not accentual, is as original as it is clarifying.

Yakovlev's generalization that Old English meter was morphological is both descriptively adequate and theoretically illuminating, but it does remain a generalization about a meter with at least three recognizable principles of organization: morphological, quantitative, and accentual. The Introduction summarized the importance of quantity in Old

English meter: in this meter, the difference between a quantitatively long syllable and a quantitatively short syllable is metrically significant in the case of stressed syllables. Old English verse also shows a minor impulse toward accentual meter alongside the major impulse toward morphological-quantitative meter. The occasional metrical promotion of function words in order to make up the requisite four positions, e.g., *Beowulf* 22a *þæt hyne on ylde*, is one expression of an incipient accentual meter.[1] Moreover, the morphological and accentual principles overlap in determining which words are eligible for metrical stress, since both principles can rely on the same hierarchy of grammatical class membership, in which content words outrank function words. The remainder of this section, along with Chapter 3, describes the formal processes by which a morphological-quantitative metrical system with minor accentual features developed into an accentual-quantitative metrical system with remnants of morphological organization. Chapters 4 and 6 move this narrative forward to the fourteenth, fifteenth, and sixteenth centuries, when alliterative meter left quantity behind in the process of becoming more accentual. Thus the accentual principle represents a form of continuity in alliterative verse history, albeit one expressed much more forcefully in the second half of that history. For now, it is important to note that the evolution of metrical modalities in the alliterative tradition was more fluid than a single label ('accentual,' 'morphological,' or 'quantitative') can convey. Keeping this caveat in mind, the labels remain useful as schematic representations of long-term trends in versification.

Yakovlev's decoupling of Old English metrical form from Old English linguistic form enables him to trace a developmental arc from the *Beowulf* meter to the *Brut* meter (and beyond: see Chs. 3 and 4). This accomplishment, too, had been unthinkable in previous statements of meter. Yakovlev finds five metrical patterns in the b-verses of the *Brut*, which are strongly reminiscent of the Old English patterns (p)Sx(x . . .)Sx, x(x . . .)SxS, and x(x . . .)S(p)Sx (Types A, B, and C in Sieversian notation), where 'p' marks a verbal prefix or negative particle omitted by the prefix license:

OE (Yakovlev/Sievers)		EME (Yakovlev)
pSx(x . . .)Sx (A)	=	xSx . . . xSx (1)
x(x . . .)SpSx (C)	=	x . . . xSxSx (2)
Sx(x . . .)Sx (A)	=	Sx . . . xSx (3)
x(x . . .)SxS (B)	=	x . . . xSxS (4)
x(x . . .)SSx (C)	=	x . . . xSSx (5)

The innovative five-position pattern x ... xSxSx (Yakovlev Type 2) could also have arisen by ignoring metrical resolution in the Old English patterns x(x ...)SrSx and x(x ...)SxSr (Types B and C), where 'Sr' marks a lift under resolution. Around 65 percent of Lawman's a-verses take one of the five forms, as well, but the others are bound by few principles. Therefore, the following discussion focuses on b-verses.

Once connected with a morphological Old English meter, Lawman's meter reveals processes of selection in alliterative verse history. The two-lift Old English patterns ((p)S(x ...)xSx, x(x ...)SxS, and x(x ...)S(p)Sx; Sievers Types A, B, and C without 'secondary stress') are precisely the ones used by Lawman in the b-verse, with expansion of one expandable dip (Types 1–5). The decline of clashing stress in alliterative meter, long remarked upon by metrists, turns out to be a red herring. It was not clashing stress *per se* that was deselected from alliterative meter after 950, but b-verses with three or four lifts. The only logically possible four-position pattern with exactly two clashing stresses (x(x ...)SSx, Sievers Type C) survived in the b-verses of Middle English alliterative poetry as Type 5. In the fourteenth and fifteenth centuries, Type 5 appears as a vestige of a morphological meter in a metrical system that had long since become accentual. Metrical vestige as a "historical residue" constitutes another of Yakovlev's contributions to the conceptual vocabulary of early English metrics. "Given the rare opportunity to observe a cross-section in the history of a poetic tradition," writes Yakovlev, "we always see 'a work in progress'; the picture observed will always be inherently dynamic."[3] In building upon Yakovlev's evolutionary model throughout this book, I seek to lend further specificity to the perception of an "inherently dynamic" configuration of metrical patterns in each phase of alliterative verse history.

A second newly visible "historical residue" is the appearance in post-950 alliterative verse of half-lines with three lifts and more than four metrical positions. In addition to the five two-lift patterns, Yakovlev finds that Lawman also composed three-lift verses constrained only by the avoidance of final long dips (as in all Old English patterns) and a minimum (but no longer a maximum) of four positions. Three-lift patterns occur commonly as a-verses and rarely as b-verses in the *Brut*. For the first time in the study of alliterative meter, three-lift verses in late Old English, Early Middle English, and Middle English alliterative verse can be explained as vestiges of a metrical system that counted positions rather than accentual stresses. Middle English metrists have always debated whether verses with three content words, e.g., *Gawain* 2a *Þe borȝ brittened ond brent*, should be scanned with two or three lifts. The proponents of two-lift scansion have made their arguments on a more or less synchronic basis, occasionally gesturing toward two-lift theories of Old English meter. Yakovlev settles the debate in favor of a three-lift scansion by engaging a historical perspective on the problem. He presents a non-beat-counting Old English meter and a non-beat-counting Middle English a-verse meter, but unlike proponents of a two-lift norm he also directly connects these two systems, and Lawman's meter, in one centuries-long *catena* of metrical practice.

In what follows, I test Yakovlev's metrical model on several late Old English poems not considered by him. By triangulating between the two moments in verse history represented by *Beowulf* and the *Brut*, it becomes possible to bring into focus the development of the alliterative meter after 950. Poems from this period include many datable compositions from the Anglo-Saxon Chronicle, not all of which have always been recognized as poems. Consider the b-verses of the *Chastity of St. Margaret* (1070–71), accompanied by Sievers and Yakovlev scansions jointly (quoted from Appendix A, no. 6):

x x x x S S x	
ac he ond his men ealle	(5)
x x x S x S	
ond eac heo sylf wiðsoc	(4)
S x S x	
habban wolde	(A)
x S x S x	
geunnan wolde	(xSxSx)
S x x S x	
5 mihtigan drihtne	(3)
x x x Sx S x	
on þisan life sceortan	(2)
S x S x	
cweman mihte.	(A)

Chastity, composed more than 100 years before the *Brut*, partakes of aspects of both synchronic systems represented by Sievers's and Yakovlev's metrical typologies. The lines characterized here as Types 3, 4, and 5 could be described, respectively, as the Old English patterns Sx(x . . .)Sx, x(x . . .)SxS, and x(x . . .)SSx (Sievers Types A, B, and C). But the tendency toward the two-lift, one-long-dip b-verse is already taking hold. The verbal prefix *ge-* in

4b may be omitted from the metrical count, as in earlier Old English verse (for Sievers Type A), or included in the count, as in later alliterative verse. The five-position pattern with no long dip (xSxSx) is particularly symptomatic of ongoing metrical evolution: this pattern had been unmetrical in the *Beowulf* meter (because it has five positions) and would become unmetrical again by the time of the *Brut* (because it lacks a long dip). The pattern xSxSx, which bears a certain similarity to the French-, Italian-, and Latin-influenced deductive English meters that had yet to be invented in the 1070s, was a pattern of avoidance in the b-verse for most of alliterative verse history. For a relatively short period, however, it was one way of resolving the conflicting demands of the outgoing four-position principle and the incoming lift-and-dip system.

Compare the first ten b-verses of the earlier *Death of Alfred* (1036–45) (quoted and numbered from *ASPR 6*):

$$x \quad x\,x\,x \quad S \quad S\,x$$
and hine on hæft sette   (5)

$$x \quad x \quad x \quad S\,x(x)\,p \quad S$$
and sume mislice ofsloh   (4)[4]

$$x \quad x \quad S \quad x(x)p \quad S \quad x$$
sume hreowlice acwealde   (2)

$$Sr \quad x \quad x \quad S \quad x$$
sume hi man blende   (3)

$$x \quad x \quad S \quad S\,x$$
10 sume hættode   (5)

$$x \quad S \quad x \quad x\,x \quad S \quad x$$
gedon on þison earde   (1)

$$x \quad x \quad S \quad S\,x$$
and her frið namon   (5)

$$x \quad x \quad S \quad x \quad Sr$$
to ðan leofan gode   (4)

$$S \quad x \quad x \quad S\,x$$
bliðe mid Criste   (3)

$$x \quad S \quad x\,x\,x \quad S \quad x$$
15 swa earmlice acwealde.   (1)[5]

The metrical system evident in *Alfred* is very similar to that in the *Brut*. Expansion of exactly one dip has become obligatory. The desuetude of the four-position principle, coupled with the reinterpretation of verses with formerly omissible prefixes in anacrusis (11b), has caused the Old

English pattern Sx(x . . .)Sx (Sievers Type A) to acquire an optional third dip, either short with long medial dip (15b) or long with short medial dip (8b). Unlike the later *Chastity, Alfred* lacks the conservative Old English pattern SxSx (Sievers Type A) in the b-verse. Taken together, *Chastity* and *Alfred* furnish evidence of the synchronic diversity of metrical styles. Fifteen late Old English poems omitted from *ASPR*, including *Chastity*, are scanned in Appendix A. Each of these poems exhibits a dynamic mixture of more conservative and more innovative metrical features.

The formal trajectory running from the *Beowulf* meter to the *Brut* meter belies the perception of decline and decay after 950. All of the "defective verses" that R. D. Fulk identifies in *Durham* (1104–1109) are metrical when viewed from the diachronic perspective developed in this chapter, e.g.:

	S S x S x	
4a	ea yðum stronge	(three lifts)
	S x S Sr x	
7b	wilda deor monige	(three lifts)
	x x x x Sx S	
9a	Is in ðere byri eac	(4)
	x x x S x p S x	
20a	ðær monia wundrum gewurðað.[6]	(2)

The "anomalous" anacrusis that Fulk notes in the *Battle of Maldon* (*c*. 991) and the "[e]xtraordinary anacrusis" he discerns in *Durham* are also characteristic of the emergent system, e.g.:

	x Sr x x S x	
Maldon 32b	mid gafole forgyldon	(1)
	x S x x S x	
Maldon 66b	to lang hit him þuhte.	(1)
	x S x x S x	
Durham 5b	on floda gemonge.[7]	(1)

Occasional lack of metrical resolution of short, stressed syllables (as in *Durham* 9a *by-* in *byri* 'town') is one predictable result of the destabilization of resolution and the four-position principle. The acceptability of Type 2 (*Durham* 20a) is another.

The metrical developments surveyed thus far mark the disintegration of a set of interdependent structures typified by the *Beowulf* meter: the four-position principle, metrical resolution, the prefix license, and a morphological basis for metrical stress. Yet the same metrical developments also herald the incipient normative force of a new set of interdependent structures typified by the *Brut* meter: exactly two lifts in the b-verse, exactly one long dip in the b-verse, decreasing symmetry of a-verse and b-verse patterns (Ch. 3), and an accentual basis for metrical stress. The second point is the crucial one missed by all commentators before Yakovlev. Hence the standard judgment that late Old English and Early Middle English alliterative meter is 'irregular.' We are now equipped to say that the net change in regularity from Old English to late Old English to Early Middle English alliterative meter was effectively zero: to the extent that one synchronically coherent configuration of metrical norms began to be effaced, a new configuration began to take shape. The meter of *Maldon* and *Durham* is only "defective," "extraordinary," or "anomalous" from the perspective of a typologically earlier moment in verse history.

The formal differences between undated and late Old English poetry reflect ongoing metrical evolution. More precisely, the observable evolution of the alliterative meter after 950 implies the unobservable evolution of the alliterative meter before 950. It is only the organization of Old English metrics around *Beowulf* at one end and the Norman Conquest of England (1066) at the other that creates a monolithic 'classical' line in the first place. The long metrical evolution narrated in this book offers a counterweight to the prioritization of the *Beowulf* meter in Old English metrics. Like the *Beowulf* poet, late Old English poets practiced metrical styles in use at the time. And like the *Beowulf* poet, they were successful. In the late tenth and eleventh centuries, more innovative metrical styles included more long dips, less metrical resolution, and innovative metrical patterns, not because poets were losing touch with a static tradition, but because they were engaged in a dynamic one.

To summarize the arguments of this section thus far: an improvement in understanding of the *Beowulf* meter and the *Brut* meter ensures an improvement in understanding of late Old English meter and alliterative verse history from Old to Early Middle English. We can go further. These four schemes – the *Beowulf* meter, late Old English meter, the *Brut* meter, and the evolutionary arc that connects them – are best conceptualized as four expressions of the same historical formation, the alliterative tradition. Each of the four schemes gains its fullest historical significance when we are able to observe the way in which it interlocks all three of the others. Correspondingly, in much prior scholarship, isolated and synchronic focus on the *Beowulf* meter, the dim view of late Old English meter, the perception of irregularity in the *Brut* meter, and the narrative of metrical death and decline after 950 are four facets of the same misapprehension about a poetic tradition. Yakovlev's dynamic theory of Old English and Early Middle English alliterative meter facilitates a new formalization of late Old English meter, presented in this chapter and in Appendix A; this formalization, in turn, confirms Yakovlev's reconstruction and supplies a deeper and broader evidentiary basis for it.

The survival of a number of datably late Old English poems enables us to create new and powerful evidence of metrical evolution and synchronic diversity between 950 and 1100. Figure 1 compares fifteen post-950 poems that are closely datable on non-metrical grounds. *Terminus post quem* (y-axis) is graphed against six purely metrical features that were unmetrical or rare before 950 but gradually became metrical or common after 950 (x-axis).

The six innovative features are, in descending order of weight: (1) more than 90 percent of b-verses with long dip; (2) Type 2 in the b-verse; (3) Type 1 and/or xSxSx in the b-verse; (4) a-verses with non-b-verse patterns; (5) three-lift b-verses with more than four metrical positions; and (6) complete avoidance of metrical resolution and/or lack of resolution of short, stressed syllables as in *Durham* 9a *byri*. In the next section, I contend that the shape of alliterative verse history before 950 remains unknowable in the absence of closely datable poems. Conversely, the date of *Beowulf* and other long poems remains uncertain without a clearer understanding of developments and trends in alliterative composition before 950. Figure 1 represents the history of alliterative verse as instantiated in several closely datable poems over 150 years. It is against this representation that hypotheses about earlier alliterative verse history should be measured.

Verse History and Language History

Old English metrists have devised a variety of comparative tests for Old English poems, most of which suggest that *Beowulf* is especially conservative.[8] Yet inasmuch as so-called classical Old English meter has been extrapolated from *Beowulf* to begin with, comparative testing risks exaggerating the poem's conservatism or typological primacy. Some tests propose to avoid circularity by correlating metrical history with language history. Such efforts are equivocal, however, for at least three reasons. First, in some cases linguists reconstruct early sound changes from the meter of putatively early poems like *Beowulf* – more *circulus in probando*. Second, in proposing to test a 'text,' ostensibly composed at one time by one poet,

940s	· Capture				
950s					
960s					
970s	· DEdg	· CEdg	· Second DEdg	· YEd · Accession	
980s					
990s		· Maldon			
1000s				· Sweyn Forkbeard	
1010s	· Thureth				
1020s					
1030s				· Death of Alfred	
1040s					
1050s			· Return of Edward		
1060s	· Death of Edward				
1070s				· Chastity	
1080s					· Death of William
1090s					
1100s			· Durham		
closer to Beowulf					**closer to the Brut**

Accession = Accession of Edgar the Peaceful (975–1051)
Capture = Capture of the Five Boroughs (942–55)
Chastity = Chastity of St. Margaret (1070–71)
CEdg = Coronation of Edgar (973–78)
Death of Alfred (1036–45)
Death of Edward (1066)
Death of William = Death of William the Conqueror (1087–1121)
DEdg = Death of Edgar (975–78)
Durham (1104–1109)
Maldon = Battle of Maldon (c. 991)
Return of Edward = Return of Edward the Exile (1057–61)
Second DEdg = Second Death of Edgar (975–1051)
Sweyn Forkbeard = Sweyn Forkbeard Razes Wilton (1003–45)
Thureth (c. 1011)
YEd = Young Edward the Martyr (978–1051)

For the Chronicle poems, *termini post quem* correspond to the dates of the events, being the date of entry except for *Accession* and *Young Edward* (975 and 978, respectively, since they speak of the reigns of Edgar and Edward with the past tense marker *on his dagum*), *Death of Edward* (*recte* 1066), *Chastity* (*recte* 1070), and *Death of William* (*recte* 1087). *Termini ad quem* are given by the date of the hands of the earliest witnesses, fixable with some precision due to scribal changeovers: Ker, *Catalogue*, items 39, 188, 191, 192, and 346; *ASPR* 6, pp. xxxii–xxxvi; and the introds. to *ASCCE* 3–7. Ker identifies seven relevant stints: MS A to 955; MS C to 1045 and to 1066; MS D to 1051, to 1061, and to 1071; and MS E to 1121. MS B was likely copied between 977 and March 978, since Edward's regnal years are left blank in a genealogy in the same hand. *Thureth* was composed after the Council of Enham (1008–11), whose canons follow *Thureth* in the MS to which the poem presumably refers: *ASPR* 6, pp. lxxxviii–xc. The handwriting of the text of *Thureth*, dated 's. x/xi' by Ker, *Catalogue*, item 141, sets a close upper limit for both poem and MS. For the date of *Durham* see *ASPR* 6, pp. xliv–xlv, disputed now by O'Donnell, "Old English *Durham*."

Figure 1. Datably Late Old English Poems in Alliterative Verse History

metrists must rely on historically inappropriate conceptions of authorship and textual transmission. When multiple copies of a single poem survive, it is evident that scribes often felt free to revise their exemplars, not in violation of metrical principles, but in accordance with them. Different degrees of scribal interventionism could skew evident linguistic-metrical differences between received texts. Third, as I will argue, metrists have been overly optimistic in assuming that metrically significant linguistic form mirrors contemporary linguistic form except in poetic formulas or identifiable instances of conscious archaizing. On the contrary, the linguistic forms encoded by alliterative meter were pervasively conservative. Phantom syllables, absent from contemporary speech but present in the meter, persisted well beyond ossified formulas or synchronically recoverable linguistic forms. In order to emphasize the independence of verse history from language history, I refer to metrically significant linguistic form as 'metrical phonology.'

That alliterative meter encodes conservative linguistic forms has long been recognized. For example, metrical resolution recapitulates equivalences that are hypothesized to have obtained in prehistoric Old English, when quantity played a larger role in linguistic phonology. Yet resolution remained a regular feature of alliterative meter as late as *c.* 1200 (in Lawman's *Brut*). Recent work in Middle English metrics finds twelfth- and thirteenth-century final *-e* alive and well in fourteenth-, fifteenth-, and even sixteenth-century alliterative meter (Chs. 4 and 6). In *Beowulf* one encounters uncontracted forms of words that had lost intervocalic *-h-* as in *gan* and *seon* ('non-contraction'), lack of vowel parasiting in historically monosyllabic words like *morðor* and *tacen* ('non-parasiting'), compensatory lengthening of vowels following loss of *h* without subsequent analogical shortening in inflected forms of words like *feorh* and *mearh*, a distinction between historically short and historically long unstressed syllables for the purposes of metrical resolution ('Kaluza's law'), an 'elliptical' dual (2002b *uncer Grendles*), *i*-stem genitive plurals in *-ia*, uninflected infinitives after *to*, and weak adjectives without determiners. *Beowulf* also has contracted forms, vowel parasiting, analogical shortening of vowels in inflected forms of words like *feorh*, *i*-stem genitive plurals in *-a*, inflected infinitives after *to*, and weak adjectives with determiners, establishing that the composition of the poem postdates these linguistic developments.[9]

Most of these linguistically conservative metrical features appear, though less frequently, in datably late poetry. *The Battle of Maldon*, for example, has three possible instances of non-parasiting (130b *wæpen*, 202b *ealdor*, and 282a *broðor*, the last two unetymological), one instance of compensatory lengthening (239b *meare*), and complete adherence to Kaluza's law (but only three relevant verses: 61a, 262a, and 322a). Finally, in *Death of Edgar* 11 (975–78), *Maldon* 256, and *Death of Edward* 12 (1066), velar and palatal *c-* alliterate together, whereas the two phonemes had diverged in the Old English language by the ninth century at the latest.[10] Clearly, their co-alliteration in some poems was a poetic convention, not a reflection of linguistic reality. Co-alliteration of velar and palatal *c-* is therefore irrelevant to dating, unless the desuetude of the poetic convention itself could be precisely dated – wholly a matter for metrics in that case, not linguistics. And so on for each metrical feature that encodes older linguistic forms.

Thus the effect of linguistic change on meter is always mediated by historical processes within the metrical system. This claim is more general than the usual objection that poets could have had antiquarian sentiments or special linguistic knowledge. Archaizing is only one of many rhetorical strategies that poets might effect through available metrical techniques; and poets need not have understood, e.g., the linguistic phenomenon of contraction in order to understand that *don, gan, hean*, etc., could notionally occupy two metrical positions. Sometimes poets can be caught getting etymology wrong, as in *Beowulf* 2894a *morgenlongne dæg*, with monosyllabic *morgen-*, a word that was historically disyllabic.[11] At other times, a poet's linguistic belatedness is concealed in poetic convention, as when the *Maldon* poet versified in accordance with Kaluza's law, which corresponds to a phonological opposition that had vanished from the spoken language centuries prior. The point to make is not only that poets' practice was far more sophisticated than contemporary understandings of that practice could have been, but also that this state of affairs obtained both before and after linguistic change. So for example the mental processes that encode *don* as a disyllable in Old English meter were as abstract and notional before as after the contraction of *don* in the Old English language. The precise means by which metrical competence passed from generation to generation have only just begun to attract the attention of metrists and literary historians, but the effects of metrical hysteresis, or what might be called the stickiness of meter, are everywhere apparent.

The methodological problem with linguistic-metrical testing lies in what I have called a category mistake: treating metrical evolution as though it were a type of linguistic evolution. Metaphors drawn from historical linguistics have been so thoroughly internalized in Old English metrics that they have ceased to be perceived as metaphors. Metrists speak of the 'rule' of the coda, the 'conditioning' of Kaluza's 'law,' etc., purporting to have described linguistic regularities affected directly by linguistic change. So Fulk states that "[Old English] poets attempted to be as conservative as possible" and that "Old English verse is more like everyday speech" than like later English poetry.[12] Both programmatic statements illustrate the reduction of verse history to language history, the neutralization of the momentum of a poetic tradition, queried in the present chapter and throughout this book.

In a purely metrical perspective, one might ask why features like non-parasiting should be chronological criteria to begin with. Such features may have served as stylistic ornamentation, used more heavily by some poets than by others. One need not lapse into "an essentially post-Romantic view of the poet as Genius" in order to believe that Old English poets had an intuitive sense of poetic style, however attenuated by traditionality.[13] For example, while *Beowulf* has a more extensively conservative metrical phonology than many other poems, this is true both of etymologically justified non-parasiting as in 2742a *morðorbealo maga* and of faux or unetymological non-parasiting as in *morgenlongne dæg*. Twelve possible instances of faux non-parasiting occur in *Beowulf*, as compared with eight possible instances in most of the rest of the corpus combined.[14] The proper conclusion is not that *Beowulf* is earlier. Any poet familiar with non-parasiting could have drawn the etymologically false analogy *morgen : morgne :: tacen : tacne*, and some did. Rather, the proper conclusion is that our poet aimed for an elevated metrical style. Whether metrical tradition had preserved for him etymological or unetymological linguistic values seems to have been of no concern whatsoever to the *Beowulf* poet. Style is the obvious explanation for the concentration of verses like *morgenlongne dæg*, and it remains a plausible explanation for all the other metrical features more common in *Beowulf* than elsewhere. For the existence of non-parasiting in alliterative verse, historical explanations must be sought; but for the treatment of non-parasiting in any given poetic text, stylistic explanations remain compelling.

The difficulties inherent in linguistic-metrical approaches to poetic chronology have encouraged a peculiar sort of wordplay, whereby 'archaic' means 'old' or 'conservative' as needed. *Klaeber's Beowulf* contains over sixty references to "archaic" features and "archaisms." When the editors speak of "[t]he linguistic changes that the poem's archaic features would seem to precede," it is unclear whether the features are old or conservative, or whether they only "would seem to," or really do, belong to an earlier era. When the editors offer evidence that "the poem's language is archaic because the work was composed early," "archaic" must mean 'old.' Yet the concession that "O[ld]E[nglish] poetic language is archaic by nature" requires "archaic" to mean 'conservative.'

Equivocation is the predictable result of an approach that fails to establish a necessary relationship between language history and verse history. The *Beowulf* poet's fidelity to Kaluza's law is held to indicate that "the distinction between the relevant long and short final vowels had not yet been eliminated when *Beowulf* was composed, or at least," the editors quickly add, "had only very recently been eliminated (as the poet's strict conformity to the law would seem to suggest)."[15] If conformity to Kaluza's law can only "seem to suggest" a date "recently" after *c.* 725, then a fortiori it cannot establish a date before *c.* 725. How "recently" is "recently" is a question that linguistics by itself cannot answer, for all the reasons given above. Recall that metrical resolution, which recapitulates prehistoric Old English phonology, survived into the thirteenth century. Or again, twelfth- and thirteenth-century linguistic -*e*'s are used correctly and extensively in fourteenth-, fifteenth-, and even sixteenth-century alliterative meter (Chs. 4 and 6). Datably post-950 Old English poems exhibit the phenomena described by Kaluza's law less frequently than *Beowulf*, but no less regularly. To date a metrical feature by dating a linguistic feature that it encodes, or once encoded, is to mistake one kind of historical form for another.

In my view, a more methodologically sound approach would be to develop purely metrical tests based on changes in the meter itself, as in Figure 1. Because there are good empirical and theoretical reasons to connect them with metrical evolution, the six criteria used in Figure 1 directly measure formal conservatism in a way that linguistic-metrical criteria would not. If the fifteen poems in Figure 1 show considerable synchronic variation in even these most structurally significant features, then, a fortiori, incidental features like non-parasiting will not provide the smooth, century-by-century progression that metrists seek. Instead of stipulating a constant and universal rate of metrical change a priori, Figure 1 maps the metrical conservatism of individual poems against time.

As is to be expected, Figure 1 shows a clear direction of development from the earlier, *Beowulf*-like poems to the later, *Brut*-like ones. Nevertheless, some poems diverge considerably from the metrical mainstream. What may be one of the oldest, the *Accession of Edgar* (975–1051), is among the most metrically innovative of the group, while one of the youngest, *Death of Edward*, is the most metrically conservative of the group (along with the earlier *Capture of the Five Boroughs*, 942–55; *Death of Edgar*; and *Thureth, c.* 1011).

The variation evident in Figure 1 argues for a wide range of metrical styles in use at any one time. If *Beowulf* was as conservative as the *Death of Edward* relative to its own verse-historical moment, then it could have been composed long after its style of meter occupied the mainstream. Figure 1 shows that alliterative meter evolved in broadly identifiable ways, but it does not hold out much hope for dating any given text on a metrical basis. Were it possible to create a graph like Figure 1 for the period 700–950, in and of itself this would not date *Beowulf*, but it would at least fix a sense of scale and directionality to earlier metrical developments. As it is, none of the six innovative features represented in Figure 1 can distinguish *Beowulf* from *Capture of the Five Boroughs, Death of Edgar, Thureth*, or even as late a poem as *Death of Edward*. Figure 1 demonstrates the tenuousness of modern judgments about alliterative verse history. Had only *Accession, Sweyn Forkbeard Razes Wilton* (1003–45), *Return of Edward the Exile* (1057–61), and *Death of Edward* (seventy-five lines in all) happened to survive, scholars might have concluded on a metrical basis that the *Brut* predated *Beowulf* (Fig. 2)!

If this seems like an idle thought experiment, consider that there exists far less uncontroverted evidence for alliterative meter before 850 (twenty-one lines in all).[16] The problem with metrical testing, then, is not only that *Beowulf* might be conservative vis-à-vis the metrical mainstream, but also that the metrical mainstream itself cannot be reconstructed in any usable detail for the decades before 950.

If the dates of *Accession* and *Death of Edward* could not be fixed on internal evidence, metrical tests would place them the wrong way round in literary history by a century or more. This should be considered a failure of a most fundamental kind, because it is symptomatic of a reductive conception of verse history. The proposition that metrically more conservative poems are invariably and proportionally earlier than metrically more innovative poems is false for the poems in Figure 1. It is also false for later alliterative poems. For example, recent studies find that *Sir Gawain and the Green Knight* (late fourteenth century) has an extensively conservative metrical phonology, which counts nearly all historically justified final -*e*'s, while *Piers Plowman* (c. 1370–90) appears to have a moderately conservative metrical phonology, which sometimes discounts some historically justified -*e*'s. Comparison to post-950 alliterative poetry implies a far more complex verse-historical situation before 950 than proponents of metrical tests for chronology had hoped.

The charts drawn up by Geoffrey Russom, in which Old English poems rate 'bad,' 'so-so,' 'good,' or 'best,' and 'early,' 'middle,' or 'late,' represent one of the more nuanced attempts to establish a poetic chronology on metrical grounds. Russom starts from a summary of "expert judgments" about the date and literary quality of each poem, based on the proportion of "anomalous verses" or "metrical faults" in each.[17] He then sifts through dating criteria in search of those that uphold the "expert judgments" within the context of his word-foot theory of Old English meter. Poems with few "metrical faults" are judged 'best' and 'early' by the experts, and the best dating criteria are those that reinforce this judgment. By design, Russom ignores criteria that would point in other directions, either to conservative 'late' poems, e.g., *Death of Edward*, or to "anomalous verses" in 'best' poems, e.g., innovative five-position patterns in *Beowulf*. "Diachronic studies of meter," Russom explains, "begin with the hypothesis that language change makes it increasingly difficult to compose in a traditional form." Yet the word-foot theory abstracts the "traditional form" of Old English meter precisely by equating linguistic and metrical units. The ostensible correspondence between language history and verse history then acts as a fundamental principle of analysis as well as a historical zero-point. While Russom usefully adopts a diachronic perspective, reference to "anomalous verses" and "metrical faults" still implies a static metrical system gradually effaced by linguistic change.

In a purely metrical perspective, it is not obvious why Russom's chosen criteria should represent chronological change to the exclusion of generic, stylistic, or diatopic variation. Even if Russom's criteria are chronologically significant, a 'bad'-to-'best' scale seems insufficiently fine-grained to capture the kind of fluid synchronic variation evident in Figure 1. Indeed, literary quality may not be the most important synchronic variable. *Sir Gawain and the Green Knight* and *Piers Plowman* are both excellent compositions, and both date from the late fourteenth century, but their metrical phonologies are dissimilar. Russom stipulates that "all other things being equal, the earlier of two poems should exhibit the stricter versecraft."[18] This may be a generally valid deduction, but it is unclear how one might determine whether "all other things" are "equal" in any given comparison. The evolution of a dynamic metrical tradition is not likely to be reducible to a chart like Russom's under the best of circumstances. Figure 1 shows that, on average, innovative features occur more frequently in later poems. That much is by definition: I identified metrical features as 'innovative' precisely by observing how they change over time across a corpus of independently datable poetry. Yet Figure 1 also discourages the expectation that each individual poem will represent the mainstream.

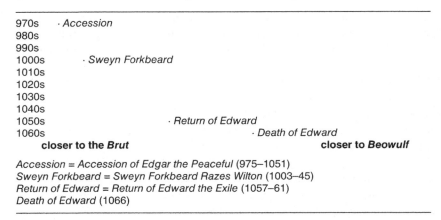

970s	· Accession	
980s		
990s		
1000s	· Sweyn Forkbeard	
1010s		
1020s		
1030s		
1040s		
1050s	· Return of Edward	
1060s		· Death of Edward
closer to the *Brut*		**closer to *Beowulf***

Accession = Accession of Edgar the Peaceful (975–1051)
Sweyn Forkbeard = Sweyn Forkbeard Razes Wilton (1003–45)
Return of Edward = Return of Edward the Exile (1057–61)
Death of Edward (1066)

Figure 2. Select Datably Late Old English Poems in (Reverse) Alliterative Verse History

A subsidiary problem faced by any comparative approach to poetic chronology is the problem of scale. It is strictly speaking impossible to derive an absolute chronology from a comparison of undated poems. Even if "anomalous verses" and lateness were held to correlate absolutely, at best Russom's argument would deliver a relative chronology. *Beowulf* and *Exodus*, labeled 'early' by Russom, could in that case be products of the 850s; *Andreas* and the Cynewulf corpus, labeled 'middle,' could hail from the 910s. The chronological spread of Russom's 'early,' 'middle,' and 'late' is not an effect of his own argumentation. As he is careful to note, it is adopted from a summary of previous scholarly consensus assembled (and challenged) by Cable in 1981.[19] The architects of the previous consensus presupposed that the extant corpus covered the Old English period more or less democratically and that metrical development plodded along at a constant pace for four centuries. Neither assumption is supported by comparison with later and more firmly datable alliterative verse. The majority of extant post-1300 alliterative poems fit in a slender 75-year window, 1350–1425. And the a-verse changed more rapidly between 1250 and 1350 than previously or subsequently: a-verse/b-verse symmetry dropped from *c.* 95% to 65% between 950 and 1250, but it dropped from *c.* 65% to 5% between 1250 and 1350.

One final consideration requires a theoretical excursus. It has been urged that, if a very early date for *Beowulf* cannot be *proven*, it can be rendered more *probable* than any alternative. The quibble on Latin *probare* conceals a misapprehension of the scientific method. In experimentation, a conclusion is valid only when extraneous variables have been ruled out ('controlled'). Otherwise, the results tend to represent a melange of factors in unknown proportion ('confounded'). Yet the fragmentary nature of the Old English poetic corpus makes it quite difficult to control for non-chronological variables.

Take conservatism, for example. If *Beowulf* is metrically conservative, it will test earlier than it is. This is so, regardless of the quantity or variety of recognizably conservative features it contains, since a density of conservative features is exactly what would be expected in a conservative poem. To control for conservatism, one would have to measure *Beowulf* against comparably conservative poems. However, the metrical conservatism of undated poems cannot be ascertained. Some metrical features, e.g., non-parasiting, might reasonably be identified as conservative in advance of speculation about dating. Yet the degree of their conservatism in a given poem depends on dating: non-parasiting in a tenth-century poem is a more conservative feature than non-parasiting in an eighth-century poem. Moreover, there may occur other, subtler conservative features that do not appear as such to metrical analysis until a date has been determined for the poem in question – the more so if, as I have recommended, the metrical features under discussion are purely metrical, like the four-position principle, rather than linguistic-metrical, like non-parasiting.

Other potential confounding factors are genre, geographical origins, and scribal revision. To extrapolate from metrical phonology to poetic chronology, metrists must proceed as though non-chronological factors had little or no effect on metrical practice. This is the meaning of Russom's provisional "all other things being equal." No sooner is the provision made, however, than pre-Conquest England becomes a colorless world, where perfectly average poets plug away at perfectly average poems ad infinitum. Figure 1 contradicts this portrait. Whether style, genre, geography, or (probably) some combination of these factors, it is plain that something other than the passage of time caused considerable variation in the handling of meter.

Nor do regularities in the distribution of conservative features across the corpus reveal that synchronic variables had a negligible effect.[20] Rather, it may be the synchronic variables that caused the regularities. Distribution of metrical features along stylistic, generic, or geographical lines, or in accordance with the tastes of a poetic community or a program of metrical revision by editor-scribes, is not a remote possibility. It is the predictable (and after 950 observable) result of literary fashions, genre conventions, cultural formations, and textual *mouvance*. There is every indication that the extant corpus is not drawn democratically from all regions and all centuries, but that it reflects the tastes and resources of those few who compiled it, *c*. 950–1025. For example, one of the few securely identifiable groups of Old English poems – the Cynewulf corpus – is not scattered throughout the manuscript record but clustered in two codices. Or again, ninety-six of the ninety-seven texts of Old English riddles are contained in a single codex. One of the longest Old English poetic compositions, the *Meters of Boethius*, is a revision of the corresponding portions of the Old English prose *Boethius* and thus may not be metrically comparable to poems composed from scratch. The extant poetic corpus can be expected to overrepresent certain literary fashions, compositional procedures, or scribal-editorial programs of whose very existence we remain ignorant.

More particularly, datable poems are almost always datable because they refer to proximal historical events. Inasmuch as there exist no datable long Old English poems set in the distant past, metrical testing cannot control for genre. (On length and historical setting as genre criteria, see the next chapter.) The datably late poems may overrepresent a less formal metrical style felt to be appropriate to contemporary events or falling within the competence of less talented chronicler-poets. Statisticians refer to such phenomena as 'sampling bias.' The potential for sampling bias associated with a tiny and mostly undated corpus constitutes yet another factor whose effect is unknowable, and for which, therefore, metrists have not even the theoretical ability to control. Notwithstanding Fulk's insistence that "scientists *must* decide which is the most likely hypothesis," the scientific method does not require practitioners to draw conclusions when all hypotheses are very tenuous.[21] The term reserved by the scientific community for complex effects without isolable causes is 'not well understood.'

The few surviving datably early Old English poems differ in material context from the bulk of Old English verse. Their value as anchor-texts for literary history is therefore limited. Fulk interprets datably early poems found in late manuscripts as evidence that some of the undated poems must be early.[22] Yet *Cædmon's Hymn* (late seventh/early eighth centuries), *A Proverb from Winfrid's Time* (eighth century), and *Bede's Death Song* (eighth/ninth centuries) are all incidental to Latin prose works, which proliferated for reasons quite unrelated to Old English verse.[23] (The same material conditions account for the survival of dozens of copies of a few Middle English alliterative poems. I discuss one such embedded snippet in Ch. 5.) The Franks Casket inscription (eighth century), recorded in runes on a whalebone box, is even less materially analogous to anthologized manuscript texts like that of *Beowulf*.

The synchronic variety of poetic styles and the uneven survival of evidence for poetic communities come together in a recent book-length study by Emily Thornbury. By combining Old English and Anglo-Latin evidence, Thornbury rebuts the presumption that 'poet' and 'poem' were privileged, transcendental categories whose meanings changed little over time and across space. Instead, she posits contemporaneous "poetic sub-dialects" corresponding to various communities, real or imagined.[24] Crucially, Thornbury's "sub-dialects," while modeled on linguistic dialects, refer to interpretive rather than linguistic communities. Most notably, Thornbury discerns the contours of a 'Southern mode' of late ninth- and tenth-century Old English poetry, marked by a modernized lexicon, Latinate style, and southerly provenance. Metrical differences between *Beowulf* and poems of the Southern mode, such as the *Meters of Boethius* and the *Paris Psalter*, serve as important points of comparison in many dating arguments. Yet these metrical differences may primarily register the fact that *Beowulf* is not in the Southern mode. It belongs to some other poetic sub-dialect, as yet unidentified, unplaced, and undated. Thornbury does not address the contentions of metrists, but the implications for verse history are there to be drawn out. She concludes her discussion of the Southern mode with a pointed caveat: "Accidents of preservation have made the tenth and eleventh centuries better known to us than earlier ones: but there is no reason to believe that late Anglo-Saxon England was alone in having multiple poetic modes simultaneously available."[25] By checking hypotheses about pre-950 alliterative verse history against Figure 1, I mean to raise the same caveat from a metrical perspective. Figure 1 lends empirical support to the intuition that the historical development of metrical systems is always complex.

In sum, metrical testing for chronology is fraught with several kinds of difficulty. It explicitly assumes the reality of controverted theoretical concepts, such as 'foot,' and it implicitly assumes the value of unknown quantities, such as the conservatism of *Beowulf*.[26] Most significantly, I have contended that using any preconceived model of pre-950 verse history in order to discover the date of *Beowulf* amounts to *ignotum per ignotius*. Tethering verse history to language history begs the question, for the relationship between metrical form and linguistic form is mediated by structures and processes within verse history. Research at the intersection of metrics and linguistics has achieved a succession of theoretical and empirical accomplishments in Old English studies, especially in recent decades. Metrical features such as the prefix license and resolution are clarified and historicized with the insight that they recapitulate familiar linguistic structures. Interdisciplinary research in this field, however, has almost always proceeded by stipulating a priori the relationship between what I characterize as two independent historical formations, verse history and language history. In my view, judgments about the historically mediated interactions of these two formations should be informed by, but must never be built into, procedures of metrical analysis.

Beowulf and the Unknown Shape of Old English Literary History

The uncanny power of *Beowulf* lies in its attentiveness to its own multivalent past. The specially ambiguous adverb/conjunction *syððan* 'later; ever since' crops up at key moments to connect story to backstory, as in the introduction of Scyld Scefing (quoted from *Klaeber's Beowulf*, ed. Fulk, Bjork, and Niles; translation mine):

> Oft Scyld Scefing   sceaþena þreatum,
> monegum mægþum   meodosetla ofteah,
> egsode eorl[as],   syððan ærest wearð
> feasceaft funden.

("Often Scyld Scefing took mead-benches from troops of enemies, from many a tribe – frightened warriors, ever since he was discovered, a foundling.") (4–7a)

The pivot from past to origins is characteristic. In *Beowulf*, events never just happen. There is always baggage. The poet uses *syððan* to point up epochal events – Sigemund's dragon-slaying (886a), the Flood (1689b), the death of Ongentheow (2996b) – that, like Woodstock or the Battle of Gettysburg, evoke foundational eras.[27] Even the future has depth, as in the long feud foretold by the Geatish messenger (2911a "orleghwile" "period of war"). The poet takes pains to convey the passing of time between each of Beowulf's feats (1257b "lange þrage" "for a long time" and 2200b "ufaran dogrum" "in later days"), suggesting triple peaks of heroism protruding from obscurer lowlands. The poet was an expert in the Old English equivalent of montages and flashbacks. At times the building up of temporal perspective becomes intensely idiomatic, and *syððan* means something like 'when':

> No þæt læsest wæs
> 2355 hondgemot(a)   þær mon Hygelac sloh,
> syððan Geata cyning   guðe ræsum,
> freawine folca   Freslondum on,
> Hreðles eafora   hiorodryncum swealt.

("That was not the smallest meeting of arms, where Hygelac was killed, when the Geatish king, offspring of Hrethel, generous lord of the people, died by sword-drinks, in the press of battle, in Frisian territory.") (2354b–58)

"Where Hygelac was killed, when the Geatish king ... died" sounds redundant to modern ears, but the two dependent clauses achieve different poetic effects. First the poet recounts the battle in Frisia, then the frame of reference opens outward to include the stretch of years between Hygelac's death and Beowulf's dragon-fight. The poet serves up the raid on Frisia in short view and long view, making clear, without condescending to explain it, the connection between digression and action.

Given this recursive attention to origins within the poem, every aspect of the poem's style should be suspected of contributing to its historicist aesthetic. Words in *Beowulf* singled out by modern scholars as 'archaic' are likely to refer to some burnished thing, lost to time in the poet's own day. One recent argument for a very early *Beowulf* is Dennis Cronan's argument from lexis.[28] Cronan's list of simplexes occurring uniquely in *Beowulf* and one other poem reads like a list of fancy words for distant worlds. In the distant past, a king is not only a *cyning*, but a *þengel* (1507a) and an *eodor* (428a, 663a, and 1044a); a ship is not only a *scip*, but a *fær* (33b); a sword is not only a *sword*, but a *heoru* (1285a). These words occur a handful of times, as if someone had tried to spice *Beowulf* with as many exotic flavors as possible. The simplexes found only in *Beowulf* and a group of poems suspected early by Cronan (*Daniel, Exodus, Genesis A, Maxims I,* and *Widsith*) are certainly striking evidence of overlapping wordhoards. As against a generic explanation for the co-occurrences, Cronan objects that "[t]he poems in question belong to a range of genres, including heroic epic, gnomic verse, catalogue verse and biblical history." Yet these are modern categories denoting kinds of subject matter, not medieval categories denoting kinds of poem. The next chapter uses formal evidence to extrapolate a more organic typology of Old English poems, in which, incidentally, *Beowulf* is grouped with *Daniel, Exodus, Genesis A,* and *Widsith*. Cronan also doubts a stylistic explanation for the shared words. "It is possible that these poems belong to a local tradition or school of poetry," he reasons. "But we know nothing of such schools – not even if they existed – and explaining this conservative diction through an unknown is poor methodology."[29] I have argued that Figure 1 and other evidence supports the presumption of "poetic sub-dialects" before 950. The diversity and robustness of pre-950 verse history is only "an unknown" in the evidential sense that it cannot be directly observed, not in the ontological sense that it may not have obtained. Whether poems with similar wordhoards constitute dedicated "schools" or merely register the pressure of other historical formations (audience, genre, geography, contact with Old Norse literature, etc.) must remain an open question.

The caution that one should avoid explaining phenomena through an unknown quantity applies no less to chronological arguments than to other kinds. Without assuming beforehand the poetic chronology one means to discover, it is impossible to measure the lifespan of any given lexical item. Very few of the simplexes discussed by Cronan appear in prose or glosses of any period, suggesting the pervasive conservatism of the alliterative poetic lexicon throughout its history. Indeed, Cronan begins by defining 'poetic simplex' as "any simple word ... whose occurrence is either completely restricted to poetry, or whose use in prose or glosses seems to be exceptional in some way," a selection procedure reified by his subsequent argument that "the complete absence of *suhtriga* from prose of any period coupled with its use in poetry and its preservation in a series of archaic glosses makes it clear that this is a word which became obsolete early in the Anglo-Saxon period."[30] A more obvious explanation for the rarity of *suhtriga* 'brother's son' is that nephews rarely appear in Old English poetry: the more prosaic synonyms *broðorsunu* 'brother's son,' *broðor bearn* 'brother's child,' and *nefa* 'nephew' together occur in only four poems (*Beowulf, Genesis A, Riddle 1*, and *Return of Edward*). The two longest of these, *Beowulf* and *Genesis A*, also contain forms of *suhtriga*.

Rare poetic words for more common things, like *fær* 'ship,' may well have flourished more in one century, region, community, genre, or level of formality than another; but rarity by itself cannot serve to distinguish diachronic variation from the many other kinds of variation within poetic tradition. As a feature of style, poetic lexis characterizes the alliterative tradition from Old to Middle English. In 1066 the *Death of Edward* poet was still rhapsodizing about a *wel geþungen* 'well-thriven' ruler (9a and *Beowulf* 1927a), *oretmægcum* 'champions' (11b and *Beowulf* 332a, 363b, and 481b), *hagestealde* 'young warriors' (14b and *Beowulf* 1889a), and a *þeodkyning* 'national king' (34b and *Beowulf* 2a, 2144a, 2694b, etc.). On the eve of the Norman Conquest, the old language of the *comitatus* was still just the right thing for eulogizing kings in conservative poetry. The relationship of *Beowulf* to newer and older lexical sets will have been no less mediated by the (unknown) contours of its verse-historical moment.

Beowulf has a way of creating its historical context, Tennessee-jar-like. A second recent argument for a very early *Beowulf* is Leonard Neidorf's argument from cultural change. Neidorf shows how a tale of the heroic yesteryear would have appealed to an Æthelredian audience, only to argue that the heroes themselves had "fallen out of cultural memory" by 1000. "[A]t a time when the past, including the migration-era past, had acquired newfound urgency and importance," English audiences set a high price on "unfamiliarity and antiquity." In the eleventh century, Neidorf explains, "it did not matter if characters were unknown or allusions were befuddling," so long as the events took place *in geardagum* 'in the days of yore' (1b).[31] There is something odd about all this. Surely English audiences did not give up understanding literary allusions on the eve of the second millennium. Stripped of any meaning, the numerous digressions in *Beowulf* make for hard going. Moreover, from the opening scene of a pagan ship burial through the fight with an ancient fire-breathing dragon, "unfamiliarity and antiquity" are integral to the poetic project of *Beowulf* and will have contributed to its appeal at any given moment in literary history. The very existence of the *Beowulf* manuscript, then, problematizes any cultural cataclysm of the kind postulated by Neidorf. In dating *Beowulf* by reconstructing early literary and cultural history, Neidorf projects cultural change as a totalized and irrevocable boundary separating monolithic historical periods that coincide with monolithic periods of literary production. As against such a schematic historicism, the example of the *Death of Edward* shows how cultural knowledge is preserved and refracted through the prism of poetic style.

In a series of essays with overlapping arguments, Neidorf also attributes chronological significance to scribal errors of proper names in the *Beowulf* manuscript. According to Neidorf, "the collective presence of scribal errors of proper names in the *Beowulf* manuscript indicates that the scribes were largely unaware of the heroic-legendary traditions constituting *Beowulf;* that these traditions were no longer in widespread circulation by the time the manuscript was copied out ... and perhaps well before then."[32] Of thirty-seven errors listed by Neidorf, most are of an assuredly mechanical nature, e.g., MS *wereda* 'troops' at 2186a for presumptive *Wedera* 'Weders.' Some bespeak misprision of meter and syntax without misrecognition of the names, e.g., MS *fres cyning* 'Frisian king' (nominative singular) at 2503b for presumptive *Frescyninge* (dative singular). Six may not be errors at all.[33]

Neidorf's analysis presupposes that scribes would not or could not miscopy names of figures known to them or their contemporaries. Evidence to the contrary is not far to seek. In an important study of Old English scribal *habitus*, Kenneth Sisam noted multiple scribal errors of biblical names in the Exeter Book and the Junius MS (both late tenth century).[34] The text of *Genesis A*, the poem closest in length to *Beowulf,* contains two scribal errors of biblical names noted by Sisam (*leoht* for 1938b *Loth* and *leohtes* for 2402b *Lothes*) and at least eleven others not mentioned by him (186a *Eve* omitted, *sedes* for 1133b *Sethes*, *cain* for 1155b *Cainan*, *caines* for 1160a *Cainanes*, *cham* for 1617a *Chanan*, *ne breðer* for 1628a *Nebroðes*, *carram* for 1747b *Carran*, *siem* for 1783a *Sicem*, 2216a *Sarran* misdivided *sar ran* with an erasure, *agan* for 2252b *Agar*, and *sarran* for 2715b *Sarra*). Scribe A of the *Beowulf* manuscript or an earlier scribe mishandled the name Cain in both of its occurrences (the first later corrected).[35] Yet no one has interpreted these errors as evidence that biblical traditions "were no longer in widespread circulation" by the late tenth century. As might be expected, scribes had difficulty with proper names in general. And textual errors, once committed, tend to persist: if the received text of *Beowulf* is the end result of several transcriptions, each contributing a negligible number of errors of proper names, this would mitigate the impression that late scribes "were largely unaware of . . . heroic-legendary traditions." The equation of textual corruption with cultural change is difficult to justify, because the former occurs routinely without the latter.

If the *Beowulf* scribes did suffer from a case of "cultural amnesia," it must have been very selective, for they copied hundreds of other proper names without incident.[36] The names copied correctly by the scribes include 17 of the 27 names that appear in Neidorf's 37 errors: (-)Dene, Finn, Fres-, Grendel, Heardred, Heathobeard, Hrethric, Hygelac, Ohtere, Ongentheow, Scilfing, Scylding, Sigemund, Sweon, Weder, Weohstan, and Wonred(-). It is tendentious to count the errors but discount the successes. Surely the point to make, by the numbers, is that Scribes A and B were exceedingly familiar with the Northern world of *Beowulf*. Other late scribes, too, successfully transcribed the names of legendary heroes. A few decades earlier, the Exeter Book scribe copied over 200 proper names in the text of *Widsith*, including names found also in *Beowulf*, with as few as 3 evident errors.[37] The scribe of the unique manuscript of Æthelweard's *Chronicon* (copied early eleventh century) managed to spell 'Ingild,' 'Fin,' 'Geat,' 'Beo,' 'Scyld,' and 'Scef.' Beow, Heremod, Scyld, and Scef appear together, with a grand total of one scribal error, in the unique manuscript of Asser's *Vita Alfredi* (*c.* 893, copied *c.* 1000), in Cotton Tiberius B.v (early eleventh century), twice in the 'Textus Roffensis' (1115–24), and in William of Malmesbury's *Gesta regum Anglorum* (*c.* 1142, copied in the twelfth century and later).[38] Insofar as transcriptional accuracy corresponds to cultural knowledge, these legendary figures seem to have been well known to literate audiences around the time of the copying of *Beowulf* and later.

Finally, even if one concludes from such equivocal evidence that "the scribes were largely unaware of the heroic-legendary traditions constituting *Beowulf*," this conclusion itself has no necessary chronological implications. Surely it is an oversimplification to equate the cultural knowledge of two individuals with the "cultural memory" of England for two centuries. If the mistranscription of proper names in the text of *Beowulf* bears witness to a differential in cultural knowledge, it could just as well point to the diversity of ninth-, tenth-, and eleventh-century interpretive communities as to a 300-year cultural chasm separating the poet from the scribes. The impossible word division in MS *mere wio ingasmilts* at 2921 for presumptive *Merewioingas milts* 'the Merovingian's favor' sums up the problems with the argument from scribal error. Either the scribe misdivided a name he in fact knew, or he was ignorant of a name that was demonstrably familiar to late authors.[39] Scribal error is weak evidence for scribal ignorance; and scribal ignorance is even weaker evidence for a long-standing, universal loss of cultural knowledge.

If no sure signs of "cultural amnesia" can be found in the scribal performance, then perhaps given names might be made to talk. Some years ago Patrick Wormald, reasoning that *Beowulf* was written for the aristocracy, looked for plutocrats named Wiglaf, Ingeld, etc., and found more in the eighth century than later.[40] Neidorf repeatedly represents Wormald's work as having shown "that many of these names are prevalent in documents prior to 840, but rare or nonexistent afterward."[41] In fact, Wormald excluded non-aristocratic names from his tallies. His goal was not to demonstrate the desuetude of heroic legend among the Anglo-Saxons generally, but to point to a time when the upper classes might have been receptive to a poem like *Beowulf*. Had Wormald considered landowners to be a potential audience for poems about ancient heroes, he would have found no less than thirty-four relevant names attached to hundreds of historical persons in Domesday Book (1086) (approximate number of individuals, Old English alternatives, and Old Norse and Old High German equivalents in parentheses): Ægelmund/Æthelmund (three; OE Ealhmund), Ælfhere (five–six; ON Álfarr), Ælfwine (dozens; OE Æthelwine, Ealdwine, Ealhwine), Beowulf (one; ON Bjólfr),[42] Bil (one; ON Bíldr), Eadwine (hundreds), Finn (three–four; ON Finnr), Folcwald (two), Froda (one; ON Fróði), Garmund (one), Hagena (one; ON Högni), Healfdene (dozens; ON Hálfdan), Hemming (one; ON Hemmingr), Hoc (one or two), Hrothmund (one), Hrothulf (three–five; OHG Radulf, ON Hrólfr), Hun (one; OE Huna, ON Húni), Hungar (two), Ingeld (three; ON Ingjaldr), Offa (three; OE Uffa), Ordlaf (one), Sæferth/Sæfrith (one),

Sceaf(a) (one; ON Skeifi), Sigeferth/Sigefrith (one–two; ON Sigfrøðr), Sigemund (three or four; ON Sigmundr), Swerting (one; ON Svertingr), Theodric (ten), Wada (three; OHG Wado), Weland (one), Wiglaf (one), Wudga (one), Wulf (dozens; ON Úlfr), Wulfgar (ten), and Wulfhere (three or four; ON Úlfarr). Eight of these names Wormald listed as "recorded only poetically (i.e. in poetry but not in historical sources)": Healfdene, Hemming, Hungar, Sæferth, Swerting, Weland, Wudga, and Wulf.[43] Ten others appear either once or not at all in the pre-840 historical documents canvassed by Wormald: Ælfhere, Bil(ling), Finn, Folcwald, Froda, Garmund, Hagena, Hrothmund, Ordlaf, and Sceaf(a). Inasmuch as name-giving correlates with knowledge of legend, the eleventh century seems as hospitable to *Beowulf* as the eighth.

However, as Wormald was careful to emphasize, the connection between name-giving and legends is speculative. A spate of heroic-legendary given names does not necessarily indicate familiarity with legend, just as a decline in the popularity of those names does not necessarily indicate ignorance of legend. People tend to be named after family members, or they are given a name from among the socially acceptable ones. The apparent desuetude of some heroic-legendary given names from the seventh to the tenth centuries may reflect parents' increasing reliance on a standardized pool of name elements ('themes'), e.g., Beorht-, Ead-, -wine, -wulf. As name-giving fashions shifted away from naming children after family members (or heroes), exotic names like Ætla and Eadgils would have gradually disappeared as a matter of course. That Wormald found ninety-four men whose names begin with 'Hyge-' before 840 and none thereafter means only that 'Hyge-' became unfashionable as a first name element ('prototheme') after 840. This development almost certainly had nothing to do with the name Hygelac in particular, much less with "cultural amnesia" about Hygelac the legendary king. Names found in legend and composed of less common themes, such as Eadgils and Widsith, are at least as likely to have dropped out of the onomasticon through normal processes of cyclical fashions as through the influence of changing cultural knowledge. Finally, if the *Beowulf* poet endeavored to recreate a remote time and place, the choice of heroes whose names had already gone out of style as given names could have enhanced the effect. Whether or not one is prepared to believe that an Old English poet could have made this kind of conscious literary choice, it remains the case that poets and parents bestow names for irreducibly different reasons. The argument from onomastics cannot sidestep the vexed question of the *Beowulf* poet's rhetorical priorities.

The arguments from cultural change, scribal error, and onomastics all rely on an overdetermined identification of cultural traditions with literary traditions. Thus Neidorf takes as his object of study "the heroic-legendary traditions constituting *Beowulf*." In an analogous argument for a very early date of composition for *Widsith*, he seeks to subordinate the "present *Großform*" of that poem to its "content."[44] Such perceptions amount to another category mistake. Throughout this book, I argue that meter and poetic style are the only historical materials "constituting" alliterative poems. Poetic form is precisely that historically variable structure through which forms of culture are amplified, focalized, refracted, or even coined in verse. To treat cultural traditions and poetic "content" as interchangeable entities is to ignore the matrix of expectations and conventions that divide the one from the other. To cast aside the "*Großform*" of a poem, it seems to me, is to cast aside the poem as such.

In his epoch-making 1936 lecture, J. R. R. Tolkien deprecated in the scholarship of his predecessors and contemporaries "the belief that [*Beowulf*] was something it was *not* – for example, primitive, pagan, Teutonic, an allegory (political or mythical), or most often, an epic, or . . . disappointment at the discovery that it was itself and not something that the scholar would have liked better – for example, a heathen heroic lay, a history of Sweden, a manual of Germanic antiquities, or a Nordic *Summa Theologica*."[45] Tolkien's impassioned plea for "the understanding of a poem as a poem" has lost none of its relevance for *Beowulf* scholarship.[46] The five methods of dating *Beowulf* reviewed in this chapter can succeed only to the extent that they reduce verse history to some other historical series, whether language, lexis, culture, textual transmission, or name-giving. Each of the methods finds it necessary to posit a historical moment when poetic tradition was simply continuous with another form of history: a moment when metrical phonology mirrored linguistic phonology; conservative poetic lexis was not yet conservative or poetic; the content of imaginative compositions embodied the "cultural memory" of an entire island; scribal accuracy, scribal knowledge of literary figures, and cultural knowledge of legendary heroes overlapped completely; and the literary circulation of poems coincided with the historical circulation of given names featured in those poems. Each of the methods goes on to measure the antiquity of *Beowulf* by estimating the distance between this hypothesized moment and the knowable literary-cultural situation of the late tenth century.

My intervention has been to assert the independence of verse history from each of these other kinds of historical reconstruction. Because the lineaments of pre-950 verse history cannot be ascertained, I suggest, the relationship of putatively pre-950 verse to language, lexis, culture, scribal transmission, and name-giving cannot be assessed. Reconstructions of a very early *Beowulf* will continue to be implausible so long as they continue to reduce poetic meter and poetic techniques to some other kind of better-understood historical material. The observable diversity, diffusion, and conventionality of English literary culture after 950 is not evidence of the decay of a once monolithic, consolidated, and naturalized poetic tradition; rather, it implies the unobservable diversity, diffusion, and conventionality of English literary culture before 950. In this chapter, I have contended that metrical and other arguments for a very early *Beowulf* are either logically invalid, i.e., proceeding from true premises but failing to arrive at necessary conclusions, or logically unsound, i.e., arriving at necessary conclusions but proceeding from false premises. In either case, the arguments reviewed in this chapter fail to establish an early date for *Beowulf* because they fail fully to reckon with a poem as a poem and verse history as history.

The conclusions of this chapter, then, are negative. The next chapter builds a preliminary model of Old English poetic genres and poetic communities on what I take to be the best available evidence, the form and style of the poems themselves. I develop a typology of prologues to long Old English poems, with special emphasis on the undated poems. The interpenetration of individual types of prologue across the Old English poetic canon provides further support for the presumption of a robust history of alliterative verse before 950, unsettles modern notions of Old English poetic kinds, and contextualizes the style of *Beowulf* in a new way.

CHAPTER 2

Prologues to Old English Poetry

Old English poems come in two varieties, which, in the absence of native terms, may be designated 'long' and 'short.' The cutoff falls at roughly 100 lines, but the difference is generic, not mathematical.[1] Long poems are distinguished by a prologue, which takes the form of a precis, a call for attention, or a dramatization of theme. Prologues are distinct from verse prefaces, which constitute separate compositions and have their own conventions.[2] As in late medieval *accessus ad auctores*, whose forms were categorized by R. W. Hunt and then discerned in Middle English writing by Alastair Minnis, prologues to long Old English poems cluster in a few distinct groups, defined by keywords and recurrent *topoi*.[3] In addition to heading long poems, prologues are sometimes placed in the mouths of characters, reifying dramatic speech as a poetic object. More commonly, they appear in the bodies of poems without ascription to a speaking character. Such 'inset prologues,' as I will call them, may have been meant to mark the junctures between rhetorical units comparable to the *fitt* or section.

Prologues may be the closest thing to a vernacular *ars poetica* that the Anglo-Saxons have left us. As prominent stylistic gestures, prologues offer a rare opportunity to understand how Old English poets perceived poetic style and to discover affiliations between undated, unlocalized, and anonymous texts. The 'days-of-yore' prologue found in *Beowulf* and other poems is especially promising as historical evidence, because it connects Old English historical verse to Middle English (alliterative) romance (Chs. 3, 4, and 5). After surveying the types of prologue and their use in individual compositions, this chapter concludes by exploring the implications of the prologue typology for historicizing the style of *Beowulf*.

Old English Prologues and Old English Poetic Styles

Prologues to Old English poetry are chiefly of four types, which I term (in descending order of frequency) the 'we-have-heard' prologue, the

'I-will-tell' prologue, the 'days-of-yore' prologue, and the 'let-us-praise-God' prologue (Fig. 3).

The 'we-have-heard' prologue asserts the familiarity of the narrative materials to an *us*, to a representative *me*, or, less commonly, to mankind en masse.[4] The key verbs *(ge)frignan* 'learn of' and *hyran* 'hear of,' and the related adjective *gefræge* 'known to,' occur in twenty-five of the thirty-two prologues or inset prologues of this type. These verbs appear to function as *termini technici* for the kind of cultural sophistication that the 'we-have-heard' prologue projects onto its audience. The education of the audience is nearly always presented

---

'we-have-heard'
Andreas (+ 'days-of-yore')
Beowulf (+ 'days-of-yore')
*Christ and Satan**
Christ I 78 ff. (+ 'days-of-yore')
Christ I 301 ff. (+ 'days-of-yore')
Christ II 586 ff.
Daniel
Deor 14 ff.
Deor 21 ff.*
Elene 397 ff. (+ 'days-of-yore')*
Elene 670 ff.
Elene 852 ff.
Exodus
*Fates of the Apostles**
Fates 23 ff.
Fates 42 ff.*
Fates 63 ff.
Genesis A 939 ff.
Guthlac A 108 ff.
Guthlac B
Instructions for Christians 131 ff. (+ 'days-of-yore')
Juliana (+ 'days-of-yore')
Menologium 189 ff. (+ 'days-of-yore')
Meters of Boethius 9*
Panther 8 ff.
(*Partridge*)
Phoenix
(*Riddle 67*)
Seasons for Fasting 25 ff.
Seasons 176 ff. (+ 'days-of-yore')*
Solomon and Saturn II (+ 'days-of-yore')
Widsith 10 ff.

Figure 3. Prologues to Old English Poems
Parentheses indicate poems under 100 lines that begin with prologues. Asterisks denote the absence of the keywords discussed in Ch. 2.

'I-will-tell'
Aldhelm 5 ff.
Andreas 644 ff.
Andreas 851 ff.
Battle of Maldon 216 ff.
Beowulf 2069 ff.
Christ I 317 ff.
Deor 35 ff.
Dream of the Rood
Guthlac B 494 ff.
(*Husband's Message*)
Judith 152 ff.
Juliana 132 ff.
Meters of Boethius Proem 8 ff.
(*Meters of Boethius* 13)
Meters of Boethius 25.37 ff.
Meters of Boethius 26
Order of the World 23 ff.
Paris Psalter 65.14.1 ff.
Riddle 42 5 ff.
Riddle 55 7 ff.
Seafarer
Seasons for Fasting 208 ff.
(*Whale*)
Widsith 54 ff.
(*Wife's Lament*)

'days-of-yore'
Andreas (+ 'we-have-heard')
Beowulf (+ 'we-have-heard')
Christ I 78 ff. (+ 'we-have-heard')
Christ I 301 ff. (+ 'we-have-heard')
Dream of the Rood 28 ff.
*Elene**
Elene 397 ff. (+ 'we-have-heard')
Guthlac A 40 ff.
Instructions for Christians 131 ff. (+ 'we-have-heard')
Juliana (+ 'we-have-heard')*
Menologium 189 ff. (+ 'we-have-heard')
(*Meters of Boethius* 1)
Meters of Boethius 26.4 ff.
Order of the World 11 ff.
Phoenix 570 ff.
Seasons for Fasting
Seasons 42 ff.
Seasons 176 ff. (+ 'we-have-heard')
Solomon and Saturn II (+ 'we-have-heard')
(*Vainglory*)
Vainglory 57 ff.
(couplet in Regius Psalter)

'let-us-praise-God'
(*Cædmon's Hymn*)
Genesis A

Figure 3. (cont.)

(*Kentish Hymn*)
(*Paris Psalter* 65)
Seasons for Fasting 39 ff.

remainders (long poems only)
Azarias
Christ II
Christ III
Descent into Hell
Instructions for Christians
Judgment Day I and *II*
Maxims I
Menologium
Meters of Boethius 11
Meters of Boethius 20
Order of the World
Resignation
Riddle 40
Solomon and Saturn I
Soul and Body I and *II*
Wanderer
Widsith

Figure 3. (cont.)

in the past or perfect tenses, as though to emphasize the preconditions for some new transaction with the material. The opening of *Exodus* is typical (unless otherwise noted, quotations of Old English poems are from *ASPR*; translation mine):

> Hwæt! We feor and neah   gefrigen habað
> ofer middangeard   Moyses domas,
> wræclico wordriht,   wera cneorissum, –
> in uprodor   eadigra gehwam
> 5   æfter bealusiðe   bote lifes,
> lifigendra gehwam   langsumne ræd, –
> hæleðum secgan.   Gehyre se ðe wille!

("Lo! We have heard near and far, across the world, the decrees of Moses, wondrous commandments, announced to the sons of men, to each of the blessed ones in heaven, rescue from life after the terrible journey, perdurable counsel for each living being, for each man. Listen, he who wishes!")

The use of *we* delimits and invites an audience of insiders well versed in the biblical account, while the postposition of the passive infinitive *secgan* pointedly connects the "we" of the audience to the "wera cneorissum . . . eadigra gehwam . . . lifigendra gehwam . . . hæleðum" who have heard the commandments handed down by Moses. The metaphor of oral transmission functions on three levels (in ascending order of abstraction from the biblical account): (1) mankind has been informed about the commandments ("wordriht," "secgan"), (2) the audience has heard about the dissemination of the commandments ("gefrigen"), and (3) "listen up!" ("Gehyre se ðe wille!"). Such an opening is hardly conceivable outside the context of a community of shared cultural horizons, whether material or imagined. Some iterations of the 'we-have-heard' prologue focus more explicitly on the moment of revelation, e.g., *Christ and Satan*: "Þæt wearð underne | eorðbuendum" ("It was revealed to the denizens of the world"). In their totalizing vision of announcement and reception, these poems present a crude theory of informatics. Important things occur, and then everyone knows. Presumably poetry itself was felt to participate in the same process.

The notion of unfolding received truth, of making important events "underne," resonates with the narrative style of these Old English poems and many others. It was natural, then, for poets to place the 'we-have-heard' prologue in the mouths of exceptionally wise characters, such as St. Helen (*Elene* 670 ff. and 852 ff.) and Widsith (*Widsith* 10 ff.). In *Elene*, the process of discovery is dramatized using the key verb *(ge)frignan*:

>   ond þa frignan ongan
> 850 on hwylcum þara beama   bearn wealdendes,
>   hæleða hyhtgifa,   hangen wære:
>   "Hwæt, we þæt hyrdon   þurh halige bec
>   tacnum cyðan. . ."

("And then [the queen] began to ask/discover on which of the crosses the son of God, giver of joy to men, was hanged. 'Lo, we (have) heard through holy books that it was made known by signs. . .'") (849b–53a)

Here *frignan* refers most immediately to Elene's question to Judas Cyriacus (856b–58), but also to the divine inspiration that results soon enough in the discovery of the True Cross (883b ff.). In this latter sense, *frignan* corresponds not so much to an action as to a state of being. For God's deputies, to ask (*frignan*) is to find out (*frignan*). The wages of righteous investigation, and the proper means of expressing public knowledge, are clear. Cynewulf was particularly fond of the 'we-have-heard' prologue. It appears at least once in all four of his signed compositions, and nine times overall in his *oeuvre*. *Guthlac B*, acaudate and lacking a signature but sometimes attributed to Cynewulf, begins with a 'we-have-heard' prologue. The 'we-have-heard' prologue also occurs in all four poems found in the Junius MS, while only one other prologue occurs in that volume (a single 'let-us-praise-God' prologue in *Genesis A*). The way in which the 'we-have-heard' prologue (re)constitutes a community of listeners may go some way to revealing the intentions and the resources of the Junius compiler.

The 'I-will-tell' prologue rearranges the dynamic of the 'we-have-heard' prologue by locating the moment of communal education performatively in the present rather than memorially in the past. The keywords *(ge)cypan, (ge)(and)reccan, (ge)secgan,* and *(ge)sprecan* 'tell,' always in the infinitive after auxiliary verbs, appear in all twenty-five prologues or inset prologues of this type. The poems that begin with the 'I-will-tell' prologue have often struck scholars as especially intimate or confessional, including some of those periodically designated (with no basis in Old English vocabulary) 'elegies.' Consider the opening lines of the *Seafarer*: "Mæg ic be me sylfum | soðgied wrecan, / siþas secgan" ("I mean to spin a true tale about myself, to tell of my travels"). Unlike the other three prologues, the 'I-will-tell' prologue appears mostly in poems of middling length. None of the seven poems beginning with the prologue exceeds 160 lines, though the prologue occurs within the body of longer poems. Perhaps the poems beginning with the 'I-will-tell' prologue were felt to be equivalent to *fitts* or sections of longer works. The opening of the *Whale* would in that case take on added significance: "Nu ic fitte gen | ymb fisca cynn/ wille woðcræfte | wordum cyþan" ("Now concerning the race of fish I will declare in words, by the power of poetry, in a *fitt*"). Like other words for prose and poetry in Old English, *woðcræft* is an unstandardized term of general application. On the other hand, in the context of the 'I-will-tell' prologue *fitt* may refer specifically to a kind of didactic poem or speech of medium length. The word *fitt* crops up in another 'I-will-tell' prologue, as well (*Meters of Boethius* Proem 9a). As an inset prologue in narrative poems, the 'I-will-tell' prologue occurs mostly in speeches, e.g., *Andreas* 644 ff., *Battle of Maldon* 216 ff., *Beowulf* 2069 ff. Elsewhere, it gravitates toward poems spoken by named or otherwise embodied narrators, e.g., *Deor, Dream of the Rood, Husband's Message, Seafarer, Wife's Lament*. Apparently the prologue sounded idiomatic and personal to Old English poets. Its appearance in the mouths of less obviously embodied narrators, e.g., *Whale, Order of the World* 23 ff., serves as a reminder that the modern distinction between omniscient narrators and speaking characters may not do justice to Anglo-Saxon ideas about literary voice.

The 'days-of-yore' prologue emphasizes the antiquity of the narrative materials. The keywords *ær- eald-, fyrn-, gear-,* and *iudagas* 'days of old,' always in the dative, and the related adverbs *geara* and *iu* 'of old,' occur in twenty of the twenty-two prologues or inset prologues of this type. Though the typecast nature of the prologue permitted poets to gesture cursorily toward an undifferentiated long ago, more sophisticated expressions of historical imagination were possible as well. At its simplest, as in *Meters of Boethius* 1, the 'days-of-yore' prologue gives the Anglo-Saxon equivalent of once-upon-a-time: "Hit was geara iu..." ("It was long ago..."). The prevalence of such tags toward the beginnings of poems implies consciousness of a genre or mode of poetry whose Old English name, if there ever was one, has not survived: the long historical poem.

Other poets used the 'days-of-yore' prologue to point up not merely the antiquity of the setting, but the antiquity of the narrative, as in the opening of *Vainglory*:

> Hwæt, me frod wita   on fyrndagum
> sægde, snottor ar,   sundorwundra fela.
> Wordhord onwreah   witgan larum
> beorn boca gleaw,   bodan ærcwide.

("Lo, an old sage in the days of yore, a wise messenger, told me many special wonders. He disclosed his word-hoard in wise teachings, a man learned in books – the old sayings of a herald.")

The same sense of oral revelation that marked the 'we-have-heard' and 'I-will-tell' prologues is here brought to bear on the distant past ("frod," "fyrndagum," "ærcwide"), with the same conflation of source and text. The "me" of the first line is the speaker, informed by a "frod wita"; but it is also the poem speaking for itself, like the "halgungboc" in *Thureth* (early eleventh century), the translation of Gregory's *Dialogues* in the *Metrical Preface to Waerferth's Translation, &c.*, and the "Biblos" in *Aldhelm* (with which *Vainglory* shares the a-verse *beorn boca gleaw*). In a neat analogy in which nothing of substance is lost between telling and retelling, the "wordhord" belongs both to the aged scholar and to the text of *Vainglory* itself as it unfolds ("onwreah"). It scarcely needs to be pointed out that in referring their subject to ancient sources Old English poets heightened the authority of their work. The conventional Anglo-Saxon equation between age and wisdom applies to texts as well as persons. As in the 'we-have-heard' prologue, the texts are figured as oral narratives ("sægde ... word-hord ... ærcwide"). A two-line 'days-of-yore' prologue glosses Psalm 17:51 in the Regius Psalter (mid tenth century): "Wæs mid Iudeum | on gearda-gum/ ealra cyninga gehwelc | Cristus nemned" ("In the days of yore, every single king among the Jews was called Christ").[5] The glossator may be equating the psalms of David to an ancient narrative, which forms the 'text' for the prologue. The didactic historicism of the gloss illustrates well the function of the 'days-of-yore' prologue: to unlock the secrets of the past. The appearance of a poetic prologue as a solitary gloss offers some insight into poetic aptitude. Perhaps the glossator was an accomplished poet or was citing from memory an Old English poem now lost; or perhaps the ability to cast off a historical prologue in meter was par for the course in literate circles in the middle of the tenth century.

Taken singly, their generic implications are fairly well defined, but the 'we-have-heard' and 'days-of-yore' prologues must not have been considered mutually exclusive, for nine poems, including *Beowulf*, combine them. No other combination of prologues occurs, suggesting that the 'we-have-heard'/'days-of-yore' prologue was a specific stylistic phenomenon. Consider the opening of *Andreas*: "Hwæt! We gefrunan | on fyrndagum/ twelfe under tunglum | tireadige hæleð, / þeodnes þegnas. | No hira þrym alæg" ("Lo! We (have) heard of twelve men under the stars in the days of yore, glorious warriors, servants of their Lord. Their glory did not subside"). The clustering of several words from the first two lines of *Beowulf* (*hwæt, gefrunan, fyrndagum* beside *geardagum, þeodnes* beside *þeodcyninga,* and *þrym*) contributes to the traditional view that the *Andreas* poet drew upon the more famous work. Yet one must make allowances, too, for the restricted vocabulary of the 'we-have-heard' and 'days-of-yore' prologues. A statement of communal knowledge about the distant past evidently appealed to a variety of poets, and it crops up in some decidedly un-Beowulfian contexts, e.g., as a transition between sections of the pervasively didactic *Instructions for Christians,* usually considered a very late composition (quoted from Rosier, "'Instructions,'" p. 15): "Hwæt, we þæt gehyrdon | hæleða secgan, / þæt iudagum | Iacob hæfde/ and Moyses eac | micele speda" ("Lo, we (have) heard men say that in the days of yore Jacob and Moses had great success," 131–33). The *Instructions* poet's *iudagum* is no further from the *Beowulf* poet's *geardagum* than was *fyrndagum* in *Andreas; sped* in this context is the virtual equivalent of *þrym* in *Beowulf* and *Andreas;* and the *Instructions* poet even offers the compound *þeodland* (139a), with its connotations of the old Heptarchy and beyond that the *comitatus* ideal. Or again, compare an inset prologue in the *Menologium* (late tenth century): "We þa æþelingas/ fyrn gefrunan" ("We (have) heard about the noblemen of old," 189b–90a).[6] The compounds in -*dagas* and a related constellation of valorizing vocabulary seem to have served as buzzwords for a particular kind of poetry, or at least a recurrent attitude toward the value of historical poetry in a community.

The last and least popular type of prologue is the 'let-us-praise-God' prologue. Forms of *herian* 'to praise' appear in all five prologues of this type. *Cædmon's Hymn* (late seventh/early eighth centuries) gives the blue-print of the prologue, and may be the direct inspiration for it. The opening of the *Kentish Hymn* (tenth century) certainly seems infused with Cædmonian language, though perhaps no more than should be expected if the 'let-us-praise-God' prologue came outfitted with certain keywords: "Wuton wuldrian | weorada dryhten/ halgan hlioðorcwidum, | hiofenrices weard" ("Let us glorify with holy chants the lord of hosts, the guardian of the kingdom of heaven"). By now the reference to a communal "we" should be familiar as a symptomatic feature of poetic prologues, which set poetic narrative in the context of the knowledge and expectations of an audience in solidarity. The 'let-us-praise-God' prologue stands apart, however, in its hortative address to the community. It is probably no accident that it is the one prologue with definite generic limitations. It occurs only in poems that explicitly celebrate God and His powers. The call to perform an essential task rather than merely to listen attentively seems to have been least easily adaptable to long narrative poems, but the 'let-us-praise-God' prologue may therefore reveal the most about the communities that produced it and heard it. The prologue does not appear in the Nowell Codex, the Exeter Book, or the Vercelli Book, as if inapposite for those poems or unknown to those compilers. The use of *Cædmon's Hymn*-like language as a prologue in later poems reveals either one vector of the reception of the *Hymn* or, more intriguingly, a hitherto unnoticed aspect of the genre of the *Hymn* itself. If the 'let-us-praise-God' prologue already existed as a convention at the turn of the eighth century, then Cædmon's *carmen* is less a poem in the modern sense than a preface to the life's work catalogued but not quoted by Bede (*Historia ecclesiastica* 4.22). The most significant dimension of the *Hymn* for Cædmon's audience, as for Bede's, may not have been the words it contained but the specific kind of attention it demanded for what followed.

The *Paris Psalter* poet managed to squeeze two different types of prologue into his translation of Psalm 65. In the opening of the psalm he expands "iubilate Deo omnis terra" to a 'let-us-praise-God' prologue, while "venite & audite me · & narrabo. . ." quite naturally becomes an 'I-will-tell' prologue (65.14.1 ff.).[7] One might suppose that Psalm 65 particularly impressed the poet with its universal address ("omnis terra"), prompting him to embellish it with two kinds of familiar rhetorical set-pieces from the vernacular poetic tradition. Like modern "Let us give thanks" or "Hear ye, hear ye," the Old English prologues invite a certain kind of attention and make certain promises.

There is no special reason why Old English poets would have used four and only four types of prologue. Other openings to Old English poems may be set prologues that have not chanced to survive in numbers. This is probably the case with the opening of the *Gifts of Men*: "Fela bið on foldan | forðgesynra/ geongra geofona" ("There are on earth many new and visible gifts"). If *Guthlac A* 1–29 as laid out in the Exeter Book and printed in modern editions belongs instead to the end of *Christ III*, then *Guthlac A* begins with a similar invocation of the multiplicity of God's creatures: "Monge sindon | geond middangeard/ hadas under heofonum" ("Many across the world are the kinds under heaven," 30–31a).[8] The opening and closing of the *Panther* are almost identical: "Monge sindon | geond middangeard / unrimu cynn" ("Many across the world are the innumerable species," 1–2a) and "Monigfealde sind | geond middangeard / god ungnyðe" ("Many across the world are the abundant benefits," 70–71a). The opening of *Meters of Boethius* 31 is cut from the same cloth:

> Hwæt, ðu meaht ongitan,   gif his ðe geman lyst,
> þætte mislice   manega wuhta
> geond eorðan farað   ungelice;
> habbað blioh and fær,   þu ungelice,
> 5   and mægwlitas   manegra cynna
> cuð and uncuð.

> ("Lo, you may perceive, if you wish to take heed of it, that many living things walk the earth, variously and diversely; they have a form and a means of life, diverse kinds of dwellings, and species of many families, known and unknown.")

The 'many-in-the-world' prologue, if such it be, works on quite different rhetorical principles from the others examined above, and it is exponentially more mysterious for its scarcity. It occurs mainly in the first two booklets of the Exeter Book as defined by Patrick Conner in "The Structure of the Exeter Book Codex." Like a half-heard echo, this and other minor types of opening may bespeak micro-communities of poets, audiences, and compilers too obscure, too short lived, or too ill attested even to be legible as such today. Finally, recognition of the literary value of prologues must intensify our dismay at the acephalous long poems such as the *Battle of Maldon, Judith*, and (presumably) *Waldere*. Who knows what essential information or suggestive affiliations might have been extracted from the lost openings of these poems?

Hunt's discussion of academic prologues of the twelfth and thirteenth centuries brims with the kind of assured chronological deductions about which Old English specialists must remain diffident. One cannot assume about Old English prologues, as Hunt convincingly demonstrates about certain types of academic prologue, that they were "in vogue for a comparatively short space of time."[9] Old English specialists lack almost everything that Hunt had in spades: named, dated authors who studied under well-known masters and wrote datable texts for knowable communities, drawing on each others' ideas in traceable ways. Only one class of evidence remains securely from what must have been equally complex and specific relations between Old English poets and audiences, and that is the style and substance of the prologues themselves. The intuition of robust and time-bound poetic communities scattered across England only heightens one's sense of the paucity of supplementary evidence. In discussing the use of academic prologues and academic terminology by vernacular authors, Minnis had the advantage of plentiful manuscript sources, named and dated authors, and, above all, the ability to distinguish borrower from lender. The cultural authority of the Latin prologues to the *accessus* was obvious; Minnis demonstrated that Middle English writers appropriated this authority for vernacular literary undertakings. By contrast, Old English specialists may never know how or why Old English poets acquired the combined 'we-have-heard'/'days-of-yore' prologue. Further research may or may not be able to determine whether the prologues represent the appropriation of Latinate authority or whether they are the products of a wholly vernacular evolution of poetic style. We are ignorant, and shall remain ignorant, of the who (*causa efficiens*) and the why (*causa finalis*) of most Old English poetry. We are left to deduce these from the what (*causa materialis*) and the how (*causa formalis* or *modus tractandi*). We can be confident that each of the types of prologue expresses some organizing principle in literary culture, but the evidence that would enable us to contextualize these principles, and so to appreciate the *causa finalis* of a work like *Beowulf*, has vanished.

All the same, Old English specialists have been too prone to imagine pre-Conquest England as a totalized zone of poetic production, in which poets' aims, attitudes, and audiences remained static across the entire island for four centuries. The normalization of the poetic corpus in *ASPR*, corresponding roughly to New Critical assumptions about the production and reception of verse, conceals the perceptible variety in the meaning of 'poem' as a category of imaginative expression. Although ingrained traditionalism and the possibility of direct literary borrowing confound attempts to construct a chronology of Old English prologues such as Hunt derived for academic prologues, the lexical and stylistic similarities within each type of prologue may point to the contours of more localized, specialized, and therefore hypothetically datable poetic communities. Emily Thornbury's *Becoming a Poet in Anglo-Saxon England* is a thoroughgoing demonstration of the importance of poetic communities for literary history and the analysis of poetic style. The uneven distribution of prologues throughout the poetic corpus provides rare clues about what alliterative meter meant to specific poets working in specific contexts. If Cynewulf, whose *floruit* Conner assigns to the late ninth or tenth century, could combine the 'we-have-heard' and 'days-of-yore' prologues as adroitly and with as much fanfare as the *Beowulf* poet (*Elene* 397 ff.), this amounts to double evidence that *Beowulf* and *Elene* belong to some more restricted school or mode than 'Old English poetry.'[10] Whether composed under similar conditions or at a great remove, *Beowulf* and *Elene* seem to belong to a genre of long narrative poems about the distant past, which has, alas, left no firmly datable or localizable representatives. The problem with dating Old English poetry, then, is not only an evidentiary one (the lack of datable poems between *Cædmon's Hymn* and the *Battle of Brunanburh*, c. 937) but a generic one (the lack of datable narrative poems about the distant past). Scholars' habitual comparison of *Beowulf* to *Deor* (a brief *de casibus* poem with refrain), *Widsith* (an anthropological romp), and the *Battle of Brunanburh* and *Battle of Maldon* (c. 991) (battle chronicles) under the rubric 'heroic verse' probably reveals more about our own priorities in segregating the 'Christian' from the 'Germanic' than it does about the production and reception of Old English poems by and for Anglo-Saxons.

Dividing the Old English poetic corpus by prologue rather than by content unsettles the received view of Old English literary landscapes. In addition to the long narrative poems that might be expected to begin by invoking the distant past (*Andreas, Beowulf, Dream of the Rood, Elene, Guthlac A, Juliana, Phoenix*, and *Solomon and Saturn II*), the 'days-of-yore' prologue appears in a number of shorter didactic or devotional works that command less critical attention (*Christ I, Instructions for Christians, Menologium, Meters of Boethius, Order of the World, Seasons for Fasting*, and *Vainglory*). The combination of the 'we-have-heard' and 'days-of-yore' prologues is as common in the latter group as in the former, occurring five times in the celebrated poems (*Andreas, Beowulf, Elene, Juliana*, and *Solomon and Saturn II*) and five times in the ignored ones (*Instructions, Menologium, Seasons*, and twice in *Christ I*). If the subheadings in anthologies and bibliographies are anything to go by, modern scholars do not think these two sets of poems have much to do with each other. Indeed, the two groups are normally studied in mutually exclusive terms. The former, for the most part, are thought to be early, sophisticated, polysemous, and interesting; the latter, when they are thought of at all, are assumed to be late, pedantic, simplistic, and boring. In their *History of Old English Literature*, R. D. Fulk and Christopher Cain describe the *Menologium* and *Vainglory* as "the unlikeliest material" for poetry.[11] Old English poets and their audiences clearly did not share this opinion. Evidently they perceived the life of Christ, ancient Scandinavia, the exploits of early saints, and the wisdom embodied in orthodox doctrine as various manifestations of the same sort of historical knowledge. To draw an analogy to Hunt's discussion, these fifteen poems would all furnish the same answer to the question *cui parti philosophiae supponitur?* 'to what part of philosophy does it belong?'

Measured by prologue, the most flamboyant Old English poem by far is *Seasons for Fasting* (?tenth/eleventh centuries), which packs 7 prologues, including all 4 types of prologue and a combined 'we-have-heard'/'days-of-yore' prologue, into a scant 230 lines.[12] No other poem can boast such density or diversity. The *Seasons* poet uses the prologues to lend gravitas to his theme and to punctuate a precocious stanza structure (prologues begin stanzas 1, 4, 6, 23, and 27). For an audience immersed in poetic convention, his efforts could have struck home. It is a disturbing thought that a poem so perfectly soporific (to us) might have been perceived by contemporaries as an especially apt embodiment of poetic discourse. *Seasons for Fasting* takes itself extremely seriously as poetry, and we are in no position to conclude that its original audience did not. The presence of all four types of prologue in *Seasons* discourages the notion that any of them had died out by the tenth or eleventh century, even if their use in that poem strikes us more as bravura than poetic achievement.

Thornbury places *Seasons* in what she terms the 'Southern mode' of late, Latinate, southern Old English poetry, which she provocatively describes as "the apotheosis of Old English verse" and "the apex of Old English as a language of high culture."[13] Four other poems in Thornbury's Southern mode contain prologues (*Kentish Hymn, Menologium, Meters*, and *Paris Psalter*). The Southern mode cuts a curious swathe through the four types of prologue, accounting for a proportionally higher percentage of the less well-attested varieties (four of thirty-two 'we-have-heard' prologues, six of twenty-five 'I-will-tell' prologues, six of twenty-two 'days-of-yore' prologues, and three of five 'let-us-praise-God' prologues). It is as if the Southern mode represents a particular take on the poetic tradition, a canny reprioritization within a shared framework of formulas.

Thirteen poems over 100 lines contain no prologues at all: *Azarias, Christ III, Descent into Hell, Judgment Day I, Judgment Day II, Maxims I, Meters of Boethius* 11 and 20, *Resignation, Riddle 40, Solomon and Saturn I,* the *Soul and Body* texts, and the *Wanderer.* Apparently these are to be grouped with shorter *catenae* of pious or sententious sayings, like *Maxims II* and *Alms-Giving,* rather than sustained narratives, like *Beowulf* and *Andreas.* Nine of them appear in the Exeter Book, where they blend in with surrounding short works. To Anglo-Saxon ears, these thirteen probably sounded like longish short poems, not shortish long ones. They address their audiences with more candor and fewer rhetorical fireworks, like self-help guides as opposed to novels. To judge from the scant evidence of manuscripts that have happened to survive, Anglo-Saxons preferred the self-help guides six to one. Four of the thirteen poems with no prologues (31 percent) occur in multiple contemporary versions (*Azarias* 1–75 beside *Daniel* 279–364 and the newly discovered inscribed silver object from Lincolnshire,[14] *Judgment Day II, Solomon and Saturn I,* and *Soul and Body*), as opposed to two of the forty-four poems with prologues (5 percent) (*Cædmon's Hymn* in numerous manuscripts, but only within Bede's *Historia ecclesiastica,* and the *Dream of the Rood* beside the Ruthwell Cross and Brussels Cross inscriptions).

Indeed, poems with prologues form a minority of Old English poetic output by poem, even if they form a majority by volume. The composition of poetic prologues with their hints of literary self-consciousness, which seems to us such valuable evidence of literary communities, was a very specialized activity. By means of poetic prologues, poets applied ancient communal wisdom to acts of versification, but many audiences, it would appear, did not need or expect such overtures.

The recognition that medieval poets and their audiences did not exercise modern taste is an important first step in reconstructing Old English literary scenes from fragmented remains. The picture will never be complete, but I have argued that poetic style can provide more precise answers to literary-historical questions than subject matter or perceived literary worth.

The *Beowulf* Prologue and the History of Style

Relating the opening lines of *Beowulf* to other prologues in a systematic way raises the dating question once again. At the head of the poem in search of a date is a prologue in search of a date. When did the mid to late sixth century become *geardagas*? Though the issue is rarely treated directly, the de facto consensus has been that a late seventh- or early eighth-century date for *Beowulf* provides enough time for sixth-century Scandinavian history and legend to assume heroic proportions. Indeed, those still committed to the study of Germanic antiquity (G *germanische Altertumskunde*) maintain that *Beowulf* preserves a pan-Germanic heroic ethos emanating from Migration Age Germania. In this view, the *Beowulf* poet's sense of the past is merely a faithful reproduction of a fifth- or sixth-century sense of the present. The proposition that poetic style and historical consciousness remained static for centuries should never have seemed very appealing. To begin with, it is profoundly untrue of other, better-documented heroic traditions. In the later Middle Ages the Arthurian cycle can be seen proliferating, adding and dropping elements, over time and between languages. It is one thing to believe that some of the *Beowulf* material has some distant basis in sixth-century conditions (as some scholars believe about Arthurian legend); it is quite another to project later material back into prehistory in its entirety, detail by detail and epithet by epithet, like a reverse time capsule (as no scholar would dream of doing for the chivalrous King Arthur). The foregoing discussion represents an attempt to situate *Beowulf* in its contemporary literary culture: broadly, Anglo-Saxon England. As regards its prologue, at least, *Beowulf* belongs with other Old English poems of the historical period.

Even assuming the earliest possible dates of composition, the other twenty-one 'days-of-yore' prologues refer to pasts between 375 and thousands of years removed from author and audience.[15] A related type of prologue in Middle English alliterative poetry (see Ch. 4) reaches back between 700 and thousands of years prior to composition. The earliest proposed date for *Beowulf, c.* 685, comes a mere 155 years after the death of the historical Hygelac as reported in the *Liber historiae Francorum* (mid eighth century), and Beowulf's dragon-fight is said to occur 50 years later.[16] Even a more modest early date of *c.* 750 places the dragon-fight only 170 years in the past. And even if the prologue is taken to refer only to the deeds of Scyld Scefing and his ancestors, the gap between past and present increases a mere 60 years or so, counting backward 3 legendary generations from Hrothgar (Scyld – Beow – Healfdene – Hrothgar). In addition to the prologue itself, the casual way in which the *Beowulf* poet skips over half a century indicates that life "Scedelandum in" "in Scandinavia (poetic)" (19b) was felt to be comfortably ancient. Modern historiography and modern media have sharpened our sense of the shape of the past, but there is no reason to deny Old English poets the ability to appreciate the

broad difference between the society and events of seven to nine generations prior and those of 350 years or of an incalculably remote long ago.

The authors of the other 21 'days-of-yore' prologues managed to avoid
applying the prologue to the proximate past, even though plenty of recent
history was ripe for versifying. As Nicholas Howe documented in
Migration and Mythmaking in Anglo-Saxon England, the story of the
adventus Saxonum (fifth/early sixth centuries) quickly grew into a pervasive
cultural myth. Yet the *adventus* is not explicitly mentioned in surviving
vernacular verse for hundreds of years, until it crops up in a tenth-century
West-Saxon propaganda piece (*Battle of Brunanburh* 70 ff.). The
Gregorian mission (597), fount of Anglo-Saxon Christianity, does not
feature in an extant English-language poem until the end of the ninth
century (*Metrical Preface to Gregory's Pastoral Care* 1–10). By the late
medieval period (Lawman's *Brut* 18, c. 1200; *St. Erkenwald* 12, late four-
teenth/mid fifteenth centuries), it has taken on almost messianic overtones.
The names of prominent seventh- and eighth-century Anglo-Saxons like
Boisil, Bede, and Cuthbert are not intoned in the poetry known to us until
the twelfth century (*Durham* 10–15 and *First Worcester Fragment* 1), and
then with a wistfulness that reminds one of *Beowulf* but not of *Maldon*.[17]
Britain acquired ancient Trojan origins in the ninth century (*Historia
Brittonum, c.* 829), but Brutus of Troy is not alluded to in an extant
English-language poem until the turn of the thirteenth (Lawman's *Brut*
151 ff.). The evident delay of several centuries between the inauguration of
cultural traditions and their expression and amplification in vernacular
poetry is doubtless due in part to the paucity of surviving textual evidence.
Nevertheless, a clear pattern emerges from these examples: poets observed a
certain historical decorum, expressed as thematic conservatism. The
Beowulf poet probably did not know the precise date of the Frisian raid.
Yet by the time the details of Hygelac's death reached the poet, by
irretrievable oral channels and/or reference to the *Liber historiae
Francorum*, they wore the trappings of old age.

Comparison to other premodern literary traditions confirms that a long
temporal delay between historical setting and historical poem is the rule
rather than the exception. Late medieval romances of the so-called Matter
of England, e.g., the Anglo-Norman *Gui de Warewic* (early thirteenth
century) and the Middle English *Athelston* (late fourteenth century),
open onto vaguely tenth-century landscapes. The Old Norse Icelanders'
Sagas (ON *Íslendingasögur*) and Legendary Sagas (ON *fornaldarsögur*) of
the thirteenth and fourteenth centuries take place in the ninth, tenth, and
early eleventh centuries and before the late ninth- and early tenth-century

settlement of Iceland, respectively, while the so-called Contemporary Sagas (ON *samtíðarsögur*) treat events of the early twelfth and thirteenth centuries. Between the two groups of sagas lie *c.* 125 years of history not felt suitable either for historicizing or for contemporary narrative. The Old High German *Hildebrandslied* (*c.* 800) postdates by some 350 years the birth of the historical Theodoric/Dietrich, who was probably better known to Germans after 800 than before. The Old Irish *Táin Bó Cúailnge*, even if it was composed as early as the seventh century, lies at a considerable remove from the mythical first-century world it depicts. The tradition of Old French *chansons de gest* set in the reign of Charlemagne (*fl.* late eighth/early ninth centuries) evidently commenced with the *Chanson de Roland* (late eleventh/early twelfth centuries). Homer's *Iliad*, to which *Beowulf* has been compared more than once, was composed some 400 years after the Bronze Age Greece in which it is set. Vergil's *Aeneid*, another favorite literary model for *Beowulf*, picks up on a minor character already legendary in the mouth of Homer, who predeceased Vergil by seven or eight centuries. The Old Babylonian *Epic of Gilgamesh* (eighteenth century BCE), possibly based on Sumerian epics of the twentieth century BCE, postdates the death of the historical king by between seven and nine centuries. The Persian *Shahnameh* (late tenth/early eleventh centuries) celebrates the ancient history of the Persian empire, ending with the fall of the Sassanid empire (mid seventh century). Building history into legend takes time. Premodern poems composed relatively soon after the historical setting tend to deify contemporary heroes understood to inhabit the contemporary world, like *Maldon* but unlike *Beowulf*. Two examples are the Anglo-Norman prose *Fouke le Fitz Waryn* (early fourteenth century), containing traces of a late thirteenth-century Anglo-Norman metrical version and concerning events of the first quarter of the thirteenth century, and the Castilian *Cantar de mio Çid* (mid to late twelfth centuries), concerning Rodrigo Díaz de Vivar (*fl.* late eleventh century). It is certainly possible that *Beowulf* is an outlier in this regard as in so many others. But inasmuch as one would want to contextualize its attitude toward the past, these are the relevant comparisons.

What has seemed striking above all about *Beowulf* is its insistence on the antiquity of the past it describes. The poet's effort "to paint the past as though it were something other than the present" is everywhere in evidence.[18] The conclusion that the grandiloquence of its opening was spent on events of relatively recent vintage would pose a challenge to prevailing appraisals of the poem's greatest literary effect. If, as several scholars have argued, *Beowulf* as we have it was composed before *c.* 750, then the poet used the 'days-of-yore' prologue quite differently from all other alliterative poets. This is entirely conceivable. *Beowulf* is unique in many ways, not only in the Old English poetic corpus but also in the field of early medieval poetry more generally. In that case, the preceding analysis has the effect of setting *Beowulf* apart from ninth-, tenth-, and eleventh-century English poetic communities. If, however, *Beowulf* was composed at some time between *c.* 750 and the copying of its unique surviving manuscript witness *c.* 1000, then the preceding analysis has the effect of demonstrating a point of contact between *Beowulf* and its broad literary context. This, too, is entirely conceivable. *Beowulf* shows many other points of contact, large and small, with English poetry of the ninth, tenth, and eleventh centuries, while recent arguments for an eighth-century date have been framed in probabilistic rather than dispositive terms (Ch. 1). It is not my purpose to use the *Beowulf* prologue to adjudicate between these possibilities. Rather, I seek to emphasize that surviving late and undated Old English poems should be the corpus of first recourse in any effort to historicize the style of *Beowulf*, and vice versa.

The distinction between long and short poems, the attention to prologues as stylistic evidence, and the emphasis on poets' sense of history in this chapter will inform the literary-historical arguments of Chapters 3, 4, and 5. The next chapter extends the metrical history from Chapter 1 and the analysis of prologues from this chapter into the twelfth and thirteenth centuries, with focus on Lawman's *Brut*, far and away the longest Early Middle English alliterative poem. I show that Lawman inherited a traditional meter and a traditional historical style from what is now known as 'Old English poetry,' but that adopting a conservative style in alliterative poetry in the late twelfth century did not require antiquarian knowledge or motivations.

CHAPTER 3

Lawman, the Last Old English Poet and the First Middle English Poet

Alliterative poetry of the late eleventh, twelfth, and thirteenth centuries rarely refers to the Norman Conquest of England (1066). Every sour note has been wrung for maximum effect in modern criticism, but the implied contrast with pre-Conquest poetry is unconvincing. *The Death of William the Conqueror* (1087–1121) is alone in criticizing the Normans, which it does in a ham-fisted way that calls to mind a few spoiled monks, not the righteous indignation of the peasantry. The sense of a way of life coming to an end in *Durham* (1104–1109) and the *First Worcester Fragment* (late twelfth century) has precedents in a variety of Old English poems. It is superfluous to add contemporary politics to the list of reasons why poets employed the *topos*. The pivotal event for post-1066 alliterative poetry was not the Conquest, but the publication of Geoffrey of Monmouth's *Historia regum Brittaniae* (*c.* 1138). To judge from the extant corpus, alliterative poets' fascination with the Arthurian past began in a Worcestershire priest's massive verse translation of the *Historia* material, extant in two copies and now known as the *Brut* (*c.* 1200).

Scholars have always had the impression that the *Brut* is metrically "loose" in comparison with earlier and later alliterative poetry.[1] In what follows this impression will be rejected. Careful study of alliterative meter yields a clear developmental arc connecting *Beowulf* to the *Brut* and the *Brut* to *Sir Gawain and the Green Knight* (late fourteenth century). The new account of the evolution of alliterative verse advanced in this book challenges the view of Early Middle English poetry as the refuse of a more glorious tradition. When metrical change is seen as the predictable result of the passage of time rather than a symptom of decadence, alliterative meter can be appreciated as a dynamic institution rather than a gradually eroded edifice. This chapter clarifies recent scholarship on the meter of the *Brut* and extends it to other Early Middle English alliterative poetry. I show Lawman's meter to be highly organized, directly related to Old English and to Middle English alliterative meter, and distinct from Ælfric of Eynsham's 'rhythmical alliteration.' Through consideration of particular words and passages, the second section demonstrates how Lawman's conservative style resembles that of his Old English predecessors, how the two manuscript versions of the *Brut* represent two different visions for the future of alliterative verse, and how Lawman's treatment of the Arthurian past anticipates Middle English romance. By implicating Lawman and other Early Middle English alliterative poetry in a long verse history, I seek to answer recent calls for a revaluation of the twelfth century in English literary history.[2]

Lawman and the Evolution of Alliterative Meter

Whether Ælfric wrote verse, and what influence he may have had on Lawman, are questions of some moment. Thomas Bredehoft urges that Ælfric's saints' lives are rhythmically identical to late Old English and Early Middle English alliterative poems.[3] However, Bredehoft's metrical model is hyper-accommodating. He defines the half-line as one or two unstressed syllables or any one of fourteen foot patterns, plus any one of the fourteen foot patterns again. Either foot can be preceded by any number of unstressed syllables, and foot boundaries need not coincide with word boundaries. Bredehoft's system can be made to describe more or less any text. For instance, the prose of the Old English translation of Bede's *Historia ecclesiastica* (quoted from *Old English Version*, vol. 1.i, ed. Miller, p. 2):

> Ic Beda Cristes þeow and mæssepreost
> (x)Sx/SxS   x/SxS
> sende gretan   ðone leofastan
> Sx/Sx   xx/Sxx *or* xx/SSx
> cyning Ceolwulf   ond ic ðe sende þæt spell
> Sx/Sx   (xxx)Sxx/S

or the opening of Charles Dickens's *Tale of Two Cities* (1859):

> It was the best of times, it was the worst of times,
> (x)xx/SxS   (x)xx/SxS
> it was the age of wisdom, it was the age of foolishness.
> (xxx)Sx/Sx   (xxx)Sx/Sxx

Bredehoft's system scarcely equips readers to distinguish anything from anything. If late Old English poetry could take all the forms he allows it, the study of alliterative verse is in a terrible muck.

A more restrictive and more dynamic theory of alliterative meter mitigates the impression that Ælfric's rhythms anticipate Lawman's. In his study of the alliterative meter, Nicolay Yakovlev found no "specific rhythmical connection between the patterns of Ælfric ... and those of Layamon."[4] For example, Lawman consistently uses metrical resolution to avoid a long dip at the end of half-lines.[5] By contrast, there is no attention to resolution at the end of Ælfric's 'half-lines,' and long dips often occur there, e.g., *St. Eugenia* 1b *be þam halgan mædene* (xxSxSxx). Yakovlev finds five metrical patterns in Lawman's b-verses, which derive from the Old English patterns Sx(x ...)Sx, x(x ...)SxS, and x(x ...)SSx (Types A, B, and C in Sieversian notation) and, just as obviously, lie behind the Middle English b-verse patterns described by Thomas Cable in the 1980s. Here 'p' marks a verbal prefix or negative particle omitted by the prefix license:

OE (Yakovlev/Sievers)		EME (Yakovlev)		ME (Cable)
pSx(x ...)Sx (A)	=	xSx ... xSx (1)	=	xSx ... xSx
x(x ...)SpSx (C)	=	x ... xSxSx (2)	=	x ... xSxSx
Sx(x ...)Sx (A)	=	Sx ... xSx (3)	=	Sx ... xSx
x(x ...)SxS (B)	=	x ... xSxS (4)	=	x ... xSxSx
x(x ...)SSx (C)	=	x ... xSSx (5)	=	x ... xSSx

It is worth spelling out why metrists and literary historians should find evidence of formal continuity in these metrical equivalences (also printed in the front matter of this book for ease of reference). Each phase of the alliterative tradition inherited most of the metrical patterns from the previous phase but regularized them according to new principles of organization. From Old to Early Middle English, the four-position principle gradually gave way to a norm of two lifts and one long dip in the b-verse. From Early Middle English to Middle English, the one remaining b-verse pattern without a final short dip (Type 4) was gradually eliminated by regularization. The evolution of metrical form narrated in this book should be persuasive in the same ways as human evolution or the evolution of the English language. For example, Middle English is acknowledged as the descendant of Old English and the ancestor of Modern English because it stands at the midpoint of a linguistic evolution. In a similar way, Yakovlev's description of the *Brut* meter has provided the evolutionary missing link between the *Beowulf* meter and the *Gawain* meter.

Because of the increasing metrical constraints on the b-verse in post-950 alliterative verse and the concomitant decreasing metrical constraints on the a-verse, this chapter, like Chapter 1, focuses on b-verse patterns. To a large extent, the b-verse becomes the locus of metricality in post-950 alliterative verse. However, this development itself furnishes more evidence of formal continuity, Old to Middle English. Around 65% of the a-verses in the *Brut* obey Yakovlev's two-lift b-verse typology, while the other 35% have some other pattern, including all three-lift patterns. This makes good developmental sense. Whereas in Old English meter virtually every pattern can appear in either half-line (*c.* 95% symmetry), in fourteenth-century alliterative meter the patterns of the a- and b-verse are almost mutually exclusive (*c.* 5% symmetry).[6] The *Brut* is much less symmetrical than *Beowulf* but still much more symmetrical than *Sir Gawain and the Green Knight*.

Embedded in a comprehensive evolutionary model for alliterative meter, Yakovlev's typology of Early Middle English alliterative b-verse patterns proves to be a powerful diagnostic. All five patterns occur in Ælfric's 'b-verses,' but so do other, disallowed patterns, e.g., *St. Eugenia* 6b *cómmodus* (one lift). In the first twenty 'lines' of *St. Eugenia* there are at least six 'b-verses' that would be unmetrical in both *Beowulf* and the *Brut*; the figure for *St. Basil* is nine; for *St. Julian*, five; for *St. Sebastian*, seven; for *St. Maur*, five; for *St. Agnes*, three.[7] Extrapolating from this sample, over one-quarter of Ælfric's 'b-verses' would be unmetrical in alliterative verse of any period. Nor do the divergences from alliterative meter point to any other sort of regularity. Ælfric's 'b-verses' fail to scan as alliterative b-verses for every possible reason. In short, Ælfric's 'lines' frequently disappoint expectation of alliterative metrical features and patterns (not to mention poetic lexis and syntax), while there exists no independent evidence that any non-alliterative verse form was available in English during Ælfric's lifetime or for 150 years following his death *c.* 1010. It should be crystal clear where Ælfric fits in.

In Chapter 1, I identified the meter of late tenth- and eleventh-century alliterative verse as a dynamic mixture of the older and newer metrical patterns typified in *Beowulf* and the *Brut*, respectively. The meter of alliterative poems more nearly contemporary with the *Brut* supports the evolutionary model elaborated in this book. Consider the first ten b-verses of the *Grave* (mid/late twelfth century), accompanied by Yakovlev scansions (quoted from Schröer, "Grave"):

```
x   x x S x   S x
er þu iboren were        (2)
x   x x   S x S   x
er ðu of moder come      (2)
```

```
        x    x    S    x  p  S x
        ne þeo deopnes imeten    (2)
        x    S    x x  S x
        hu long hit þe were      (1)
        x    x    S      S x
    5   þer ðu beon scealt       (5)⁸
        x    x    S x S    x
        and þa molde seoðða      (2)
        S    x x xS   x
        healice itinbred         (3)
        x    x x S   x S  x
        þonne þu list þerinne    (2)
        S    x x x   S x
        sidwaȝes unheȝe          (3)
        x    S x  x   S
   10   þire broste ful neh.     (1 – final syllable)⁹
```

Or again, the first ten b-verses of the *First Worcester Fragment* (quoted from *Selections*, ed. Hall):¹⁰

```
        x    S x x   x  S
        on breotene mid us       (1 – final syllable)
        S       x x  x S x
        þurh weren ilerde        (3)
        x  S   xx    S x
        þe questiuns hoteþ       (1)
        x  S    x  x S
        þe deorwurþe is          (1 – final syllable)
        x    x S   x    S x
    5   þe we alquin hoteþ       (2)
        x    x  S   S  x
        and þe bec wende         (5)
        x    S  x x   S x
        ure leoden on englisc    (1)¹¹
        x       S x x x  x  S
        þeo bodeden cristendom   (1 – final syllable; stress shift *cristendom*)
        x    S  x x  S   x
        ure leodan on englisc    (1)
        x    x  S x  S
   10   ac hit fæire glod.       (4)¹²
```

As before, the correspondences to Lawman's practice are many. Six other Early Middle English alliterative poems are scanned in Appendix B.

Alliterative poets' consistency across time (and presumably space) is impressive. I have scanned the 1,331 total b-verses of the *Coronation of Edgar* (973–78), *Death of Edgar* (975–78), *Battle of Maldon* (c. 991), *Thureth* (c. 1011), *Death of Alfred* (1036–45), *Death of Edward*, *Durham*, the *Grave*, the *First Worcester Fragment*, *Proverbs of Alfred* (late twelfth century), *Soul's Address to the Body* (late twelfth century), the Middle English *Physiologus* (c. 1250), and the 21 poems in Appendices A and B.[13] Apart from the *Brut*, these are all the datably late Old English or Early Middle English alliterative poems known to me. They span the period c. 975–1250. Of the 1,331 b-verses, 270 diverge from Yakovlev's typology of Early Middle English alliterative b-verses, excluding occasional three-lift b-verses. However, fully 248 of these scan as Old English types, including the transitional pattern xSxSx but not including Types A* and D*, which primarily appear in the a-verse in Old English meter. Aside from b-verses with the transitional form xSxSx, then, only 22 of the 1,331 b-verses (<2 percent) diverge from both of the synchronic metrical systems at work in *Beowulf* and in the *Brut*. Of these non-conformant b-verses, 21 have 2 long dips; only 1 has a possible final long dip.[14] Like Lawman, the poets responsible for the 1,331 b-verses normally fill medial and final short dips with historical schwa. Finally, only 10 of the corresponding 1,331 a-verses (<1 percent) have the final long dips that Lawman so scrupulously avoids.[15]

This survey of late Old English and Early Middle English alliterative b-verses points to several conclusions, reinforcing and extending Yakovlev's summary of the *Brut* meter. I would propose that, on the one hand, b-verses with two long dips are rare but authentic in alliterative verse of this period, and, on the other hand, b-verses with a final long dip are categorically prohibited. Both conclusions match what is known of earlier and later alliterative meter.[16] Additionally, final long dips are prohibited in the a-verse of late Old English and Early Middle English alliterative meter, just as they had been in the *Beowulf* meter and as they would continue to be in the meter of *Gawain*.[17] The surprising regularity of the datably late poems demonstrates, first, that they really are alliterative poems, and, second, that the alliterative meter continued to be strict for hundreds of years after 950. More work remains to be done, especially, of course, on the a-verse, but the vitality of the alliterative tradition between 950 and 1250 need not remain in doubt.

Another kind of evidence of the health of alliterative meter, 950–1250, can be drawn from scribal treatment of alliterative verse texts. It is clear from manuscript variants that most scribes recognized the extant late Old English and Early Middle English alliterative poems as poems and could improvise new, metrically acceptable lines in the act of copying. Consider, for example, 3 variants in the text of the Anglo-Saxon Chronicle poem *Sweyn Forkbeard Razes Wilton* (1003–45) (quoted from Appendix A, no. 4):

	x x x S p S x	
6b (MS C)	ond swa þæt folc becyrde	(5)
	x x x x S p S x	
6b (MS D)	ond swa þeah þæt folc becyrde	(5)
	x x x S x S	
6b (MS E)	ond swa þet folc beswac.	(4)

Variant readings are underlined. The addition (or deletion) of *þeah* 'though' and the substitution of *beswac* 'fooled' for *becyrde* 'betrayed' (or vice versa) are metrically conformant revisions. At most one of these readings can be authorial, but meter offers no basis on which to prefer one over the others. Throughout this book, I isolate the problem of metricality from the problem of recovering authorial readings, because I regard verse history and the scribal transmission of poetic texts as two irreducibly distinct historical series. The abundance of metrical variants in multiply attested alliterative verse texts suggests how scribes' historically determined metrical expectations intercede between exemplar and copy. To reduce meter to its expression in a scribal text on the one hand or a reconstructed archetypal text on the other is thus to ignore a potentially significant layer of historical mediation. Nevertheless, it is possible to supplement verse history with documentary evidence precisely by recognizing the metrical competence implicit in scribal variants. The overwhelmingly metrical variants in the texts of the extant late Old English and Early Middle English alliterative poems corroborate the verse history narrated in Chapter 1 and in this chapter.

Triangulation between two notational systems, one designed for *Beowulf* and the other for the *Brut*, reveals the glacial rate of metrical change. The evolution of the alliterative b-verse must have been an unimaginably slow creep from the four-position system to the two-lifts/one-long-dip system. All alliterative poetry composed before 1350 falls somewhere between these two poles. On the one hand, no poem is so conservative that it lacks long dips altogether. As early a poem as *Bede's Death Song* (eighth/ninth centuries) has long dips in fully half of its verses. On the other hand, it took 700 years (*c.* 650–1350) for the Old English pattern SxSx (Sievers

Type A) to disappear from the b-verse. Poets did not have Sievers's *Altgermanische Metrik* or R. D. Fulk's *History of Old English Meter* by their sides to establish the limits of 'classical' usage and avoid 'late developments.' No poet or scribe could have perceived metrical change in his lifetime, if by this is meant a categorical change, like 'stop composing b-verses of the form SSxS' or 'from now on, only b-verses with exactly one long dip are permissible.' The view from the ground in 900, or 1066, or 1200, must have been of the diversity of metrical styles, some more conservative, some more innovative, but all located (we can now say in retrospect) on the continuum between where the meter had been and where it was headed.

It should be clear by now that the labels 'Old English,' 'Early Middle English,' and 'Middle English' designate synchronic phases of the alliterative tradition in this book as a descriptive convenience only. Any individual poem will fall somewhere in between two of the three typological moments schematized earlier. So for example the *Accession of Edgar the Peaceful* (975–1051) already employs the innovative Types 1 and 2 in the b-verse (Ch. 1); Lawman still makes use of the Old English pattern SxSx (Sievers Type A), albeit rarely (see below); and the *Conflict of Wit and Will* (late thirteenth/mid fourteenth centuries) exhibits significantly more a-verse/b-verse symmetry than other post-1250 alliterative poems (Ch. 4). It is a central tenet of this book that any purely synchronic statement of meter will be unable to accommodate the most conservative and most innovative elements of an individual moment in verse history. As discussed in Chapter 1, a recurrent problem with prior accounts of Old English meter has been the way in which they project the *Beowulf* meter as a transhistorical norm. The same problem had not arisen for the Early Middle English period, because no one before Yakovlev had worked out an adequate theory of Lawman's meter. Happily, Yakovlev's contribution to the study of the *Brut* was not an uncontextualized, synchronic statement of meter. For however important Yakovlev's description of the *Brut* meter may become for study of that poem, the clarification of a formal trajectory from *Beowulf* to *Gawain* reveals the longer history of metrical practice from which all alliterative poems variously emerge.

There can be no more talk of Lawman's "loose" meter. The vexed question of what sort of verse form Lawman inherited, and from whom, can now be answered. Lawman inherited the alliterative meter. He did not inherit this meter from anyone in particular, any more than the *Beowulf* poet had. Yet Lawman could not have composed otherwise and remained an alliterative poet. The failure of Ælfric's prose to measure up to Lawman's metrical system demonstrates how structured alliterative verse was, even if the *Brut* sounds choppy and unregulated to modern ears. It bears repeating that Lawman's meter has turned out to be every bit as strict as the *Beowulf* meter or the *Gawain* meter. In fact, to separate them is artificial. *Beowulf*, the *Brut*, and *Sir Gawain and the Green Knight* were all composed in the alliterative meter, at different moments in its evolution.

Lawman at a Crossroads in Literary History

On a broad view of a continuous alliterative tradition, to be the last Old English poet is to be the first Middle English poet as well. Lawman was both. To re-inscribe Lawman in literary history, it is necessary to disassemble the departmental apparatus that pinion him between decadence and doubtful beginnings. To appreciate his fundamental contribution to alliterative romance, it is necessary to unwrite the Old English grammars, dictionaries, anthologies, metrical theories – the whole imposing field of Old English studies, reverse engineered to turn into a pumpkin in the autumn of 1066. And to understand his use of the past as innovative, it is necessary to forget what Lawman could not have known, the efflorescence of English poetry in the late fourteenth century that has cast its long shadow over his long poem.

The *Brut* survives in two thirteenth-century copies, British Library MSS Cotton Caligula A.ix and Cotton Otho C.xiii. Because it preserves Lawman's conservative style, scholars originally believed Caligula to predate Otho by fifty years or more, but both manuscripts are now recognized as late thirteenth-century productions.[18] Each copy represents the happenstance collaboration of poet and scribe. The object of the collaboration is an impossibly long historical poem in English, elaborated from Wace's French verse translation (*c.* 1155) of Geoffrey's *Historia*. Entitled *The Brut* by modern specialists, the poem is called *hystoria Brutonum* in Caligula and *liber Brutonum* in Otho.

Those interested in the reputation of alliterative poetry after the Conquest find little to go on in the *Brut*. Lawman reels off line after line without explanation or apology – 16,095 of them, over half as many as all other pre-1300 alliterative poems combined. The prologue concerns other matters. The alliterative long line did not need defending, probably because its survival seemed to Lawman about as certain as sunrise. The battle between the English and the continental, 'native' and 'foreign,' is a modern battle, and Lawman would not have recognized his multilingual and multi-ethnic world translated into these modern terms. Belonging not to a sovereign nation but to Christendom, submitting not to government but to lordship, the poet could not have felt the proliferation of end-rhymed poetry as an invasion, in that modish sense of 'invasion' reserved for international ephemeralia. And ephemeral is what the end-rhymed meters must have seemed. In 1200, the written alliterative tradition was well into its sixth century; beyond *Cædmon's Hymn* (late seventh/early eighth centuries), it recedes into the mists of prehistory. By contrast, the syllabic meters of *Poema Morale* (*c.* 1180) and *Ormulum* (late twelfth century) had been in use in English for fewer than fifty years, if the written record can be believed.[19] There was as yet no Chaucer to promulgate a Frenchified literary standard, no Shakespeare to animate it, no sons of English gentlemen to learn it, and no Great Britain to export it. In 1200, the choice to use the alliterative meter was not an antiquarian choice, much less an iconoclastic one. It was the only reasonable choice for a 16,000-line narrative poem in English.

If the alliterative meter continued to dominate the English literary field in the twelfth century, from a multilingual perspective it must have increasingly seemed like a curiosity. In 1200 there were still two centuries to wait for a king to deliver a speech in English. There were still few French loanwords in English, not because a proud nation was refusing the oppressor's yoke, but because kings, courtiers, lawyers, churchmen, teachers, historians, and poets were pouring their energies into the Anglo-Norman language.[20] As Derek Pearsall observes with characteristic wit, "Anglo-Saxon England had its contacts with the continent, but England is now part of the continent, and not a very important part."[21] It is no coincidence that Lawman's *Brut*, which may justly be called the first English romance, dates from the time at which Arthurian verse romance was becoming *passé* in Anglo-Norman and French. The alliterative meter had survived the Conquest, not because of a stiff upper lip, but because it was of such unimportance in Anglo-Norman England.

All the same, Lawman felt keenly the pressures and privileges of the alliterative form. He opens with thirty-five lines not found in Wace, and they are some of the liveliest in all of the *Brut*. To be sure, prologues are a fixture in poems of the period. Wace's poem begins (quoted from *Wace's Roman de Brut*, ed. Weiss; translation mine):

> Ki vult oïr e vult saveir
> De rei en rei e d'eir en eir,
> Ki cil furent e dunt il vindrent
> Ki Engleterre primes tindrent,
> 5 Quels reis i ad en ordre eü
> E qui anceis e ki puis fu.

("Whoever wants to hear and to know, king by king and heir by heir, who they were and whence they came who first held England, which kings there were in order, and who came first and who came later.")

Compare the opening of the *Ormulum* (quoted from *Ormulum*, ed. Holt):

> Þiss boc iss nemmnedd Orrmulum
> Forrþi þatt Orrm itt wrohhte,
> And itt iss wrohht off quaþþrigan,
> Off Goddspellbokess fowwre;
> 5   Off quaþþrigan Amminadab,
> Off Cristess Goddspellbokess.

The two prologues signal recurrent structural concerns: for Wace, royal lineage; for Orm, didactic repetition. Lawman, too, declares his subject in his opening lines, following the contours of a quadripartite Aristotelian preface.[22] Yet the style of his prologue owes as much to the alliterative tradition that stands behind him as to the French romance tradition that stands before him or the academic Latin traditions that envelop him (quoted from *Laȝamon: "Brut"*, ed. Brook and Leslie, with editorial punctuation deleted and capitalization retained only for proper names):

> an preost wes on leoden   Laȝamon wes ihoten
> he wes Leouenaðes sone   liðe him beo Drihten
> he wonede at Ernleȝe   at æðelen are chirechen
> vppen Seuarne staþe   sel þar him þuhte
> 5   on-fest Radestone   þer he bock radde
> hit com him on mode   ond on his mern þonke
> þet he wolde of Engle   þa æðelæn tellen
> wat heo ihoten weoren   ond wonene heo comen
> þa Englene londe   ærest ahten
> 10   æfter þan flode   þe from Drihtene com
> þe al her a-quelde   quic þat he funde
> buten Noe ond Sem   Iaphet ond Cham
> ond heore four wiues   þe mid heom weren on archen
> Laȝamon gon liðen   wide ȝond þas leode
> 15   ond bi-won þa æðela boc   þa he to bisne nom
> he nom þa Englisca boc   þa makede Seint Beda
> an-oþer he nom on Latin   þe makede Seinte Albin
> ond þe feire Austin   þe fulluht broute hider in.

Lawman could have adopted Wace's prologue, if he had considered it suitable for alliterative verse. Instead, in thirty-five lines there is only one echo of Wace (8–9 = *Roman de Brut* 3–4). Where Wace, following Geoffrey, forefronts genealogy, Lawman holds with earlier and later alliterative poets in tying his material to distant, epochal events. In the space of forty lines he mentions the Flood (10–11), Noah's voyage on the ark (12–13), the Gregorian mission (18), and the fall of Troy (38 "þa Grickes hefden Troye | mid teone bi-wonen" = *Roman de Brut* 10). As in *Beowulf* and *St. Erkenwald* (late fourteenth/mid fifteenth centuries), in the *Brut* the distant past is lit up against an even more distant past. A sense of the multivocality of the past is not to be found in Geoffrey or Wace, for whom history is an endless parade of battles and kings. Geoffrey's *Historia* unfurls, like a roll chronicle; Lawman's prologue turns and returns.

Lawman's final additions to Wace are likewise aimed at achieving extra historical depth. Regarding Cadwalader, Wace and Geoffrey say only that he was buried splendidly, and that his soul ascended to heaven. Lawman elaborates:

> his ban beoð iloken faste   i guldene cheste
> and þer heo scullen wunie   þat þa daȝes beon icumene
> þa Merlin ine iuurn daȝen   vastnede mid worden. (Caligula 16076–78)

With *iuurn daȝen* 'olden days' (<OE *fyrndagas*), Lawman reminds the audience one last time of the antiquity of the Arthurian past. Cadwalader's bones are set on an equally massive time-scale, one embracing both the present and the future. The gesture – even the wording – comes straight from the Old English 'days-of-yore' prologue (Ch. 2).

In over sixty other places throughout the poem, Lawman pauses to relish *longues durées* not mentioned by Wace or Geoffrey.[23] Sometimes, e.g., 2997 ff., Lawman effects a cinematographic fast-forward, previewing at length the action to come. At other times, e.g., 3936 ff., events of the poem are dramatically recalled later in the narrative, to emphasize the layers of time or the historical consciousness of the characters themselves. The *Beowulf* poet made extensive use of both strategies, as did the authors of *Morte Arthure* (late fourteenth/early fifteenth centuries), *Sir Gawain and the Green Knight*, *St. Erkenwald*, etc. Thus Lawman's poem, with its prologue, inset prologues, and recursive return to the distant past, documents stylistic as well as metrical continuity in alliterative verse history.

Wace translated Geoffrey's *Historia* into a romance, but Lawman adapted Wace's poem into an alliterative romance, a new fusion of form and genre, of which the *Brut* is the first known instance. Lawman fitted to the *Roman* a frame familiar from what we now call Old English poetry, but filled that frame with altogether new content (the Matter of Britain), thereby anticipating the major thematic concern of what we now call Middle English alliterative poetry. Though a thoroughly traditional poem, the *Brut* was also a fresh beginning. To judge from later alliterative poems, it was a successful one.

The two texts of the *Brut* have equal status in the reconstructed manuscript stemma.[24] Their syntax is similar, and they both conform to the principles of Early Middle English alliterative meter.[25] Before the discovery of a coherent metrical structure in the *Brut*, scholars were wont to imagine the Otho reviser modernizing Lawman's language *ad libitum*, like a censor. Yakovlev's analysis reveals that the reviser took pains to render new, metrical half-lines after deleting or rewriting what he found objectionable. For example, Caligula 3b *at æðelen are chirechen* (Type 1, resolution of *chirech-*) becomes Otho *wid þan gode cniþte* (Type 2), invented in order to avoid the obsolescent adjective *æðele* 'noble' and the poetic inversion of the adjective and the indefinite article *are*. The metricality of both texts of the *Brut* is compelling evidence for knowledge of the alliterative meter between the *Physiologus* and *William of Palerne* (1336–61) (Ch. 4). It also has implications for the status of alliterative poetry in the period. In the second half of the thirteenth century, what seemed confusing or old-fashioned about Lawman's poem was the language, but not the meter.

Faced with a conservative poem, the Otho and Caligula manuscripts enact divergent programs for the future of alliterative verse. The Caligula scribe was a reactionary, committed to preserving the *Brut* in a difficult but historically authentic form. His modern descendants are the textual scholar and the rare-book dealer. The Otho reviser sought to bring Lawman's conservative style up to date, while preserving its metrical form. In this he might be compared to William Langland. The Caligula scribe's vision for alliterative poetry corresponds more closely to Lawman's own agenda, but the Otho reviser's attitude is another possible response to late thirteenth-century English literary culture.

At this early stage, the polar extremes of antiquarianism and modernization did not include rewriting the poem into a different meter. By comparison with the rhyming meters of the Harley Lyrics (late thirteenth/early fourteenth centuries), *Pearl* (late fourteenth century), and the *Awntyrs off Arthure* (late fourteenth/early fifteenth centuries), even Otho seems old-fashioned. During the course of the thirteenth century, the alliterative meter ceased to be the default choice for long poems in English. By 1300, many poets evidently came to believe what the author of *Poema Morale* had intuited a century earlier, that an upwardly mobile English poetry must have end rhyme. The demotion of the alliterative meter marks a sea change in literary history. It was one step in the internationalization of English language and literature. For the first time, mainstream English poetry moved beyond alliterative verse, to meters directly inspired by Anglo-Norman, Latin, and continental verse forms. The only non-alliterative English poems of any length datable before 1250 are *Poema Morale* and *Ormulum* (both in septenary) and, controversially, the *Owl and the Nightingale* (tetrameter).[26] Only five of Carleton Brown's thirteenth-century lyrics certainly date from the first half of the century. After 1250, there is an explosion of metrical romances and short religious pieces, and the *South English Legendary* is begun.

What happened in the thirteenth century was a schism between alliterative verse and English poetry *tout court*, a development that had been brewing since the invention of new English meters at the end of the twelfth century. Alliterative meter became visible in a new way within the English literary field as a specific form with specific regional and topical affinities.

The production of poetic manuscripts mirrors the revolution of poetic form. Before 1250, English poetry was laid out as prose. Exceptions are Cambridge Trinity College MS B.14.52 (*c.* 1200) and Oxford Bodleian MS Digby 4 (early thirteenth century), two early copies of *Poema Morale*, lineated in the French and Latin fashion.[27] The other early text of *Poema*, in Lambeth Palace Library MS 487 (*c.* 1200), was laid out as prose. Variable treatment of *Poema* implies that syllable-counted English meters were perceived as extremely innovative around the time the *Brut* was composed. One scribe opted to subsume the text of *Poema* under the older convention, no doubt on the basis that it was in English. Two others adopted a new, Latin-influenced verse format for the new, Latin-influenced verse form, one departure from tradition answering to the other.

After 1250, English poetry was increasingly lineated in the modern way. Lineation became the default by 1300, in lockstep with the promotion of French- and Latin-influenced English meters. However, some English poetry, especially alliterative poetry, continued to be laid out as prose. In Caligula, for instance, the *Brut* is in prose format whereas the *Owl and the Nightingale* is lineated. In Oxford Jesus College MS 29 (late thirteenth century), the alliterative *Proverbs of Alfred* is in prose format whereas *Poema Morale* and the *Owl and the Nightingale* are lineated. Apparently metrical form was the deciding factor for these scribes. The unique text of the *Physiologus* in British Library MS Arundel 292 (*c.* 1300) was laid out as prose (as was the text of the alliterative *Satire on the Blacksmiths*, added a century later). Because the *Physiologus* is composed of many meters, the meaning of the format of Arundel 292 is unclear. Probably the scribe chose the prose format because much of the *Physiologus* is in the alliterative meter, but it is also possible that in 1300 the prose format was still felt to be suitable for an English poem *per se*. Of the earliest fourteenth-century manuscript texts of free-standing alliterative poems, most are lineated, but two were laid out as prose: *Joseph of Arimathie* in the Vernon MS and the six scraps containing fragments of the *Conflict of Wit and Will*.[28] A few other poetic texts were laid out as prose in the fourteenth and fifteenth centuries, most notably the text of *Piers Plowman* in Oxford Bodleian MS Digby 102 (early fifteenth century) and some of the alliterating (but non-alliterative) Harley Lyrics (copied *c.* 1330).[29] However, the final decades of the thirteenth century mark the end of the older, prose format as the standard for poetry in English. The sporadic retention of the prose format for alliterative poems after *c.* 1250 is another symptom of the demotion of alliterative verse.

The *Brut* was composed and copied before these tendencies had settled into a status quo. On a long view, the Caligula scribe's vision came to pass. Within three centuries, alliterative poetry would be reduced to an antiquarian curiosity. But Otho stands as a reminder that the marginalization of alliterative verse did not seem inevitable in the late thirteenth century. To one reviser, at least, it seemed possible that alliterative poetry would appropriate continental manners and continue to dominate the English literary field. The two copies of the *Brut* thus emblematize two opposed trends within alliterative writing. These two trends can be summarized by the titles of two essays by David Lawton, "The Unity of Middle English Alliterative Poetry" and "The Diversity of Middle English Alliterative Poetry." On the one hand, alliterative poets grew conscious of the marked status of alliterative verse, and responded with stylistic specialization. Caligula anticipates the 'unity' trend. On the other hand, alliterative poetry never gave up on its pretensions to occupy center stage in the translation of authority into the vernacular. After 1300 it continued to borrow freely from Latin, Anglo-Norman, and continental sources. The alliterative meter is used, in an unselfconscious way, as a vehicle for political critique in *Piers Plowman* (*c.* 1370–90), *Mum and the Sothsegger* (early fifteenth century), etc. Otho was an early contribution to the 'diversity' trend.

What is striking about the turn of the fourteenth century is that the center of power shifts so decisively between these two characteristic attitudes. Caligula makes no apologies for its difficult style. It is Otho that sticks out as a modernization. In the thirteenth century, alliterative poetry was still largely synonymous with English poetry in general. Lawman harbored "antiquarian sentiments," but he took his cue from alliterative poetry itself, which had always emphasized the distant past and striven to preserve a traditional style.[30] When the unrhymed long line reappears in the written record in the fourteenth century, the shoe is on the other foot. No special explanation is needed for the topical content of the so-called *Piers Plowman* tradition. In Middle English, poems of political complaint are legion. Rather, the question is why poets continued to use the alliterative meter at all – a question that would have puzzled Lawman.

The relationship between Otho and Caligula, then, is not that of original text to bowdlerized copy, but of one to another programmatic use of the alliterative style. As Christopher Cannon has stressed, the similarities between the two texts are as striking as the differences.[31] The Otho reviser retained many battle set-pieces with minimal alteration (407–11, 766–69, 2076–79, 3727–30, etc.) and occasionally replaced one traditional word for 'man' with another (940b *scalkas* > *kempes* and 11377b *kempen* > *leode* but in the sense 'people'). To Caligula's unparalleled *here-gumen* 'war-warriors' (7254a, 9563a, and 10106b), Otho answers with *hired-gomes* (9563a, also Caligula 6132a), a distinct coinage modeled on *hired-man* 'retainer,' and equally appropriate in context. The reviser preserved, and at least twice augmented (1930aa and 3617b), Lawman's references to *longues durées*.

Comparison of passages with more discrepancies, however, illustrates the different goals of the two versions. Consider the opening of a battle in the Arthurian section:

> alle dæi þer weore   duntes swiðe riue
> folc feol to uolden   and fæie-sið worhten
> græmende segges   gras-bæd isohten
> gullen þa helmes   ȝeoumereden eorles
> sceldes þær scenden   scalkes gunnen reosen. (Caligula 11720–24)

> alle dai þar weren   duntes swiþe riue
> folk ful to folde   and þane grunde sohte
> ȝolle þe helmes   ȝeomerede eorles. (Otho, *ibid.*)

By omitting two lines and rewriting 11721b/11722b, the Otho version manages to suggest the intensity of the fight without getting bogged down by the poetic diction found in Caligula. Certainly the retention of *fæie-sið, segges, gras-bæd,* and *scalkes* in Caligula is a boon for modern philologists.[32] But the Otho passage is effective as poetry in its own right. It is entirely possible, in fact, that Lawman himself authored these and other revisions to the text attested in Caligula.[33] If so, the *Brut* would refer to an A text and a B text, like *Piers Plowman*.

What is at stake in the revision, whether it is the author's or the scribe's, is poetic idiom. In Otho the more indulgent tendencies of the alliterative style are pared away for a pithier account. Yet the persistence of marked stylistic elements in later alliterative poems means that they remained part of the living alliteration tradition, even as it drifted further away from the mainstream. The Otho revision registers the extent to which conservative poetic lexis was falling out of fashion. The Caligula version, by contrast, seems totally uninterested in fashion, devoting energy instead to a self-contained set of transpositions: death is a 'doom-journey,' knights are 'sedges,' the battlefield is a 'grass-bed,' etc. Scholars may bemoan the anesthetization of poetic language in Otho. But if the 'diversity' partisans had had their druthers, the alliterative tradition would have continued to occupy a central position within the English literary field, and Chaucer and Shakespeare might have been alliterative poets.

If Otho and Caligula are at odds over the meaning of alliterative verse, it is because Lawman's use of alliterative style poses the question *avant la lettre*. Consider another battle set-piece:

```
2580  to-gædere come þeos kinges     mid heore here-ðringes
      ferde whit ferde       feon-liche feu[ð]ten
      Scottes ond Bruttes    bei[ene] to-gaderes
      Belin here læuerd      heom biforen wende
      Brennes bisides    mid his folke of Burguine
2585  heo smiten to-gædere   helmes þere gullen
      breken brade sperren    bordes þer scænden
      redde blod scede    rinkas feollen
      þer wes muchel gristbat      þer wes cumene fæl
      weoren þa hulles and þa dæles    iwriȝen mid þe dæden. (Caligula 2580–89)
```

Perhaps fittingly, given the reviser's aversion to such verbal pyrotechnics, Otho is illegible here. Few internal rhymes and a concentration of alliteration are two hallmarks of a purple passage. Lawman is using every tool in the box. The passage has many clear connections with Old English poetics, including formulas (*ferde whit ferde:* cp. *Beowulf* 440a *lað wið laþum* 'enemy against enemy'; *bei[ene] to-gaderes:* cp. *Beowulf* 1043b *bega gehwæþres* 'of either of the two'; *heom biforen wende:* cp. *Exodus* 93a *him beforan foran* 'travelled in front of them'; *breken brade sperren:* cp. *Elene* 122a *bræcon bordhreðan* 'the shield-bucklers broke'), poetic lexis (*here-ðringes:* a *hapax legomenon*, but cp. OE *geþring* 'crowd' and *herepreat* 'war-troop'; *helmes* <OE *helm* 'helmet'; *bordes* <OE *bord* 'shield'; *rinkas* <OE *rinc* 'warrior'), traditional battle verbs (*gullen:* cp. *Andreas* 127a *guðsearo gullon* 'war-gear sang out'; *feollen:* cp. *Maldon* 111b *beornas feollon* 'warriors fell'), inverted syntax (*heom biforen* 'in front of

them'), verse-internal rhyme (*redde blod scede*: cp. *Beowulf* 1422a *flod blode weoll* 'the water welled up with blood'), and even the conservative metrical pattern SxSx (Sievers Type A) (2587b).

Verses with two lifts and no long dip are extremely rare in the *Brut* (*c.* 1% of verses), so it may be tempting to interpret 2587b as a self-conscious homage to Old English poetry.[34] However, it is doubtful that Lawman knew, or could have expected his audience to know, the first thing about Old English poems.[35] The pattern SxSx crops up from time to time in other Early Middle English alliterative poetry, including compositions on contemporary topics. The pattern remained metrical through to the *Conflict of Wit and Will* (Ch. 4), and there is no need to ascribe sentimental value to it. Vestige is a feature of traditional meters and an expression of metrical hysteresis, or the way in which the history of form resists complete systematization. As Yakovlev observes,

> [t]he average time span between major prosodic upheavals appears to be less than that required to eliminate any remains of the previous restructuring . . . [T]he number of asystemic patterns, i.e. patterns that are not produced by general metrical rules . . ., may be greater or smaller at any given point in poetic history, but it will hardly ever be zero.[36]

If the Old English long line never died, Lawman can hardly be mourning it with verses like *rinkas feollen*. Battle scenes were a traditional strength of alliterative poetry, and so it makes sense that they should attract traditional phraseology. This is as true of the *Brut* as it was of *Beowulf*. In 1200, *rinkas feollen* was still the right way to describe the losers of an ancient battle immortalized in conservative poetry. Lawman did not use the phrase as an outsider, in an attempt to revive a Golden Age of literature. He used it unselfconsciously, one in a long line of poets.

Evident coinages like *here-ðring* and *gristbat* (both peculiar to the *Brut*) show that what modern scholars call 'Old English' poetic language was still a manipulable thing for Lawman. He would not have considered his poem antiquarian, because antiquarianism implies a death of poetic tradition – either the 'death' of Old English poetry, which is an artifact of modern subdisciplinary boundaries, or the death of alliterative verse in the sixteenth century, of which Lawman suspected nothing. The copying and glossation of Old English texts by the so-called Tremulous Hand of Worcester toward the middle of the thirteenth century may be more relevant for understanding the motivations of the Caligula scribe late in the century than those of Lawman in 1200. The dichotomy of archaism and neologism, sharpened in the fourteenth century and dominant today, was less pointed for Lawman. Of course the *Brut* was an old-fashioned poem, even in 1200. But in 1200, old-fashioned was still hip. The *Brut* owes its attitude toward the past to a durable poetic tradition, not to one priest's excursion through a pile of manuscripts.

Lawman's difficult style is above all an idiomatic poetic style. The combination of alliterative meter and historical romance is his lasting legacy, yet the *Brut* also gives a clear impression of a writer steeped in tradition. Lawman's materials would be turned to new ends in the second half of the century. Neither Caligula nor Otho is the poem that Lawman wrote, for each copyist was responding to new developments in literary culture that quickly, and permanently, changed the stakes of alliterative writing. Lawman is the last Old English poet because he wrote the last long alliterative poem before the ascendancy of new, non-alliterative English verse forms. He is the last poet not to have contended with the marginalization of alliterative verse. He is the first Middle English poet because his original treatment of Arthurian legend laid a foundation for Middle English romance. The point to make about Lawman's two hats is that they are really one hat. The eventual death of alliterative poetry casts over the whole tradition a desperate pallor, of which Lawman naturally was ignorant. Until the invention of printing, the prestige of alliterative poetry did not completely dry up, though it was channeled more stringently after 1250. So it is in the truest sense that Lawman belongs both to the Old and to the Middle. These are after all our divisions, not his. Lawman's "ambivalence toward the past" parallels his ambivalence between two possible futures for alliterative verse.[37] The inheritor of a poetic tradition he did not consider outdated, Lawman contributed to a new English genre whose wild success he could scarcely have imagined.

By way of conclusion, I would like to draw an analogy between the terms used to discuss metrical traditions in this chapter and the terms used to discuss language traditions in Sheldon Pollock's wide-ranging study of Sanskrit, *The Language of the Gods in the World of Men*. Pollock introduces the key concept of 'vernacularization,' defined as "the historical process of choosing to create a written literature, along with its complement, a political discourse, in local languages according to models supplied by a superordinate, usually cosmopolitan, literary culture."[38] Vernacularization occurs in two stages, for which Pollock coins the terms 'literization,' or the process of committing a language to written form, and 'literarization,' or the elaboration of a written language into a literary tradition. A related concept introduced by Pollock is 'superposition,' or the way that culturally powerful language traditions inflect the development of their less culturally powerful neighbors. Scholars of medieval English literature have been interested in vernacularization for some time now. Pollock's terminology may help refine critical understanding of the processes by which a spoken language becomes a written language, a written language becomes a vernacular literary tradition, and a vernacular literary tradition becomes a 'cosmopolitan vernacular,' the fifth and last of Pollock's key terms. Pollock defines cosmopolitan vernacular as "that register of the emergent vernacular that aims to localize the full spectrum of literary qualities of the superposed cosmopolitan code."[39] In two dedicated chapters, "A European Countercosmopolis" and "Europe Vernacularized," Pollock himself capitalizes on the power of his theoretical frame to clarify the development of premodern European literary traditions.

Much more could be said about the theoretical capacity of Pollock's framework in general and his treatment of the medieval English situation in particular. Most relevant for the present purposes is Pollock's insight that "[a] prevalent feature in the vernacularization process is the time lag between literization and literarization."[40] Substituting metrical traditions for language traditions, we can say that the literization of non-alliterative English meters occurred approximately one century before their literarization. In the second half of the twelfth century, it became newly possible to compose English poetry in non-alliterative meters, but I have argued that it was not until c. 1250 that non-alliterative meters were consolidated into metrical traditions to rival the alliterative tradition. The earliest extant long syllable-counted English poems, *Ormulum* and *Poema Morale*, are workmanlike in comparison with much contemporary and earlier alliterative verse. Lawman should be understood as working in the time in between the literization and the literarization of the first new English meters. Hence the absence in his poem of any apology for or indeed acknowledgment of his metrical choice; hence his ambivalence in diachronic perspective; hence the stylistically charged reception of his poem in two late thirteenth-century manuscripts.

The literarization of syllable-counted English meters c. 1250 may well be the defining event in the vernacularization of English literature as a whole. This is one way of glossing Cannon's challenging study, *The Grounds of English Literature*, which recovers the richness of Early Middle English literature by examining the paths taken and not taken in the development of later English literary forms and genres. Pollock's terminology makes it possible to follow through on Cannon's project from a new angle. Comparison to other European vernaculars and South Asian vernaculars enables us to gauge the durability and cultural status of the English alliterative tradition. Alliterative verse enjoyed an exceptionally early literarization under the superposition of Latin literature from at least the ninth century. The alliterative tradition resisted (for 100 years) and then survived (for 300 more) the promotion of English meters inspired by metrical traditions in more culturally prestigious languages. Situating Early Middle English literature within (or against) this longer trajectory of verse craft further historicizes the *English Literature* of Cannon's title.

The displacement of Pollock's terminology onto the metrical traditions of a single language prefigures the convolutions of metrical form in the more densely populated fields of fourteenth-, fifteenth-, and sixteenth-century poetry. The concepts of vernacularization and cosmopolitan vernacular help pinpoint an important irony in the history of English metrical forms. While in a multilingual perspective syllable-counted meters represent a newly cosmopolitan disposition toward (English) language tradition, within the English literary field they were at first a belated curiosity. The cosmopolitanism of non-alliterative English meters vis-à-vis Anglo-Norman, French, and Latin literatures has received the full attention of literary scholars. These meters have always been understood to register the pressure on English of an ascendant Anglo-Norman/French vernacular and a durably cosmopolitan Latin literature. It was partially against the teleological force of such arguments that Cannon saw himself to be working. The isolation of developmental trajectories within the English literary field is at once his book's greatest achievement and its greatest weakness.[41] Yet the question of the vernacularization, as it were, of French- and Latin-inspired English meters vis-à-vis the alliterative meter has never been posed as such. The reason is simple: Early Middle English alliterative meter and its Old English ancestry have never before been understood in detail. Alongside the more familiar questions about Anglo-Norman/French and Latin influence on Middle English literary forms, it is now desirable to investigate how the alliterative tradition influenced the syllable-counted English metrical traditions on which it was superposed from the late twelfth to the mid thirteenth centuries.

The next chapter takes up this sensitive task. The chapter presents metrical, lexical, and textual evidence for the continuity of the alliterative tradition across the ninety-year gap in the written record (*c.* 1250–1340). It then extends the foregoing discussion of the 'unity' and 'diversity' trends within alliterative writing into the fourteenth and fifteenth centuries, with double focus, as here, on the diachronic lineage of poetic styles (especially prologues) and the synchronic interpenetrations of English, Anglo-Norman, French, and Latin literary traditions.

CHAPTER 4

Prologues to Middle English Alliterative Poetry

If Old English meter evolved directly into Middle English alliterative meter, then there was no need for the resuscitation of alliterative verse at any point in its history. Conceptualized not as a new beginning in literary history but as one phase in a durable poetic tradition, the fourteenth- and fifteenth-century alliterative corpus sheds new light on the chronological distribution of the manuscript record, the diversification of medieval English poetic forms, and the shifting relationships between Middle English, Anglo-Norman, and French.

This chapter argues that the lack of firm documentary evidence for the composition of alliterative poetry between the Middle English *Physiologus* (*c.* 1250) and *William of Palerne* (1336–61) is an accident of manuscript survival, not evidence of the death of alliterative verse and a subsequent 'Alliterative Revival.' Because the hypothesis of an Alliterative Revival remains the consensus among Middle English specialists, the first section presents metrical, lexical, and textual evidence for the continuity of the alliterative tradition across the ninety-year gap in the written record. The second section offers metrical, syntactical, and codicological evidence against the conflation of the (unrhymed) alliterative meter with alliterating stanzaic meters. The third section develops a typology of prologues to long Middle English alliterative poems, with reference to similar prologues to non-alliterative Middle English, Anglo-Norman, and French poems and with special emphasis on *Piers Plowman* (*c.* 1370–90). The typology has a twofold purpose: first, to measure prologues to Middle English alliterative poetry against the prologues to earlier alliterative poems, discussed in Chapters 2 and 3, and so to extrapolate a stylistic *longue durée* for alliterative verse; second, to measure alliterative poetry against non-alliterative poetry (especially romance), and so to gauge the position of alliterative verse in late medieval English literary culture.

The Continuity of the Alliterative Tradition, 1250–1340

The evidence that alliterative verse continued to be composed between the *Physiologus* and *William of Palerne* is chiefly metrical. It can be divided into metrical-phonological evidence and purely metrical evidence.[1] Because the metrical-phonological evidence came first in the history of the field and laid the groundwork for purely metrical theorization, I take it up first. Over the past few decades, Thomas Cable, Nicolay Yakovlev, and Ad Putter, Judith Jefferson, and Myra Stokes independently demonstrated the significance of historically justified *-e* in fourteenth-century alliterative meter. Had alliterative poets fabricated a new meter out of whole cloth, it is difficult to imagine how they could have recovered *-e* in words whose fourteenth-century spellings and pronunciation gave no clue to their ancestry, e.g., monosyllabic *skinne* (<ON *skinn* + OE *scinn*) beside disyllabic *sunne* (<OE *sunne*). Historical *-e* survived in fourteenth-century alliterative meter as a phantom syllable, absent from the spoken language, often invisible in scribal orthography and possibly inaudible in performance, yet metrically significant.

A comparison of the long-line and short-line meters of *Sir Gawain and the Green Knight* (late fourteenth century) is instructive in this regard. As Marie Borroff has shown, historical *-e* normally was not sounded in the *Gawain* short-line or bob-and-wheel meter.[2] Differential treatment of *-e* within a single poem indicates that the two meters have different histories. *Pearl* (late fourteenth century), if it was composed by the same hand as the other Cotton Nero poems, provides more evidence for divergent treatment of *-e* on a metrical basis. Unlike in *Cleanness, Patience,* or the long lines of *Gawain,* in *Pearl* historical *-e* is not counted at line end, since there occur many rhymes like *pere* 'peer' : *were* 'were' (subjunctive) (4b and 6b; *pere* <OF *per* and *were* <OE *wære*). As relative newcomers in English, the bob-and-wheel meter and template meter captured contemporary (fourteenth-century) phonology. By contrast, the alliterative meter was at least 700 years old by the fourteenth century, and so it did not immediately reflect the desuetude of *-e* in contemporary spoken English. The concept of metrical hysteresis, that is, the momentum accrued by a poetic tradition over time, helps explain how eleventh- through thirteenth-century linguistic phonology could become fossilized in fourteenth-century metrical phonology.

Complementary to the metrical-phonological evidence that Middle English alliterative meter had historical precursors is purely metrical evidence that those precursors were none other than Old English and Early

Middle English alliterative meter. Simply put, Middle English alliterative meter fits into a developmental arc beginning at Old English meter and traveling through Early Middle English alliterative meter. Recall Yakovlev's typology of Early Middle English b-verse patterns alongside the late Middle English b-verse patterns described by Cable:

EME (Yakovlev)		ME (Cable)
xSx . . . xSx (1)	=	(x)Sx . . . xSx
x . . . xSxSx (2)	=	x . . . xS(x)Sx
Sx . . . xSx (3)	=	(x)Sx . . . xSx
x . . . xSxS (4)	=	x . . . xS(x)Sx
x . . . xSSx (5)	=	x . . . xS(x)Sx

Early Middle English alliterative poets could fill the final dip with a schwa (Types 1, 2, 3, and 5) or leave it empty after a medial short dip (Type 4), whereas late Middle English alliterative poets always filled it with a schwa (x . . . xS(x)S$\underline{x}$ and (x)Sx . . . xS$\underline{x}$). In other words, fourteenth-century alliterative poets used the same b-verse patterns as their immediate predecessors, but with the tendency toward a feminine ending regularized. To suppose that they independently hit upon a b-verse repertoire so close to the one used by Lawman would be absurd. The decreasing symmetry of a-verse and b-verse (*c.* 95% in Old English, *c.* 65% in Early Middle English, and *c.* 5% in Middle English) also points to continuous development. Further, Old English meter and Middle English alliterative meter use the same prosodic hierarchy to assign metrical stress.[3] The prosodic hierarchy would have seemed very artificial by the late fourteenth century in comparison to the phrasal and rhythmically conditioned stress assignment used in deductive meters, e.g., *Canterbury Tales* I 1 *Whán that Áprille with his shóures sóote*. Here the function words *whan* and *with* receive metrical stress because of the expectation of an alternating rhythm. That Middle English alliterative meter assigned stress according to different principles was one effect of its different history.

Other evidence of continuity can be drawn from lexis. Middle English alliterative verse employs eleven poetic words for 'man,' which take the linguistic forms to be expected from direct descent from Old English or Old Norse: *bern/burn* <OE *beorn, freke* <OE *freca, gome* <OE *guma, hathel* <OE *hæleð* + OE *æðel* 'noble (adj.),' *kempe* <OE *cempa, ledel lude* <OE *leod, renk* <OE *rinc* + ON *rekkr, shalk* <OE *scealc, segge* <OE *secg, tulk* <ON *túlkr,* and *wye* <OE *wiga*. In Middle English, the eleven words are

overwhelmingly concentrated in alliterative poems. For example, the *Gawain* poet uses ten of them (hundreds of occurrences) in *Sir Gawain and the Green Knight* and *Cleanness*, and nine (forty-two occurrences) in *Patience*, but only four (seven occurrences) in the alliterating but non-alliterative *Pearl*, which is twice as long as *Patience*. Or again, William Dunbar's lone alliterative poem, the *Tretis of the Tua Mariit Wemen and the Wedo* (*c.* 1500), making up less than 10% of Dunbar's corpus by volume, contains more total occurrences of the eleven words than his other eighty-three poems combined. Metathesis in *hathel*, dialectal vowel changes in *burn*, *lude*, and *renk*, and reduction of final vowels to schwa in *freke*, *gome*, *kempe*, and *wye* are the results of well-understood linguistic processes. The eleven poetic words do not appear ever to have been part of everyday language, to judge from their almost complete absence from prose or documentary sources of any period. Therefore, their exposure to linguistic change indicates that they were continuously used in alliterative verse.

Finally, the copying of alliterative poems provides direct evidence of the circulation of alliterative verse in the late thirteenth and early fourteenth centuries and (in the form of textual variation) indirect evidence of the development of alliterative meter. Over sixty surviving texts of alliterative poems were made *c.* 1250–1350, including both copies of Lawman's *Brut* (*c.* 1200), three copies of the *Proverbs of Alfred* (late twelfth century), and dozens of copies of the ubiquitous couplet on St. Kenelm (?late eleventh/early thirteenth centuries). Although most of the texts are incidental to Latin or rhyming English texts, an abundance of metrically regular variants confirms that scribes remained familiar with alliterative meter at the turn of the fourteenth century.[4] The half-century in which the Otho reviser reworked thousands of lines of Lawman's *Brut* into correct alliterative a-verses and b-verses is not a likely period in which to locate metrical death.

If alliterative verse history continued across the gap in the record, then the extant poems closest to the gap can help give a sense of what has been lost. The ten alliterating lines found in Richard Rolle's *Ego Dormio* (1340s) may be the earliest surviving fourteenth-century alliterative poem. If Rolle is quoting an earlier work, the poem could trim the ninety-year gap even further. "Alle perisches and passes" comes closer to the meter of Lawman's *Brut* than do post-1350 alliterative poems. Yakovlev scansions accompany the b-verses (quoted from *English Writings*, ed. Allen, p. 64):[5]

```
x    S x x x    S x      x   x x   S x S
```
Alle perisches and passes þat we with eghe see   (4)

```
x   S x x x   S x  S x    x  S   x x   S  x
```
It wanes into wrechednes, þe welth of þis worlde.   (1)

```
S   x x   S  x      S x x  S x
```
Robes and ritches rotes in dike,   (3)

```
S       S  S  x   S x x x  S x
```
Prowde payntyng slakes into sorow,   (3)

```
x S x x    S x S x    S  x x  x  S x
```
5 Delites and drewryse stynk sal ful sone,   (3)

```
x   S   x    x   S  x    S x   x  x   S x
```
Þair golde and þaire tresoure drawes þam til dede.   (3)

```
x x   S x x x   S  x     S x  x x  S x
```
Al þe wikked of þis worlde drawes til a dale,   (3)[6]

```
x   x   x  S  x    S  S  x     x   S  x x x  S x
```
Þat þai may se þare sorowyng, whare waa es ever stabel.   (1)

```
x   x   x  S  xx  S x      x x x   S x   S
```
Bot he may syng of solace, þat lufes Jhesu Criste.   (4)

```
x    S  x    x  S x   S x  x x  S x
```
10 Þe wretchesse fra wele falles into hell.   (3)

Assuming 'compound stress,' or two lifts on a single word, in four instances (2a *wrechednes*, 4a *payntyng*, 5a *drewryse*, and 8a *sorowyng*), all the a-verses meet the minimum requirements of at least four positions, two to four lifts, and no final long dip. Three of the a-verses (1a, 3a, and 10a) (30%) would make acceptable two-lift b-verses – much less a-verse/b-verse symmetry than in the *Brut* (c. 65%) but still much more than in *Sir Gawain and the Green Knight* (c. 5%). (Verses 2a, 4a, 5a, and 8a have three lifts; 6a and 9a have non-schwa final short dips, with *tresoure* <OF *tresor* and *solace* <OF *solaz* both scanning Sx, regardless of scribal -*e*'s; and 7a and 9a have two long dips, with infinitive -*e* counted but not written in 9a *syng* <OE *singan*.) All ten of the b-verses would be metrical in the *Brut*, and all but two (1b and 9b) would be metrical in *Gawain*. "Alle perisches and passes" even has an example of the internal rhyme that is so characteristic of the Early Middle English poems (10 *wele* : *hell*).

Another candidate for the earliest fourteenth-century (or even latest thirteenth-century) alliterative poem is the *Conflict of Wit and Will*. Roughly 120 lines of a presumably much longer poem survive in 6 fragments, in a hand of "the middle or the second quarter of the fourteenth century."[7] The text of *Wit and Will* is laid out as prose, presumably reflecting the format of the exemplar. Prose format for vernacular poetry remained an option throughout the fourteenth and fifteenth centuries but was significantly less common after the early fourteenth century than before. The poem contains nine words not attested elsewhere after *c.* 1325, including five not attested elsewhere after *c.* 1200. These latter have a distinctly poetic tinge: B 34a *auel* 'strength' <OE *afol* + ON *afl*, D 2b *wiplaw* 'warfare' <OE *wig-plega*, D 11b *on-borne* 'incensed' <OE *onbærnan*, D 13a *diues* 'submerge (tr.)' <OE *dyfan*, and E 1b *gres-bed* 'grass-bed=battlefield' <OE *gærs-bed*. The poem also has conservative b-verse patterns, e.g., B 30b *þar he rughest was* (Type 4), B 44b *Happes fere* (Type A), and F 6b *wordes melte* (Type A). Finally, *Wit and Will* exhibits approximately the same level of a-verse/b-verse symmetry as "Alle perisches and passes" (25%). Taken together, these conservative features of textual format, lexis, and meter make possible a date as early as the second half of the thirteenth century, though such considerations are by no means conclusive. A chapter in alliterative verse history took place during the ninety-year blank in the written record, but in the absence of firmly datable texts it should be spoken of sparingly. The traceable evolution of the long line provides formal criteria for identifying any late thirteenth- or early fourteenth-century alliterative poetry that might surface. It would look much like the *Physiologus*, "Alle perisches and passes," and *Wit and Will*.

In addition to the positive evidence for the continuity of the alliterative tradition, there are other reasons to doubt both assumptions underlying the hypothesis of an Alliterative Revival. The first of these assumptions is that alliterative meter could have died suddenly in the thirteenth century; the second is that poets could have revived or reinvented it in the fourteenth. I do not believe that either of these hypothetical events is intrinsically likely to have occurred. With regard to the first, thirteenth-century metrical death, it is salutary to consider the last surviving thirteenth-century alliterative poem, the *Physiologus*. In the middle of that century, a poet rendered Theobaldus' Latin *Physiologus* (eleventh century), itself an experiment in metrical variety, into a slew of Middle English meters. The alliterative long line is given pride of place as the first meter (ll. 1–26), and it accounts for *c.* 25 percent of the poem by volume. Of 147 alliterative lines, 146 a-verses and 146 b-verses conform to the alliterative metrical system as this is known from other compositions (Ch. 3). The plurality of meters in the Middle English *Physiologus* has traditionally been seen as a sign of the impending death of the 'native' meter at the hands of 'foreign' meters. But this is to let the fortunes of manuscript survival, not to mention the boundaries of modern nations, determine literary history. The meaning of polymetricality in the *Physiologus* would be lost if alliterative verse were an obscurity *c.* 1250. To the contrary, the *Physiologus* shows alliterative meter thriving within a newly diversified poetic landscape. In the middle of the thirteenth century the alliterative meter was apparently first to spring to mind as a choice for a polymetric poem in English, perhaps because it contrasted most clearly with the other English meters in use at the time. A verse form so firmly established in poets' active repertoire would not be likely to disappear overnight.

To the alliterative tradition in its final centuries one could compare modern accentual-syllabic meters. In the first quarter of the twentieth century, Ezra Pound and the modernists announced the death of metered verse, proffering in its place a kind of poetry that claimed to be free of meter altogether. Yet here we are 100 years on, using blank verse to translate epics (as in Sarah Ruden's *Aeneid* of 2008) and limericks to satirize news items (as in the Listener Limerick Challenge on National Public Radio's "Wait, Wait, Don't Tell Me"). The form and politics of metered verse have undergone continuous change since Pound's lifetime; yet meter endures. In the previous chapter I argued that the demotion of alliterative verse in literary culture, analogous to Pound's "first heave," took place *c.* 1250. Without a foothold in the grammar curriculum of its day, the means by which alliterative verse survived generation to generation were quite different from the preservation of modern metrical forms. Yet if the alliterative tradition had half as much momentum in 1250 as metrical traditions had in 1915, when Pound began work on the *Cantos*, then it could not have died out so suddenly as proponents of an Alliterative Revival must suppose. As it happens, the two watershed moments came at almost precisely the same point in their respective metrical traditions. In 1915 the pentameter was 535–45 years old, counting forward from the 1370s, when Chaucer to all appearances invented this form on the model of French and Italian meters. By 1250 the alliterative tradition was 565 years old, counting forward from the approximate date of *Cædmon's Hymn*, the earliest datable Old English poem.

It is even harder to accept the second assumption inherent in the hypothesis of an Alliterative Revival, that fourteenth-century poets "consciously – and by gradual stages – remodeled a written tradition of alliterative composition."[8] A fourteenth-century English writer stood little chance of encountering a pre-1250 alliterative poem, less chance of understanding it, and virtually no chance of extracting from it a complex prosodic hierarchy, four and only four b-verse patterns, and eleven poetic words for 'man.' If Old English poems were the model, then surely the four-teenth-century poets would have imitated prevalent Old English patterns such as x(x . . .)SxS and xSSx while avoiding x . . . xSxSx, a pattern that was vanishingly rare before the eleventh century. They also would have written long lines with a high degree of a-verse/b-verse symmetry. On the other hand, if Early Middle English alliterative poems were consulted, whence the avoidance of internal rhyme and the absence of x . . . xSxS in the b-verse? Least credible of all would be the idea that fourteenth-century antiquarians consulted Old English and Early Middle English poems in tandem, comparatists *avant la lettre*. The difficulty of intuiting b-verse patterns from poetic manuscripts is demonstrated by the fact that modern specialists, aided by critical editions, concordances, textual corpora, and, latterly, linguistics and computers, have only recently discovered them. Moreover, metrical regularities in earlier alliterative poetry are not percep-tible in the first place without knowledge of metrical resolution and the prefix license, both defunct by the fourteenth century and without a basis in the spoken language. The more conservative Old English poems also exhibit non-contraction, non-parasiting, and a variety of other specialized metrical features. Earlier alliterative poets learned these principles implicitly, through habitual imitation of their peers and predecessors. It is difficult to believe that fourteenth-century antiquarians should have mastered such arcane rules, only to reinvent alliterative meter without them. Like modern specialists, medieval antiquarians would have faced the additional problem of having to parse poetry textualized in an unfamiliar way, as prose. Indeed, one might question whether fourteenth-century readers would have been capable of recognizing an Old English poem in manuscript as such.

A more concrete way to gauge the plausibility of the antiquarian hypoth-esis is to turn to the one richly documented example of a medieval reader who grappled with much earlier alliterative poetry. Henry of Huntingdon's Latin translation of the *Battle of Brunanburh* (c. 937) in his *Historia Anglorum* (c. 1125–40) suggests that some Old English poetic language had become obscure by the twelfth century.[9] Henry marvels at the use therein of "strange words and figures [*extraneis tam verbis quam figuris*]," and his translation shows it.[10] He mistakes 8a *cneo-* 'generation' for 'know' (*cognationum*), 16b *mære* 'famed' for 'merry' (*hilariter*), 21b *eorod-* 'troop' for 'ere' (*prius*), 25b *hælepa* 'warriors' for 'health' (*sanitas*), etc.

On the other hand, the translation reveals a remarkable facility with alliterative style. Henry handily translates 2a *beorna* 'men' (*nobilibus*), 13a *secga* 'men' (*armati*), and 50b *gumena* 'men' (*proborum*). He correctly glosses 8b *campe* 'war' (*bellis*), 6ob *hræw* 'carrion' (*carnes virorum*), 62b *hasewan-* 'gray' (*livens*), etc. He recognizes the formulaic understatement 'had no need to boast' in three occurrences with three different infinitives (39b *hreman*, 44b *gelpan*, and 47b *hlehhan*), answering with three of his own (*jactare, declamare,* and *mentiri*). Henry invents his own poetic variation (*thesauros et domos | pecunias et xenia* 'treasures and homes, monies and gifts' for 10b *hord and hamas* 'hoard and homes') and coins a metaphor (*trans maris campos* 'over the fields of the sea' for 26b *ofer æra gebland* 'over the commotion of the sea') that picks up on the formulaic system 'sea=land,' as in OE *seglrad* 'sail-road=sea.' He substitutes the Latin equivalent of a traditional synecdoche for 'ship' (*ligni* = OE *wudu* 'wood') for a poetic simplex (27a *lid* 'ship'). Henry even manages an interlingual pun (49a *campstede : campo belli* 'battlefield'). Clearly, some aspects of alliterative style were familiar to Henry in the twelfth century.

Metrically, the translation is nothing short of an English alliterative poem in Latin (Appendix C). All but one of Henry's seventy b-verses scan as alliterative b-verses, in the mixture of older and newer metrical patterns characteristic of the twelfth century, not the tenth. While the majority of Henry's b-verses have the *cursus* patterns that come so easily in Latin, Henry takes pains to compose a few Types 2 (46b *licet vérbis blándus*), 4 (60b *Ergo córvus níger*, with resolution of *níger*), and 5 (13b *ex quo sól máne*) and Sievers Types A (1b *décus dúcum*), B (52b *planxérunt súos*, with resolution of *súos*), C (27b *trans máris cámpos*, resolution of *máris*), and D (1a *Réx Ádelstàn*). Henry fares much better, in fact, than the three Old English poets who tried their hand at alliterative meter in Latin and produced only the *cursus-* and/or hexameter-compliant pattern Sx(x . . .)Sx (*Aldhelm, Phoenix* 667–77, and *Summons to Prayer*). Henry includes three-lift half-lines (2a, 15a, 37a, etc.) but concentrates them in the a-verse, like Lawman and later alliterative poets but unlike Old English poets. Like Lawman but unlike most Old English poets, Henry employs internal rhyme, correlated either syllabically in the Latin manner (14 *mícans : laetíficans*) or accentual-syllabically in the English manner (12 *corruérunt : resonuérunt*, 19 *lanceáti : Scótti*, and 70 *fugavérunt : suscepérunt*).

Extrapolating forward in time, Henry's errors imply that it would have been more or less impossible for a fourteenth-century reader to understand tenth-century alliterative poetry. Yet the translation also shows that knowledge of some specialized poetic techniques was alive and well in the twelfth century. The apparent ease with which Henry equates the *Brunanburh* poet's tenth-century alliterative metrical practice to twelfth-century alliterative metrical practice constitutes valuable contemporary testimony against a break in the alliterative tradition after the Norman Conquest of England (1066) (see Ch. 3). The successes of Henry's translation do not point to the use of Latin-Old English glosses. Errors in translation like *sanitas* for *hælepa* suggest that Henry was mentally translating into his own English before moving on to Latin. Certainly no glossary could have taught him the meter that Lawman was to use decades later. For Henry's knowledge of poetic lexis, formulas, variation, and alliterative meter, the most plausible source is a living alliterative tradition that survived from the tenth century to the twelfth century and beyond. The same argument holds for fourteenth-century alliterative poets.

If a variety of evidence implies that alliterative poetry existed in a precise metrical form *c.* 1250–1340, one might inquire why none of it has survived. Here we must discard another influential hypothesis concerning this silent century in alliterative verse history. Proponents of the continuity of the alliteration tradition, writing before Early Middle English alliterative meter was well understood, appealed to the existence of an undocumented oral tradition of alliterative poetry. To this phantom tradition they then imputed all the attitudes so conspicuously lacking in the extant corpus – patriotism, xenophobia, provincialism, antiroyalism, and the will to speak for the poor. The need for such radical speculation is greatly reduced once Early Middle English alliterative verse takes up its rightful place as a phase in the development of the alliterative tradition. It is inherently unlikely that a durable written tradition was interrupted by ninety years of oral transmission, which chanced to develop just the sort of meter and poetic lexicon that would have resulted from evolution of the written tradition before depositing the tradition back onto the page around the time of Chaucer's birth. It would be tautologous to point out that all other alliterative poetry survives in manuscript. It is because it survives in manuscript that scholars know of it in the first place. One can never rule out the existence of some other, oral alliterative tradition, but it is bad reasoning to invoke such a tradition only so as to be in a position to explain a gap in the written one.

Metrical, lexical, and textual evidence leads us to make an inference: alliterative poetry was composed and written down *c.* 1250–1340, but no manuscript containing it happens to survive. This situation should not be surprising. Undoubtedly, many more alliterative poems have been lost than survive. Nearly the whole extant Old English poetic corpus is contained in 4 codices, compiled within a 75-year period; the 2 copies of Lawman's *Brut* constitute 95 percent of the extant alliterative verse by volume for 300 years; and only 9 of the 45 extant Middle English alliterative poems appear in more than 2 manuscripts or early printings.[11] The lack of firm documentary evidence for alliterative poetry in a 90-year window is inconvenient, but it is also a statistically predictable conse-quence of the massive loss of manuscripts and the decreasing prestige of the alliterative tradition.

All the same, the disparity in the record between the first and second halves of the fourteenth century need not be an illusion. There are several reasons why alliterative poetry might have been composed and copied more widely after *c.* 1350. These include the attenuation of Anglo-Norman literary traditions, the changing prerogatives of scriptoria, the leveling effects of the Black Death, and the expansion of the bureaucratic middle class. These explanations apply as well to Middle English litera-ture in general. In other words, the uptick in the production of English alliterative poems is readily intelligible as a special case of the uptick in the production of Middle English literature. Rupture in metrical history does not appear among either the likely causes or the direct effects of the explosion of English writing after 1350. Alliterative verse history did not register in any immediate way the vicissitudes of fourteenth-century spoken English, or written English, or monastic life, or class mobility. Alliterative poets seem never to have convened to celebrate and discuss traditional verse forms, as Welsh poets did at the Eisteddfodau of Cardigan (1176), Carmarthen (1451), and Caerwys (1568). From *Beowulf* to the *Brut* to *Sir Gawain and the Green Knight*, the alliterative meter went on evolving, relatively independent of cultural, linguistic, political, and textual history. From a verse-historical perspective, the Alliterative Revival was a non-event.

Excursus: Middle English Alliterating Stanzaic Poetry

In parallel with ongoing metrical development within the alliterative tradition, a new kind of poetry began to be composed in English in the fourteenth century.[12] This new kind of poetry, typified by the *Awntyrs off Arthure* (late fourteenth/early fifteenth centuries), employed heavy allitera-tion, alliterative poetic lexis, and even alliterative rhythms in an elaborately rhymed stanza structure. Previous scholars have nearly always categorized the alliterating stanzaic poems as alliterative poems and folded them into discussions of the alliterative tradition. Much excellent literary and textual scholarship has been carried out on this basis.[13] Here I offer metrical, syntactical, and codicological evidence in support of the proposition that the (unrhymed) alliterative meter and alliterating stanzaic meters are closely related but formally distinct.

The most telling difference between (unrhymed) alliterative meter and alliterating stanzaic meters concerns stress assignment. In the *Awntyrs off Arthure*, metrical stress often seems to fall on a non-alliterating function word, e.g., *Awntyrs* 73–74 *And þis mékel mervaíle | þat Í shal of méne./ Now wol Í of þis mervaíle | méle if I móte.* In a-verses like *Awntyrs* 74a in alliterative poetry, the first metrical stress may fall on a non-alliterating function word from the initial dip ('metrical promotion'), e.g., *Beowulf* 22a *þǽt hine on ýlde* 'that . . . him in old age.' However, b-verses like *Awntyrs* 73b are studiously avoided in alliterative poetry. With no alliteration or inherent prosodic weight to guide in the placement of stress, the first lift in b-verses like *Awntyrs* 73b could be mistaken for part of the initial dip. (The ambiguity is tolerated in the a-verse because the alliterative value of the first lift cannot be predicted anyway.) There are 13 verses in the first 200 lines of *Awntyrs* like 73b or 74a (9 b-verses), as against 3 in the first 200 long lines of *Sir Gawain and the Green Knight* (0 b-verses).[14] In *Awntyrs* this type of b-verse can occur, because there is a new dimension that supplements prosodic weight as a determiner of metrical stress: the metrical beat.

The shape of the a-verse in *Awntyrs* furnishes a particularly stark contrast with (unrhymed) alliterative poems. The three-lift a-verses so common in the unrhymed corpus are hardly to be found in *Awntyrs*. In the *Awntyrs* sample there are some 22 three-lift a-verses (11%), as against 67 (34%) in the *Gawain* sample.[15] The incidence of three-lift a-verses in *Awntyrs* is significantly lower than that of any unrhymed poem except the metrically problematic *Destruction of Troy* (?late fourteenth/early sixteenth centuries).[16] In alliterative verse, the three-lift a-verse is the most inductive metrical pattern of an inductive verse form. The scant attestation of this pattern in *Awntyrs* is one effect of the introduction of deductive techniques of scansion, consequent upon the addition of end rhyme.

The *Awntyrs* meter, then, is in template meter, tending toward anapestic tetrameter. The b-verses of *Awntyrs* and similar poems very often form the same metrical patterns as their counterparts in (unrhymed) alliterative meter, but in the stanzaic poems these patterns are reified as rhythmical variations in a beat-counting meter. The alliterative *rhythm* may be in the foreground, but the anapestic *meter* jingles along in the background. Counterpoint between rhythm and meter is foundational to accentual-syllabic (deductive) meters, but it does not occur in the same way in alliterative (inductive) verse. Anapests and dactyls are the metrical units nearest to hand for poets who borrow their rhythms from the alliterative meter, as witness the translation of a portion of the *Coronation of Edgar* (973–79) into dactylic hexameter in Æthelweard's *Chronicon* (975–83), or James VI of Scotland's remark in his *Reulis and Cautelis* (1584) that alliterating stanzaic meter ("*Tumbling* verse") "hes twa short, and ane lang throuch all the lyne."[7] The same effect of alliterative rhythm overlaid on accentual-syllabic metrical expectations also occurs in the wheels of the alliterating stanzaic poems, where the opening short lines take alliterative a-verse rhythms and the closing short line takes an alliterative b-verse rhythm.[18]

Poetic syntax provides a second analytical category by which to distin-guish (unrhymed) alliterative meter from alliterating stanzaic meters. David Lawton has observed that the addition of rhyme transforms the syntax of alliterative poetry. Stichic syntax becomes strophic syntax as the focal point of the line shifts from the caesura to the line boundary.[19] The metrical and syntactical differences between the *Awntyrs* meter and the *Gawain* meter can be illustrated by a moment when the *Gawain* poet switches to the newer style for rhetorical effect: "Þay boȝen bi bonkkez | þer boȝez ar bare;/ Þay clomben bi clyffez | þer clengez þe colde" (*Gawain* 2077–78). These lines, with their hyperalliteration (a a | a a), a-verse/ b-verse symmetry (all four half-lines scan xSxxSx), chiming rhythm between lines or what might be called 'rhythm rhyme,' and syntactical parallelism, dramatize Gawain's journey to the Green Chapel and stand out clearly from the *Gawain* poet's normal metrical-syntactical practice.

Because a perceptible metrical distinction between (unrhymed) allitera-tive meter and alliterating stanzaic meters has rarely been asserted in previous studies of alliterative poetry, I supplement the preceding metrical and syntactical arguments with indirect evidence for the reality of the distinction in the minds of medieval practitioners. My evidence comes from the compilation of codices. Given the scant survival of codices containing multiple alliterative poems, three examples will have to suffice. Among the 392 poems in the massive Vernon MS (1390–1400), the 2 alliterative poems, *Piers Plowman* and *Joseph of Arimathie* (late fourteenth century), appear consecutively, while two poems in the rhyming thirteen-line stanza, the *Disputation between Mary and the Cross* (non-alliterating) and the *Pistill of Swete Susan* (alliterating), appear in sequence elsewhere in the manuscript. Among the 37 poems in British Library MS Cotton Caligula A.ii (mid fifteenth century), the 2 alliterative compositions, *Siege of Jerusalem* (late fourteenth century) and *Chevalere Assigne* (late fourteenth/early fif-teenth centuries), appear consecutively, far away from *Susan* in the same manuscript, which instead immediately precedes *Sir Eglamour of Artois*, a non-alliterating romance in a twelve-line stanza. Finally, the *Parlement of the Thre Ages* (late fourteenth/early fifteenth centuries) and *Wynnere and Wastoure* (late fourteenth century) appear consecutively in British Library MS Additional 31042 (mid fifteenth century), over 100 pages away from the *Quatrefoil of Love*, an alliterating romance in the thirteen-line stanza. Meter may not be the only relevant organizational principle in these three instances, but no non-metrical explanation by itself (genre, length, subject matter, the presence of alliteration) accounts for the compilers' disposition of materials. We can infer that the compilers recognized a formal difference between (unrhymed) alliterative poems and alliterating stanzaic poems and acted on that recognition in the process of *compilatio*.

Whether that difference was one of meter or of rhyme is a moot issue. The preceding analysis supports the traditional view that end rhyme is antithetical to the alliterative meter. End rhyme invites a deductive scansion because it performs phonological identity at perceptually regular intervals. This is why Old English poetry avoids rhyme and why Early Middle English alliterative poems rhyme irregularly and only line-internally. To exclude rhyming poems from the alliterative tradition is not to impose an arbitrary criterion, but to recognize in the unrhymed poetry what Derek Pearsall calls "a striking formal characteristic."[20] The codicological evidence serves to ground this modern judgment in medieval perceptions of metrical form.

On metrical, syntactical, and codicological grounds, then, the *Awntyrs off Arthure* and similar poems stand outside the verse history sketched in the previous section. The next section will invoke and then problematize the category of 'non-alliterative poetry,' now understood to include the alliterating stanzaic poems. I erect this admittedly incoherent category in an effort to shed comparative light on fourteenth- and fifteenth-century alliterative verse history.

Middle English Prologues, *romaunce*, and Middle English Poetic Styles

To adjudge the position of alliterative verse in late medieval English literary culture, as I propose to do by means of a typology of poetic prologues, one must confront the slippery category of romance. In the previous chapter I argued that Lawman's *Brut* anticipated Middle English alliterative romance, which I called "a new fusion of form and genre." Where Chapters 1 and 3 sought to contextualize the alliterative verse form, this section and the next chapter connect alliterative meter to the genre of *romaunce* (<OF *roman*) that loomed so large for late medieval English writers.

What is romance? The definition of the genre has provoked much critical hand-wringing. While *romaunce* certainly comes to name a literary genre with features recognizable enough to be parodied, as in Chaucer's *Tale of Sir Thopas* (last quarter of the fourteenth century), I am persuaded by Yin Liu's discussion of "Middle English Romance as Prototype Genre." Liu argues that medieval English discussions of *romaunce* imply comparisons to prototypical instances rather than absolute definitions. When Middle English writers adduced examples of *romaunce*, they turned less often to the heroes who have become most emblematic of medieval romance in the modern imagination (Lancelot, Orfeo, Tristan, et al.) than to others who figure less prominently in anthologies and critical discussion (Octavian, Guy of Warwick, et al.).[21] Liu's reorientation of the problem of the category of romance enables other revisionist arguments, like my own, that would locate influence on the genre emanating from unexpected quarters. I seek to understand *romaunce* as it is created by and through alliterative and non-alliterative poems, in order to avoid relying on an absolute definition that would predetermine the scope of my investigation. In what follows, I consider the prologues to Middle English poetry for the evidence they provide of influences between metrical traditions and across language traditions, with attention to Old English precursors on the one hand and to the genre of romance on the other.

Like other ingredients of the alliterative style, prologues were not restricted to alliterative poems. By the fourteenth century, alliterative verse had fully internalized the conventions of romance, and alliterative romances were probably received as romance first and alliterative second. It is only on a long historical view that the prologues of alliterative poetry can be treated separately from the similar openings of non-alliterative poems. However, the long historical view is the one taken in this book. Precisely because Middle English alliterative poetry was saturated with the conventions of romance, it suffices for an overview of Middle English romance to discuss prologues to alliterative poetry separately before comparing them to those of adjacent Middle English, Anglo-Norman, and French verse forms and drawing broader literary-historical conclusions. Beginning with alliterative poems aids in highlighting continuities with the prologues to earlier alliterative poems, discussed in Chapters 2 and 3. Moreover, I will identify some salient differences between the handling of individual types of prologue in alliterative and non-alliterative verse.

Before proceeding, it is worth pointing out one type of literary self-consciousness not found in earlier alliterative poetry and so not discussed in Chapters 2 or 3, but which confirms that the long poem continued to function as a discrete literary format in the English literary field after Lawman. The *Wars of Alexander* (late fourteenth/early fifteenth centuries) opens with what I will call a 'meta-prologue' (quoted from *Wars*, ed. Duggan and Turville-Petre):

> When folk ere festid & fed,   fayn wald þai here
> Sum farand þinge eftir fode   to fayn[en] þare hertis,
> Or þai ware fourmed on fold   or þaire fadirs oþir.

The representation of a courtly audience gearing up for postprandial minstrelsy is an authorizing fiction, no less than the scop scenes in *Beowulf*. But the subsequent description of themes is a crash course in the subgenres of Middle English romance: martyrology ("Sum is leue to lythe | þe lesing of sayntis," 4), courtly love ("And sum has langinge of lufe | lay[e]s to herken," 6), chivalric romance ("Sum couettis & has comforth | to carpe & to lestyn/ Of curtaissy, of knyʒthode, | of craftis of armys," 8–9), and moral *exemplum*, positive ("Sum of wirschip, iwis," 11) and negative ("And sum of wanton werkis," 12). Most importantly, the action takes place in the distant past (3). In addition to the presence of prologues *per se*, the existence of meta-prologues lends further support to the division between long and short poems observed in this book.

Prologues to Middle English alliterative poetry fall into four types, which I term (in descending order of frequency) the 'May-morning' prologue, the 'God-grant-grace' prologue, the 'olde-tyme' prologue, and the 'doughty' prologue (Fig. 4).[22]

The first of these is ultimately derived from the French *chanson d'aventure* tradition and, more proximally, Guillaume de Lorris's hugely influential *Roman de la Rose* (Lorris's portion completed *c.* 1230). The following discussion, however, begins with the Middle English poems, returning to the *Roman* and French poetry by way of conclusion. I prioritize English here for two reasons. First, this book centers on an English metrical tradition, and I mean to emphasize continuities between Old and Middle English poetry that remain invisible in a late medieval, international perspective. Second, most Middle English 'May-morning' prologues exhibit a cluster of keywords and *topoi* found in *Piers Plowman* but not Lorris's *Roman*, suggesting the value of treating the English prologues as discrete formal phenomena before restoring them to their multilingual context.

The 'May-morning' prologue locates the opening scene in season (early summer), in perspective (first person), and, usually, in space (a countryside).[23] Five of the twelve prologues or inset prologues of this type mention the month of May; eleven are narrated in the first person. The opening of

'May-morning'
(*A Bird in Bishopswood*)
Crowned King 17 ff.*
Death and Liffe 22 ff.*
Mum and the Sothsegger 876 ff.*
(*NIMEV* 1507.5)
(*NIMEV* 1564)*
Parlement of the Thre Ages
Piers Plowman
Piers Plowman B 8*
Prophesie of Waldhaue
Tretis of the Tua Mariit Wemen and the Wedo
Wynnere and Wastoure 31 ff.*

'God-grant-grace'
*Chevalere Assigne**
*Crowned King**
Death and Liffe
Destruction of Troy
Morte Arthure
*Pierce the Ploughman's Crede**
Piers Plowman B.7.203 ff.
Scottish Field
("Þanne God graunte grace…" in Trevisa's *Dialogus inter dominum et clericum*)
William of Palerne 161 ff.
William 5527 ff.

'olde-tyme'
*Destruction of Troy**
Destruction 99 ff.
Morte Arthure 13 ff.
Scottish Field 18 ff.
*Siege of Jerusalem**
Sir Gawain and the Green Knight
Gawain 2522 ff.
St. Erkenwald
Wynnere and Wastoure

'doughty'
Destruction of Troy 7 ff.*
Morte Arthure 18 ff.
*Romance of Alisaunder**
Wars of Alexander 15 ff.*

meta-prologue
Wars of Alexander

remainders (long poems only)
Cleanness
"Merling saies in his booke…" in the *Whole Prophesie*
Mum and the Sothsegger
Patience
Richard the Redeless
Vision of William Banastre

Figure 4. Prologues to Middle English Alliterative Poems
Parentheses indicate poems under 100 lines that begin with prologues. Asterisks denote the
absence of the keywords discussed in Ch. 4.

the *Piers Plowman* B Prologue is the best-known instance (quoted from *Piers Plowman*, ed. Kane and Donaldson):

> IN a somer seson   whan softe was þe sonne
> I shoop me into [a] shrou[d]   as I a sheep weere;
> In habite as an heremite,   vnholy of werkes,
> Wente wide in þis world   wondres to here.
> 5   Ac on a May morwenynge   on Maluerne hilles
> Me bifel a ferly,   of Fairye me þoʒte.
> I was wery forwandred   and wente me to reste
> Vnder a brood bank   by a bourn[e] syde . . .
>
> .   .   .
>
> [Ac] as I biheeld into þe Eest,   an heiʒ to þe sonne,
> I seiʒ a tour on a toft   trieliche ymaked,
> 15   A deep dale byneþe,   a dongeon þerInne
> Wiþ depe diches and derke   and dredfulle of siʒte.
> A fair feeld ful of folk   fond I þer bitwene. (1–8; 13–17)

The alliterative groups *somer seson . . . softe . . . sonne, May morwenynge, wery . . . wandred, bank . . . bourne* (elsewhere *bryme*) *syde*, and *deep dale* reappear in later 'May-morning' prologues.

Since *Piers Plowman* is by far the most frequently attested alliterative poem in the surviving records and among the most frequently attested Middle English poems overall, its opening is likely to have exerted significant influence on later poets. To distinguish specific borrowings from conventional alliterative formulas, however, may be impossible. The 'May-morning' prologue occurs in two long early fifteenth-century polemical poems that have been grouped within a '*Piers Plowman* tradition' (*Mum and the Sothsegger*, ll. 876 ff., and *Crowned King*, ll. 17 ff.) and five other alliterative poems that should also be so grouped (*A Bird in Bishopswood*; *Parlement of the Three Ages*; *Death and Liffe*, ?fourteenth/sixteenth centuries; Dunbar's *Tretis*; and the *Prophesie of Waldhaue* in the *Whole Prophesie of Scotland, &c.*, first printed 1603).[24] In recent years, literary scholars have been most interested in reading *Piers Plowman* as a religio-political tract, thereby emphasizing its similarity to fifteenth-century topical poems which were evidently influenced by it. But *Piers Plowman* is also an allegorical debate or *dialogus* (like *Parlement* and *Death and Liffe*), a satirical treatise (like Dunbar's *Tretis*), and a political prophecy (like the *Prophesie of Waldhaue*). The presence of the 'May-morning' prologue in later poems registers generic similarities to Langland's exceptionally popular alliterative composition.

The 'May-morning' prologue to *Wynnere and Wastoure* bears the least similarity to Langland's diction, but it includes the three basic elements (summertime, first-person perspective, a countryside) and a vision of a multitude ("In aythere holte was ane here | in hawberkes full brighte," 50, quoted from *Wynnere and Wastoure*, ed. Trigg). The correspondence to Langland's "fair feeld ful of folk" is enhanced by the detail that the armies occupy a lawn ("lande," 48; cp. *Piers Plowman* B.8.65 "launde") beside a hill ("lawe," 49; cp. *Piers Plowman* B.Prol.14 "toft"). *Wynnere and Wastoure* has been dated as early as 1352–53 on historical grounds, but more recently scholars have questioned the evidentiary basis for dating the poem much before *c.* 1370.[25] Whether composed before or just after the publication of *Piers Plowman* A, the 'May-morning' prologue to *Wynnere and Wastoure* seems to signal affiliation with a certain genre of long polemical poem. Indeed, *Wynnere and Wastoure* combines most of the genres represented by *Piers Plowman* and the other poems with 'May-morning' prologues: allegorical debate or "refreyte," as announced in the poem's title in manuscript; satirical treatise; and political prophecy, as in ll. 10–18.

The 'God-grant-grace' prologue, like the Old English 'let-us-praise-God' prologue before it, opens long poems with an invocation to the deity by a personalized *me* or, less commonly, an *us*. Eight of the eleven prologues of this type combine two or more of the alliterating keywords 'God,' 'give,' 'grant,' and 'grace.' One uses the Middle English reflex of OE *herian* 'praise,' the keyword for the Old English 'let-us-praise-God' prologue (*Crowned King* 3 *heried*). Presumably this word continued to carry solemn liturgical connotations in vernacular poetry between the tenth and the fifteenth centuries. The opening of *Destruction of Troy* is typical of the 'God-grant-grace' prologue (quoted from *Destruction*, ed. Panton and Donaldson):

> Maistur in magesté,   maker of Alle,
> Endles and on,   euer to last!
> Now, god, of þi grace   graunt me þi helpe,
> And wysshe me with wyt   þis werke for to end!

Allusion to the might ("Maistur"), dignity ("magesté"), unity ("on"), and immortality ("Endles . . . | euer to last") of God must have struck poets as an all-purpose opener. In sharp contrast to the Old English 'let-us-praise-God' prologue, the 'God-grant-grace' prologue occurs in a wide variety of genres, including chivalric romance (*Destruction of Troy, Morte Arthure,* and *Chevalere Assigne*), non-chivalric romance (*William of Palerne*), allegorical debate (*Piers Plowman* and *Death and Liffe*), treatise (*Piers Plowman* again; *Pierce the Ploughman's Crede*, last decade of the fourteenth century; and *Crowned King*), and even a victory poem (*Scottish Field*). Among the four types of prologue, the 'God-grant-grace' prologue occurs most often in poems containing multiple types of prologue (six of eleven 'God-grant-grace' prologues or 55 percent).

The 'olde-tyme' prologue, like the Old English 'days-of-yore' prologue before it, emphasizes the temporal distance separating author and audience from the matter of the poem. Seven of the nine prologues or inset prologues of this type include the keyword *sythen* 'ever since' or the key phrase *olde tyme*, which could be translated 'days of yore.' Four of them (*Wynnere and Wastoure*; *Sir Gawain and the Green Knight*; *Gawain* 2522 ff.; and *Scottish Field*, 1515–47) mention Brutus of Troy, legendary founder of Britain. The opening of *Gawain* is typical (quoted from *Poems of the Pearl Manuscript*, ed. Andrew and Waldron):[26]

> Siþen þe sege and þe assaut   watz sesed at Troye,
> Þe borȝ brittened and brent   to brondez and askez . . .
>
> . . .
>
> And fer ouer þe French flod,   Felix Brutus
> On mony bonkkes ful brode   Bretayn he settez. (1–2; 13–14)

The references to the fall of Troy (1) and the subsequent conquest of Britain (14) locate the action not merely in a glorious past, but in a past with its own prior history. One might compare the allusions to Scyld Scefing in *Beowulf* or to the Flood and the fall of Troy in Lawman's *Brut*. The 'olde-tyme' prologue may have been especially marked as vernacular in literary culture, an expression of the same cultural perception that Chaucer's Pardoner declares to the pilgrims: "lewed people loven tales olde;/ Swiche thynges kan they wel reporte and holde" (*Canterbury Tales* VI 437–38).

The 'olde-tyme' prologue occurs primarily in chivalric romance (*Morte Arthure*, late fourteenth/early fifteenth centuries; and twice each in *Sir Gawain and the Green Knight* and *Destruction of Troy*), but its appearance at the head of a debate poem (*Wynnere and Wastoure*), a hagiographic romance/*inventio* (*St. Erkenwald*, late fourteenth/mid fifteenth centuries), and a victory poem (*Scottish Field*) reveals further complexities of genre and poetic style. Because the next chapter discusses *St. Erkenwald* in detail, I focus here on the other two poems. If we are not to regard the opening allusions to "Bruyttus" (1) and the "takynge of Troye" (2) in *Wynnere and Wastoure* as "pointless" and "irrelevant," with Dorothy Everett, then we must presume that the 'olde-tyme' prologue held some particular cachet for a mid fourteenth-century poet.[27] The value of the prologue may well have lain in the way the *Wynnere and Wastoure* poet puts the Arthurian past to unexpected uses, simultaneously inverting its reputation as a storehouse of marvels ("There hathe selcouthes bene sene | in seere kynges tymes/ Bot neuer so many as nowe | by the nyne dele," 3–4) and nostalgically painting it as a Golden Age of oral poetry ("Whylome were lordes in londe | þat loued in thaire hertis/ To here makers of myrthes | þat matirs couthe fynde," 19–20). Then again, the 'olde-tyme' prologue to *Wynnere and Wastoure* may have been intended as an emblem of high seriousness. Its thematic dissonance with the poem to which it is attached signals the interpenetration of genres and the influence of alliterative romance style on other alliterative verse by the middle of the fourteenth century.

The reference in *Scottish Field* to the span of time "Sith Brute heere abode | & first built vp houses" (18) seems similarly unconnected to its immediate context, if more thematically appropriate in a poem that promises to tell "of kings | that conquered full wide, / That dwelled in this land | that was always noble" (5–6) (quoted from *Scotish Ffeilde*, ed. Oakden). The *Scottish Field* poet employed the 'olde-tyme' prologue to authorize and embellish a victory poem in the tradition of the *Battle of Brunanburh*. That a poet could do so as late as the second quarter of the sixteenth century has implications not only for our understanding of the last chapter of the alliterative tradition (Ch. 6), but also for our understanding of the poetic communities represented by the 'olde-tyme' prologue. Whether they knew the alliterative poems known to us or (more likely) many others now lost, the *Gawain* poet, the *Wynnere* poet, and the *Scottish Field* poet were habituated to the alliterative tradition at three times and in three places in which allusion to Brutus of Troy was *de rigueur* for a poetic high style.

The 'doughty' prologue was very popular as a framing device in non-alliterative romance (see below), but it occurs in only four alliterative poems, all chivalric romances. Only one of the four, the alliterative *Morte Arthure*, includes the keyword 'doughty' (quoted from *Morte Arthure*, ed. Brock):

> Herkynes me heyndly   and holdys ʒow stylle,
> And I salle tell ʒow a tale,   that trewe es and nobylle,
> Off the ryealle renkys   of the Rownnde Table,
> That chefe ware of cheualrye   and cheftans nobylle,
> Bathe ware in thire werkes   and wyse mene of armes,
> Doughty in theire doyngs,   and dredde ay schame. (15–20)

Like the *Destruction of Troy* poet, the *Morte* poet combines the 'olde-tyme,' 'God-grant-grace,' and 'doughty' prologues. No other Middle English alliterative poem contains three or more types of prologue, whether consecutive or far separated. In a genre famous for rhetorical bluster, *Destruction* and *Morte Arthure* stand out for the extreme formality of their openings.

Five long alliterative poems do not contain prologues: two theological/homiletic treatises in the *Gawain* manuscript (*Cleanness* and *Patience*), two long late political prophecies ("Merling saies in his booke. . ." in the *Whole Prophesie* and *Vision of William Banastre*, late fifteenth century), and a political satire in the *Piers Plowman* tradition (*Richard the Redeless*, early fifteenth century). As in Old English verse, the lack of a prologue seems to follow from the *modus tractandi* of these poems, which can be broadly characterized as exegetical rather than diegetical. The generic similarities of the five prologue-less poems to *Piers Plowman* illuminates, by contrast, Langland's ability to combine exegetical and diegetical poetic modes. In *Piers Plowman*, most spectacularly of all alliterative poems, the exegetical and the diegetical constitute one and the same poetic event.

In the previous chapter I identified two opposed trends in alliterative verse, which I related to the titles of two essays by David Lawton, "The Unity of Middle English Alliterative Verse" and "The Diversity of Middle English Alliterative Verse." Comparison of Figure 4 to the prologues to long non-alliterative Middle English poems (Fig. 5) illustrates both the unity and the diversity of the alliterative tradition after 1300.

'May-morning'
Amoryus and Cleopes 8 ff.
Buke of the Howlat
Buke of the Howlat 156 ff.
Buke of the Howlat 998 ff.
Canterbury Tales I 1 ff.* (*General Prologue*)
Canterbury Tales I 1033 ff. (*Knight's Tale*)
Canterbury Tales I 2483 ff.* (*Knight's Tale*)
Eneados, Prol. VIII*
Floure and the Leafe*
(*In May in a Morning*)
Isle of Ladies
Legend of Good Women 103 ff.
Quatrefoil of Love
Quatrefoil of Love 517 ff.
Romaunt of the Rose 49 ff.
Somer Sunday*
Thomas of Erceldoune 25 ff.

'God-grant-grace'
Arthour and Merlin
Athelston
Avowyng of Arthur*
Emaré*
Erle of Tolous
How Our Lady's Sauter Was First Found 13 ff.*
King and his Four Daughters
King Edward and the Hermit

Figure 5. Prologues to Select Non-Alliterative Middle English Poems
Parentheses indicate poems under 100 lines that begin with prologues. Asterisks denote the absence of the keywords discussed in Ch. 4. Alliterating stanzaic poems underlined.

Laud Troy Book*
Lybeaus Desconus*
Nativity and Early Life of Mary 9 ff.*
Octavian*
Prick of Conscience*
Reinbroun
Richard Coer de Lyon*
<u>*Ane Satyre of the Thrie Estaits*</u>
Sir Degrevant
Sir Eglamour of Artois*
Sir Gowther*
Sir Isumbras*
Sir Tryamour*
Sowdone of Babyloyne
Torrent of Portyngale
Ywain and Gawain*

'olde-tyme'
Amis and Amiloun*
Avowyng of Arthur*
<u>*Awntyrs off Arthure**</u>
<u>*Awntyrs* 714 ff.*</u>
Book of the Duchess 53 ff.
Canterbury Tales III 857 ff. (*Wife of Bath's Tale*)
Confessio Amantis*
Eger and Grime*
Erle of Tolous*
Generides 23 ff.*
<u>*Gologras and Gawain**</u>
<u>(*Gyre Carling*)*</u>
Horn Childe & Maiden Rimnild*
How Our Lady's Sauter Was First Found*
Kyng Alisaunder*
Life of St. Alexius
Nativity and Early Life of Mary*
(*NIMEV* 1209)
Octavian*
A Peniworþ of Witt*
<u>*Rauf Coilȝear**</u>
<u>*Roland and Vernagu* 5 ff.</u>
Seege of Troye
Seege of Troye 21 ff.*
Seynt Katerine 5 ff.*
Siege of Milan*
Sir Cleges*
Sir Corneus*
Sir Degaré*
Sir Degrevant*
Sir Eglamour of Artois*
Sir Isumbras*
Sir Launfal*
Sir Orfeo*
Stanzaic Morte Arthure*
Tale of Beryn
Troy Book 148 ff.*

Figure 5. (cont.)

Troy Book 195 ff.
*Wedding of Sir Gawain and Dame Ragnelle**
Þe *Wenche þat Loved þe King** (assuming extensive loss)

'doughty'
Amis and Amiloun 33 ff.
Anonymous Short Metrical English Chronicle 14 ff.
Avowyng of Arthur
*Beves of Hamtoun**
Canterbury Tales VII 712 ff. (*Tale of Sir Thopas*)
*Carle of Carlisle**
*Eger and Grime**
Gologras and Gawain
*Havelok the Dane**
Ipomydon
Laud Troy Book 11 ff.
Le Bone Florence of Rome
*Life of St. Alexius**
Lybaeus Desconus
Octavian 18 ff.
Otuel a Kniȝt
Reinbroun
Richard Coer de Lyon 28 ff.
*Robert of Cisyle**
*Roland and Vernagu**
Siege of Milan
Sir Cleges
Sir Degaré 9 ff.*
Sir Degrevant 10 ff.
Sir Eglamour of Artois 7 ff.*
Sir Gawain and the Carle of Carlisle
Sir Isumbras 7 ff.
Sir Launfal
Sir Perceval of Galles
*Squire of Low Degree**
*Stanzaic Guy of Warwick**
Tale of Gamelyn
Thomas of Erceldoune
Torrent of Portyngale
Tournament of Tottenham
The Turke and Sir Gawain
Wedding of Sir Gawain and Dame Ragnelle 11 ff.

meta-prologue
Book of the Duchess 44 ff.
Canterbury Tales VII 897 ff. (*Tale of Sir Thopas*)
Cursor Mundi
Generides
Kyng Alisaunder
Laud Troy Book 11 ff.
Lay le Freine
Richard Coer de Lyon
Richard Coer de Lyon 6723 ff.
Sir Orfeo
Speculum Vitae 35 ff.

Figure 5. (cont.)

The 'May-morning' and 'God-grant-grace' prologues to non-alliterative poetry are more or less indistinguishable from their counterparts in alliterative poems, though the 'May-morning' prologue occurs less frequently in the non-alliterative corpus (17 of 118 total prologues or 14% for non-alliterative poems, as against 12 of 36 total prologues or 33% for alliterative poems). Helen Cooper argues cogently that Chaucer modeled his *General Prologue* on the Prologue to *Piers Plowman* A. However, the 29 'May-morning' prologues gathered in Figures 4 and 5 qualify Cooper's passing remark that "[s]uch an opening is . . . rare as a beginning for long poems."[28] None of the Middle English 'May-morning' prologues certainly predates *Piers Plowman*. The conventionalized nature of the 'May-morning' prologue makes it difficult to go much further than Cooper in treating the opening of the *Canterbury Tales* as the result of specific literary borrowing. The significantly higher proportion of 'May-morning' prologues in extant alliterative poems could mean that the prologue, in its specifically Langlandian form, originated in alliterative verse; or that it was borrowed from non-alliterative (English?) verse into alliterative verse and subsequently became more popular there; or even that *Piers Plowman*-like alliterative poems have disproportionately survived in manuscript, for any number of reasons. The 'May-morning' prologue forms a point of contact between the alliterative tradition and the metrical traditions inhabited by Chaucer.

In contrast to the 'May-morning' prologue, the distribution of the 'olde-tyme' prologue demonstrates in a most immediate way the unity or distinctiveness of alliterative verse. Though 'olde-tyme' prologues occur slightly more often in non-alliterative poems than in alliterative poems (40 of 118 total prologues or 34% for non-alliterative poems and 9 of 36 total prologues or 25% for alliterative poems), none of the non-alliterative 'olde-tyme' prologues mentions Brutus of Troy (as against 4 of 9 alliterative 'olde-tyme' prologues or 44%). Only 6 of the non-alliterative 'olde-tyme' prologues use the keyword *sythen* or the key phrase *olde tyme* (15%, as against 7 of 9 alliterative 'olde-tyme' prologues or 78%). Some non-alliterative 'olde-tyme' prologues use the equivalent phrase *olde days*; more commonly, non-alliterative poets employ less ornate terms like *in the dayes of . . .*, *sometyme*, and *whilom* to mark the antiquity of their subject matter. In Chapters 1, 2, and 3, I discussed Old English and Early Middle English precedents for the 'olde-tyme' prologue, including the use in Old English verse of *syððan*, ancestor of ME *sythen*. Evidently this aspect of poetic style became marked as alliterative after the founding of non-alliterative English metrical traditions. The use of the 'olde-tyme' prologue in non-alliterative poems conceivably reflects the influence on Middle English romance of alliterative style as it developed over the centuries before the ascendance of French- and Latin-inspired English meters.

The 'doughty' prologue tells a different story again. This prologue probably originated in non-alliterative romance and was then borrowed into alliterative verse. It occurs nearly 3 times as often in non-alliterative poems (37 of 118 total prologues or 31% for non-alliterative poems, as against 4 of 36 total prologues or 11% for alliterative poems). The keyword 'doughty' appears much more frequently in the non-alliterative group than in the alliterative group (26 of 37 'doughty' prologues or 70% for non-alliterative poems, as against 1 of 4 'doughty' prologues or 25% for alliterative poems). The prologue to the alliterative *Morte Arthure*, including the word 'doughty,' suggests that alliterative poets could conceive of themselves as contributing to the most prestigious echelon of romance writing. But the paucity of 'doughty' prologues in alliterative poetry also suggests that, when composing alliterative verse, poets remained resistant to this particular aspect of the Middle English romance tradition as it developed in non-alliterative verse after *c.* 1250.

One other type of prologue prevalent in non-alliterative romance scarcely occurs at all in alliterative poetry. It might be called the 'listen-here' prologue, and it appears prominently in the openings of dozens of rhyming romances. The presentation of the narrator as a minstrel is not foreign to alliterative poems (cp. the foregoing discussion of the *Wars* meta-prologue, and *Gawain* 30–31 "If ʒe wyl lysten þis laye | bot on littel quile, / I schal telle hit astit, | as I in toun herde"). However, the 'listen-here' prologue is rare in alliterative verse and is never given pride of place in the opening lines of an alliterative poem. Like the 'doughty' prologue, the 'listen-here' prologue illustrates the unity of the alliterative tradition as against non-alliterative Middle English verse. Both of these types of prologue had become closely associated with rhyming romance by the late fourteenth century, when Chaucer could use them in tandem to satirize tail-rhyme romance in *Sir Thopas* ("Listeth, lordes," VII 712, and "Sire Thopas wax a doghty swayn," VII 724).

As in all likelihood the first extant long alliterative poem after Lawman's *Brut, William of Palerne* is of special importance to a reconstruction of the 'unity' and 'diversity' trends within the alliterative tradition. The *Brut* and *William* are both translations of French-language poems, yet whereas the *Brut* is massively and, as I have argued, characteristically absorbed in the distant past, *William* is distinguished by its total lack of interest in this category. The text of *William* is acephalous in the unique manuscript, Cambridge King's College MS 13. Though the French *Guillaume de*

Palerne (*c.* 1200) opens by describing the tale as "le fait dune anciene estoire" "the event of an ancient story" (20, text and translation from *Romance*, ed. Skeat), it is difficult to imagine the English poem beginning with an 'olde-tyme' prologue. The William who composed *William* ("haþ william | al his werke ended," 5521) crafts a romance world whose temporal distance from poet and audience is less important than its moral, political, and emotional drama.

Thus *William of Palerne* provides a limit case for the thematic argument of this book, that the alliterative tradition was characterized by an abiding interest in the distant past. When compared to the overtly historicizing style of many prior and contemporary alliterative compositions, the style of *William* shows that metrical traditions and poetic styles do not overlap automatically or completely. Recognition of the durable engagement with the distant past in alliterative poetry, in turn, provides a framework within which to historicize William's stylistic choices. Like the Otho reviser before him and Langland after him, but unlike Lawman, William actively pursued diversification and internationalization of alliterative style.

To summarize the arguments of this section thus far: the form and distribution of the 'May-morning' prologue imply the imposing influence of *Piers Plowman*, not only on other alliterative poems but on Middle English verse generally. The 'olde-tyme' prologue (positively) and the 'doughty' and 'listen-here' prologues (negatively) demonstrate the perceptibility and unity of the alliterative tradition within the wider English literary field in the fourteenth and fifteenth centuries. Finally, the 'God-grant-grace' and 'olde-tyme' prologues, including the use of the keywords *herien* and *sythen*, respectively, link the Middle English alliterative corpus with earlier phases of the alliterative tradition in a continuous chain of poetic style. The relative abundance and datability of Middle English poems in comparison with Old English poems has enabled me to extend the methods of Chapters 2 and 3 to new research questions, approaching prologues as expressions of poetic style but also as symptoms of literary influence and vectors of continuity in literary history.

Though useful as an analytical convenience for the writing of alliterative verse history, 'non-alliterative poetry' is, of course, an incoherent category. The concept of verse history already indicates the insufficiency of treating poems in various meters under one head. Therefore it should be worthwhile to disaggregate the prologues to non-alliterative poetry by meter. As a first step in this direction, in Figure 5 I have underlined those poems in alliterating twelve- or thirteen-line stanza forms. The stanzaic poems have always been held to have special relevance for the alliterative tradition.

Indeed, most scholars categorize them as alliterative; in the previous section, however, I discussed reasons for regarding the stanzaic tradition as a formally distinct offshoot of the alliterative tradition. Of fifteen prologues in alliterating stanzaic poems, fully eight are 'May-morning' prologues. Further, these eight 'May-morning' prologues comprise over half of all 'May-morning' prologues in Figure 5. Five of the remaining seven prologues to alliterating stanzaic poems are 'olde-tyme' prologues. The 'May-morning' and 'olde-tyme' prologues, like alliteration, half-line structure, and alliterative rhythms, are loci of affiliation with the alliterative tradition in these stanzaic poems. And as in the cases of alliteration, half-line structure, and rhythm, in the case of prologues the alliterating stanzaic poems simplify alliterative style. When compared to the alliterative corpus, the paucity of meta-prologues and 'God-grant-grace' and 'doughty' prologues in the alliterating stanzaic poems reveals a pattern of prosodic stereotyping. Moreover, the overrepresentation of alliterating stanzaic poems among non-alliterative poems with 'May-morning' prologues implies that the direct influence of alliterative style was more concentrated in alliterating stanzaic poetry than in other non-alliterative verse. Disaggregation of other metrical traditions from the category 'non-alliterative' could yield additional insights into formal influence within the English literary field. Ideally, such disaggregation would proceed from a more comprehensive list of prologues than Figure 5 provides.

Anglo-Norman poems contain few of the types of prologue discussed so far.[29] *Boeve de Haumtone* (late twelfth century) and some of the *Lais* of Marie de France (late twelfth century) begin with calls to attention and descriptions of valiant heroes; Marie sometimes uses *jadis* 'of old' in the opening of a *lai* in a manner similar to OE *geara* 'of old' in the 'days-of-yore' prologue; and the opening line of *Gui de Warewic* (early thirteenth century) uses *puis* 'after' somewhat like ME *sythen* 'ever since' in the 'olde-tyme' prologue. Yet surviving Anglo-Norman prologues do not employ anything like shared keywords. Marie herself offers a reason for the diversity of prologues to Anglo-Norman poetry when she states at the opening of *Milun* that "whoever would treat various tales must begin variously [*Ki divers cuntes veut traitier / Diversement deit comencier*]" (quoted from *Les lais*, ed. Rychner; translation mine).

The prologue to one Anglo-Norman romance seems more closely connected to the practice of Middle English poets. Traces of rhyme reveal that the prose *Fouke le Fitz Waryn* (1320s), the latest extant Anglo-Norman romance, was based on a prior Anglo-Norman poem in octosyllables, now lost.[30] The romance begins with an unmistakable 'May-morning' prologue (text and translation from *History*, ed. Wright):

> En le temps de Averyl e May, quant les prées e les herbes reverdissent, et chescune chose vivaunte recovre vertue, beauté, e force, les mountz e les valeys retentissent des douce chauntz des oseylouns, e les cuers de chescune gent, pur la beauté du temps e la sesone, mountent en haut e s'enjolyvent, donqe deit home remenbrer des aventures e pruesses nos auncestres, qe se penerent pur honour en leauté quere, e de teles choses parler qe à plusours purra valer.

> ("In the season of April and May, when fields and plants become green again, and everything living recovers virtue, beauty, and force, hills and vales resound with the sweet songs of birds, and the hearts of all people, for the beauty of the weather and the season, rise up and gladden themselves, then we ought to call to memory the adventures and deeds of prowess of our forefathers who laboured to seek honour in loyalty, and to talk of such things as shall be profitable to many of us.")

Much of the underlying poem can be tentatively reconstructed (quoted from *Fouke*, ed. Hathaway et al., n. to 3.1–12):

> Quant prees e herbes reverdissent,
> E mountz e valeyes retentissent,
> Des douce chauntz des oseylouns
> Pur la beauté de la sesone,
> Donqe deit home [se pener]
> Des aventures remenbrer,
> E [des] pruesses nos auncessours
> Qe se penerent pur honour,
> E de teles choses parler
> Qe a plusours purra valer.

The lost Anglo-Norman verse romance of Fulk may have been composed as early as the 1260s.[31] Of the basic elements of the Middle English 'May-morning' prologue, the opening of the prose *Fouke* lacks the first-person perspective, morningtime, and the dream; the prologue to the lost verse *Fouke*, insofar as it can be reconstructed on the evidence of vestigial rhyme, lacks in addition a reference to May.

All the elements found in the prologue to the prose *Fouke*, plus the first-person perspective and the dream, appear already in Lorris's *Roman de la Rose* (quoted from *Roman*, ed. Langlois, vol. 2; translation mine):

> Qu'en mai estoie, ce sonjoie,
> Ou tens amoreus, plein de joie,

Ou tens ou toute rien s'esgaie,
50   Que l'en ne voit boisson ne haie
Qui en mai parer ne se vueille
           .   .   .
Mout a dur cuer qui en mai n'aime,
Quant il ot chanter sor la raime
As oisiaus les douz chanz piteus.

("It was in May, this dream, in the lusty season full of joy, in the season in which everything exults, so that one sees neither bush nor hedge but it desires to be adorned [*sc.* with flowers] in May . . . He has too hard a heart who does not love to hear in May the sweet poignant songs of the birds upon the branches.") (47–51; 81–83)

Comparison of these Anglo-Norman and French 'May-morning' prologues to later Middle English 'May-morning' prologues may help clarify the specific influence of *Piers Plowman* on the Middle English poems, as well as the Anglo-Norman/French background to *Piers Plowman*. In the translation between languages and literary traditions, the prologue has undergone considerable change. Depictions of sweet birdsong in the Anglo-Norman and French 'May-morning' prologues (*Roman*: "Quant il ot chanter . . . / As oisiaus les douz chanz piteus"; reconstructed verse *Fouke*: "Des douce chauntz des oseylouns") beside references to the hearts of springtime frolickers (*Roman*: "Mout a dur cuer qui en mai n'aime"; prose *Fouke*: "les cuers de chescune gent . . . mountent en haut e s'enjolyvent") produce a very different effect from Langland's vision of "a fair feeld ful of folk." In the General Prologue to the *Canterbury Tales* Chaucer split the difference between the two varieties of 'May-morning' prologue, emphasizing that the spring season stirs the hearts of songbirds ("And smale foweles maken melodye/ . . . (So Priketh hem Nature in hir corages)," I 9–11; cp. I 1033–46 and I 2483–87) before assembling a "compaignye/ Of sondry folk" (I 24–25). A century later, in his *Morte Darthur* (1469–70), Thomas Malory adapted the Anglo-Norman/French version of the prologue in two contiguous passages ("the moneth of May . . . whan every lusty harte begynnyth to blossom and to burgyne" and "In May, whan every harte floryshyth and burgenyth").[32]

As noted above, most of the other evidence for the Anglo-Norman background to Middle English poetic prologues is negative. The Anglo-Norman poetic corpus shows that conventionalized prologues as defined in this book are not an inevitable feature of poetic traditions. While some rhetorical gestures appear at the beginnings of both Middle English and Anglo-Norman poems, the keywords and generic connotations of Middle

English prologues evidently developed before *c.* 1250 in English alliterative verse and/or after *c.* 1250 in Middle English romance (including alliterative romance). This conclusion justifies the largely monolingual approach to poetic prologues adopted in this chapter. It also returns us to the concept of verse history, for though the desuetude of Anglo-Norman romance and the consolidation of English romance are only meaningful as two aspects of the same literary-historical event, the style of ascendant English metrical traditions did not simply mimic that of more established meters in the other vernacular. In seeking for the materials with which insular poets translated the cultural authority of romance, scholars would be well advised to sift the preexisting literary forms of the ascendant language as carefully as those of the incumbent language.

By observing the relative absence of evidence for Anglo-Norman or French influence on the form of Middle English poetic prologues, I do not mean to minimize or explain away the formative role of Anglo-Norman, French, and indeed Latin literatures in the development of English literature. To the contrary, I propose to enrich prevailing accounts of these important interlingual influences with reflection on the considerable complexity of kinds of influence within the English literary field. A future study could coordinate interlingual and intralingual vectors of influence. It is surely of grave literary-historical significance, for example, that Langland, when he reached for romance, reached for the French Arthurian variety more readily than for the English alliterative variety.[33] It likewise seems significant that Chaucer combined the Anglo-Norman/ French and Middle English 'May-morning' prologue varieties at the end of the fourteenth century, while Malory could employ the Anglo-Norman/ French 'May-morning' prologue exclusively at the end of the fifteenth. Yet these points of contact with French-language writing in Langland, Chaucer, and Malory ought to be read alongside, not in place of, interconnections between English poems. In this chapter, I have tried to indicate the density of such interconnections.

To put the matter differently, comparison of Middle English poetic prologues reveals one striking way in which poets expressed the interrelationships obtaining between Middle English and other language traditions. This chapter has labored over the form of that expression, which turns out to be largely specific to English metrical traditions, but the fact of the expression only gains its full historical and cultural significance in a multilingual perspective. The long view onto fourteenth- and fifteenth-century English poetry from the perspective of the durable alliterative tradition is not the only possible view. But it is, I suggest, an important and productive one.

In recent decades, scholars of medieval English literature have endeavored to find the international in the local, that is, to situate English literature in an international literary culture. This chapter contributes to the same research program, but from the other side of the dialectic: prologues to Middle English poetry help to find the local in the international, that is, to notice how the internationalization of English literature proceeded in part from prior formal practice within the English literary field. English literary history is often narrated as the history of a vernacular becoming cosmopolitan. But it can with equal justice be narrated as the history of the cosmopolitan language becoming vernacular.

Sheldon Pollock's concept of 'cosmopolitan vernacular' captures the dialectical interplay between the local and the international in the cultural meaning of language and literature. The cosmopolitan vernacular is "that register of the emergent vernacular that aims to *localize* the full spectrum of literary qualities of the superposed *cosmopolitan* code" (my emphasis). Pollock's notion of 'superposition,' or the way that culturally powerful language traditions inflect the development of their less powerful neighbors, can aid in isolating the multiple historical pressures shaping the development of English literature. From the late twelfth to the mid thirteenth century, within the superposition of Anglo-Norman, French, and Latin literatures on English literature there obtained a smaller (as it were) but significant superposition of the alliterative tradition on non-alliterative English metrical traditions. This initial hierarchy of meters was dramatically reversed during the course of the thirteenth century (Ch. 3). The connections between alliterative and non-alliterative Middle English prologues testify primarily to the diversification and internationalization of alliterative verse after 1300, but also to the historical influence of the alliterative tradition upon a new English genre called *romaunce*. Alliterative romance emerges, of course, from the larger history of Middle English romance and the yet larger history of European romance, but I have argued in this section that Middle English romance also emerges from the larger history of alliterative verse.

Because alliterative verse preceded romance in literary history, 'alliterative romance' cannot quite be the "subclassification" that its Linnaean nomenclature promises.[34] If there is a lot of romance style in alliterative verse, it may be that there is also some alliterative style in English romance. That two of the prologues to Middle English poetry had precedents in Old English poetry certainly would not have crossed anyone's mind in the fourteenth century. Nonetheless, alliterative poets crafted such prologues with especial gusto. The elaborate openings to *Sir Gawain and the Green*

Knight and *St. Erkenwald* outmatch any of the 'olde-tyme' prologues to non-alliterative romances. It is not too much to imagine that such exceptional displays of virtuosity showed the 'olde-tyme' prologue in its first and most agreeable metrical setting. The hypothesis of an Alliterative Revival encouraged researchers to explain any connection between Old English and Middle English alliterative poetry as a coincidence or else a mystical rediscovery of native roots. But the Middle English 'olde-tyme' prologue may simply have been alliterative poetry doing what it had always done well. In this way the prologues to some alliterative poems, in addition to performing their local rhetorical duties, bear the marks of alliterative verse history. A paucity of textual evidence makes it difficult to judge the direction of influence between the alliterative tradition and the romance tradition in each case, but it stands to reason that the influence ran in both directions.

Like Chapter 2, this section was concerned with a literary form I called the 'poetic prologue.' By way of conclusion, I would like to compare the treatment of poetic prologues in this book with the significance of prologues in medieval vernacular literary theory, as explicated most fully by Alastair Minnis and the editors of *The Idea of the Vernacular*. In a brief but powerful essay in that volume, Ruth Evans traces the emergence in the fourteenth century of the Middle English words *preamble, prefacyon, prohemy,* and *prologe* and the development of the vernacular literary practices to which they refer. For Evans, prologues are "repositories of information about the English vernacular" but also "opaque entities, standing in a complex relation to the works they preface ... and to the history of the vernacular of which they form a significant part."[35] Evans's twofold definition of 'prologue' stands as a justification for the edited volume in which her essay appears.

One result of the history of poetic prologues traced in Chapters 2 and 3 and in this section is simply to remind Middle English specialists that prologues constituted a practice within the English literary field long before the emergence of Latin- or French-derived English words for them in the fourteenth century. Nor did Old English lack words to denote prefaces and prologues: compare Old English *forerim, foresaga, foresægdnes,* and *forespræc,* calques on Latin *prefatio, prohemium,* and *prologus.* Old English prologues, like Middle English prologues in Evans's account, "contribute to the problematizing of the traditional distinction between 'text' and 'preface'" and "participate in a long prolocutory tradition that has its origins in the classical period and in late antiquity." More particularly, I have sought to enrich the focus on prologues as vernacular phenomena with new focus on prologues as metrical phenomena. Within the idea of the vernacular (another concept with an often overlooked Old English heritage) there also developed a discrete idea of alliterative verse. Old English poetic prologues perform the idea of alliterative verse *avant la lettre*, at a time when the alliterative tradition occupied the entire space of 'English poetry.' Middle English poetic prologues perform the historically conditioned interplay between the idea of alliterative verse and the idea of other metrical traditions.

The *longue durée* of English poetic prologues traced in Chapters 2 and 3 and in this section, then, historicizes medieval literary theory in three ways. First, it situates fourteenth-century vernacular literary theory as one phase in a much longer history of Latinate literary thought and practice in English. Second (a corollary of the first), it identifies, in Old English literature, a third genealogy for literary theory in Middle English, in addition to the classical and medieval Latin models. Third, it suggests the extent to which metrical traditions impinge on what Evans calls the "particular discursive matrix in which the prologue plays a historically specific role in differentiating theory from practice and in authorizing the text."[36] The specifically metrical connotations of poetic prologues show why it is inadequate for research into vernacular literary theory to operate only on the level of the vernacular, or the literary, or even poetry.

The next chapter offers a case in point for the arguments of this chapter through a reading of the understudied Middle English alliterative poem *St. Erkenwald*. The style of *St. Erkenwald*, set in its long verse-historical as well as its broad contemporary contexts, demonstrates in a vivid and specific way the three general conclusions offered above: that the alliterative tradition endured from the thirteenth to the fourteenth centuries without antiquarian renovation; that alliterative verse influenced the English romance tradition even as it was influenced by it; and that alliterative style in the fourteenth and fifteenth centuries differed from non-alliterative style in some respects, for historical reasons and with consequences for the position of alliterative verse in late medieval English literary culture.

CHAPTER 5

The Erkenwald *Poet's Sense of History*

The central question of *St. Erkenwald* (late fourteenth/mid fifteenth centuries) is the central question of the alliterative tradition: how to uncover and understand the distant past. Consequently the narrative proceeds in two discrete stages, excavation (ll. 1–176) and interview (ll. 177–352). The plot can be summarized in one sentence, with a semicolon to represent the turning point between lines 176 and 177: in the seventh century, Erkenwald, bishop of London, discovers a tomb beneath St. Paul's Cathedral covered in indecipherable carvings and containing the undecayed body of a pagan judge, who begins to speak to the astounded onlookers; after interviewing him about his life and death, Erkenwald unintentionally baptizes the judge by reciting the baptismal formula while shedding a tear. Throughout the poem, the *Erkenwald* poet constructs a "many-storied long-ago" so detailed that it threatens to overpopulate the simple past tense.[1] With characteristic ambition, the poet extends the 'olde-tyme' prologue (see Ch. 4) far beyond a colorless reference to once-upon-a-time. The careful layering of historical frames in the first thirty-two lines of the poem is without peer in medieval English literature. For this poet, as for the *Beowulf* poet, the past is a foreign country that demands to be confronted. The tragedy of both poems is the intractability of history, the inevitability of loss in time. In *Beowulf*, there is always "æfter wiste | wop up ahafen" "lamentation taken up after feasting" (128; quoted from *Klaeber's Beowulf*, ed. Fulk, Bjork, and Niles; translation mine). In *St. Erkenwald*, "Meche mournynge and myrthe | was mellyd togeder" (350; all quotations of *St. Erkenwald* are from *St. Erkenwald*, ed. Savage).

This chapter reads *St. Erkenwald* as a serious meditation on history. The second section contrasts *St. Erkenwald* with some short English alliterative poems embedded in Latin prose and rhyming English verse, in an effort to infer the connotations of the alliterative meter in late medieval English literary culture. I argue that the *Erkenwald* poet's sense of history and use of alliterative style are more robust than the impression of an archaistic alliterative meter shared by some thirteenth- and fourteenth-century writers and some modern critics of *St. Erkenwald*. The third section provides reasons to doubt the traditional attribution of *St. Erkenwald* to the *Gawain* poet. I argue that, in the context of the alliterative tradition, an understanding of poetic style *per se* is both more important and more attainable than knowledge of the corpora of anonymous authors.

A Meditation on Histories

Again and again, *St. Erkenwald* returns to the ever-since, the past imagined as the swathe of time separating a foundational event from the present. The poet begins by juxtaposing the two meanings of the adverb/conjunction *sythen* 'afterwards; ever since': "At London in Englonde | noȝt fulle longe sythen/ Sythen Crist suffride on crosse, | and Cristendome stablyde" (1–2). Bishop Erkenwald's London is located in living memory ("noȝt fulle longe sythen"), but also, paradoxically, deep in Christian history. The contrast is so abrupt that Israel Gollancz replaced the first *sythen* with *tyme* in his edition of the poem, nullifying the ambiguity. The vacillations between the short view and the long view set the stage for the anachronistic resurrection to come. The bishop is introduced as "Saynt" and "þat holy mon" (4), titles that superimpose on Erkenwald's life his post-mortem history as a pilgrimage destination. From the start, present and past overlap:

5   In his tyme in þat toun   þe temple aldergrattyst
       Was drawen doun þat one dole   to dedifie new,
       For hit hethen had bene   in Hengyst dawes,
       Þat þe Saxones unsaȝt   haden sende hyder.
       Þai bete oute þe Bretons,   and broȝt hom into Wales,
10   And pervertyd alle þe pepul   þat in þat place dwellide.
       Þen wos this reame renaide   mony ronke ȝeres,
       Til Saynt Austyn into Sandewiche   was sende fro þe pope. (5–12)

To understand the rededication of the temple (5–6), one must remember the Gregorian mission (12) to convert the pagan Anglo-Saxons (7), who in turn had come to the island from Saxony (8) and conquered the Britons (9–10). The chronological contortions are so fierce that it is unclear how many Christian dedications St. Paul's is supposed to have undergone.[2] The uncertainty reflects the poem's anxieties about burying the past. The *Erkenwald* poet imagines history as a mess of renovation and apostasy, not linear but "geometrical."[3] The view is of a *longue durée*, comprehending centuries of wasted time and dead ends: "Þen wos this reame renaide | mony ronke ʒeres."

Like *Beowulf, St. Erkenwald* makes the question of history explicit by hinting at the future of the past it narrates. The world of bishop Erkenwald (d. 693) is itself remote from late medieval England, as cued by "In his tyme" (5). When he sits in the "New Werke" (38), Erkenwald occupies a cathedral church as yet unbuilt. The New Work was a Norman addition *c.* 1250 to the edifice now remembered as Old St. Paul's, itself constructed in 1087, 400 years after the death of the historical Erkenwald. The reconstruction that is the occasion of the poem (37 ff.) could be an imaginary seventh-century renovation of St. Paul's or the eleventh-century renovation and thirteenth-century addition transposed to seventh-century London. The poet's note "Þat was the temple Triapolitan" (36) might refer to a pre-Christian historical reality, the historical consciousness of the Londoners in the poem, or the historical consciousness of the late medieval audience. In a grotesque gesture that presages the discovery of the corpse, the poet has the saint preside over his own future resting place: the historical Erkenwald was buried and later enshrined in St. Paul's. During the poet's lifetime the shrine was located in the New Work, where it was to remain until the Dissolution of the Monasteries (1536–41). The invocation of the successive edifices of St. Paul's mirrors the deconstruction and reconstruction on which the narrative turns. Pagan St. Paul's haunts the seventh century, and modern St. Paul's lies in the ruins of an ancient temple, waiting to be built. The corpse doubles the historical Erkenwald, as though it were his own body that the bishop discovers.

It would be easy to identify inconsistencies in this powerful opening, but to do so would be to overlook more important symmetries. For the *Erkenwald* poet, the past is entirely implicated in the present. The aim of *St. Erkenwald* is not to achieve historical accuracy, whatever that might be, but to expose the inner workings of historical memory. Anglo-Saxon London comes to bear not only the imprints of past conquests, but, eerily, the imprints of future ones (Fig. 6).

London is detached from England, "þat toun" (5) from "this reame" (11), only to be celebrated as the crossroads of British history. The poet's own spatial relationship to London parallels the temporal paradoxes of the poem. Possibly from Cheshire, in the first line the poet plays the outsider, though the poem betrays extensive knowledge of the metropolis.[4]

If poet and audience remain aware of the antiquity of Anglo-Saxon England, the narrative itself focuses on the pre-Saxon British past. Like every other past in *St. Erkenwald*, its legacy is ambivalent. A great deal of

	Adam's original sin	ll. 295–96
	Brutus of Troy conquers Britain	l. 207
	King Belin rules the Britons	l. 213
early first century CE	Jesus of Nazareth born	l. 209
early first century	Jesus of Nazareth crucified	l. 2
fifth century	Anglo-Saxons invade Britain	l. 7–11
597	Gregorian mission to Kent	ll. 12–24
604	original St. Paul's erected	
?–693	Erkenwald, bishop of London	ll. 4, 33, etc.
c. 890	second St. Paul's erected	
962	third St. Paul's erected	
1066	Normans conquer England	
1087	Old St. Paul's begun	
c. 1138	*Historia regum Brittaniae* published	
c. 1250	New Work begun	?ll. 37 ff.
late fourteenth/mid fifteenth centuries	*St. Erkenwald* composed	
1477	British Library MS Harley 2250 copied	
1536–41	Dissolution of the Monasteries	
1666	Great Fire of London	
1711	modern St. Paul's completed	
1881	*St. Erkenwald* first edited	

Figure 6. The Pasts, Presents, and Futures of *St. Erkenwald*

Geoffrey of Monmouth's British history predates the birth of Christ, including the reign of King Belin, under whom the pagan judge says he served (213). Geoffrey presents the Britons as the rightful first owners of the island, and a good Christian people from the birth of Christ to the *adventus Saxonum*. The Saxon invaders, led by Hengist, are double-crossing heathens. At the same time, a historiographical tradition originating with Gildas's *De excidio et conquestu Brittaniæ* (sixth century) cast the Britons as a corrupt and querulous people who received their comeuppance at the hands of the Saxons. The Viking incursions of the ninth and tenth centuries were subsequently freighted with a similar moral import. The knowledge that Britain had been pagan before the birth of Christ, Christianized thereafter, re-paganized by the *adventus Saxonum*, re-Christianized by the Gregorian mission, and visited with destruction by the pagan Vikings, held rhetorical value for Bede, Alcuin, Wulfstan, and Gerald of Wales, among others.

Because medieval historians imagined Christianity on the island as a cycle, there was the potential for slippage between the pagan Britons and the pagan Saxons. Each conquest and each conversion forecasts a future one. The *Erkenwald* poet is content to assemble the elements of late medieval British historiography without organizing them into an *exemplum*. The "ambivalence toward the past" that Daniel Donoghue identified in

Lawman's *Brut* characterizes *St. Erkenwald*, too.[5] By reversing a Monmouthian *translatio imperii*, the poet has London become 'the New Troy' in the judge's mouth: "I was (o)n heire of an oye(r) | in þe New Troie, / In þe regne of þe riche kynge | þat rewlit us þen" (211–12; cp. 25). Then, as though by a translation that reverberates backwards through time, a death in New Troy causes lamentation in Troy itself: "And for I was ryȝtwis and reken, | and redy of þe laghe, / Quen I deghed, for dul | denyed alle Troye" (245–46; cp. 251 and 255). The Old Troy becomes shorthand for, or even replaces, the New. Each familiar connection – between colony and motherland, name and namesake, past and ulterior past – is emphatically drawn only so as to be just as emphatically reversed.

Like the *Beowulf* poet, the *Erkenwald* poet dwells on pagan rites:

> Þe mecul mynster þerinne   a maghty devel aght,
> And þe title of þe temple   bitan was his name;
> For he was dryghtyn derrest   of ydols praysid,
> And þe solempnest of his sacrifices   in Saxon londes. (27–30)

Beyond the condemnatory buzzwords lies a curiosity about ancient customs. The Saxon temple was named for the most important god. Its function, we are told, was sacrificial. The treatment of heathendom does not come any closer to relativism than the parallel passage in *Beowulf* (175–88). But neither is the pagan world fully eclipsed by the evangelical activities of Augustine (12–24). In seeking to finish burying the pagan past, bishop Erkenwald accidentally accomplishes the opposite. The past returns, unbeckoned, from the earth. The discussion of pagan religion is no simple denunciation, for it names an ancient world that comes hurtling back from beyond the grave, visceral and authentic.

The pagan judge was entombed with as much pomp and circumstance as Beowulf (247–56). The poet emphasizes the exotic meaning of the burial garments. What the Londoners (98) and even the narrator himself take to be royal vestments (77 "rialle wedes") are really "bounty" (248) for exceptional virtue. In "a fine display of chronological wit," the antiquarian and the anachronistic coincide: the pagan judge is buried like a late medieval justice, confusing the seventh-century Londoners.[6] The circumstances of the judge's burial indicate a pre-Christian morality, without confirming whether this morality can coincide with Christian doctrine: "Cladden me for þe curtest | þat courte couthe þen holde, / In mantel for þe mekest | and monlokest on benche" (249–50). Like another pair of superlative *m*-words hanging out at a pagan funeral (*Beowulf* 3181 *mildust* and *monðwærust*), *mekest* and *monlokest* call to mind the Christian virtues of *humilitas* and *caritas,* even as they expose the anachronism of that association. Where the *Beowulf* poet leaves the Christian exorcism of the past to the audience's imagination, the *Erkenwald* poet has the past talk back to the present directly, with a will and a moral code proper to itself. Pagans even harbor their own expectations for the future, as when the judge is deemed most virtuous "of kene justises, / Þ(at) ever wos tronyd in Troye | oþer trowid ever shulde" (254–55). This alien past is both alluring and terrifying. It invites evangelism and provokes self-reflection in equal measure.

St. *Erkenwald* comes much closer than *Beowulf* to a Christian synthesis of past and present, and the poem is often read as an allegory of salvation history. It has been compared to the popular Gregory-Trajan legend, on which it is loosely based. The poet takes pains to stay within the bounds of late medieval orthodoxy.[7] But St. *Erkenwald* is more romance than hagiography. Its overall effect is to raise historical questions, not to settle theological ones. The inscription on the judge's tomb, for example, becomes a scene unto itself:

And þe bordure enbelicit   with bryȝt golde lettres;
Bot roynyshe were þe resones   þat þer on row stoden.
Fulle verray were þe vigures,   þer avisyde hom mony;
Bot alle muset hit to mouthe: and quat hit mene shulde,
55 Mony clerke(s) in þat clos,   with crownes ful brode,
Þer besiet hom aboute noȝt,   to brynge hom in wordes.
Quen tithynges token to þe toun   of þe toumbe-wonder,
Mony hundrid hende men   highide þider sone.
Burgeys boghit þerto,   bedels ande othire,
60 And mony a mesters-mon   of maners dyverse.
Laddes laften hor werke   and lepen þiderwardes,
Ronnen radly in route   with ryngande noyce;
Þer commen þider of alle-kynnes   so kenely mony,
Þat as alle þe worlde were þider walon   within a hondequile. (51–64)

The poet packs all of London into St. Paul's, but no explanation is forthcoming. The writing is "roynyshe" "mysterious(?)," a word whose possible affiliation with Old English *run* 'mystery; runic letter' might not have been lost on poet or audience.[8] There is a decorum in this. The inscription is 'all runes' to the seventh-century Londoners, just as Anglo-Saxon runes would be inscrutable to late medieval Englishmen, and just as the origins and meaning of *roynyshe* are newly murky in modern times. Each age gets the mysterious script it deserves. Tantalized, the Londoners perceive that the writing is clear and precise ("Fulle verray"), but its meaning eludes them utterly. There is no Daniel to decipher the inscription, as in the other alliterative tableau in which curious writing is 'runish' (*Cleanness* 1545).

Nor does there conveniently appear an old man "quite erudite in scripts [*litteris bene eruditum*]," as in a similar *inventio* narrative attributed to the tenth century in Matthew Paris's portion of the *Gesta abbatum monasterii S. Albani* (early thirteenth century).[9] In *St. Erkenwald*, workmen remove the lid of the tomb, revealing the greater mystery of the undecayed body. One confrontation with the long ago has passed, but it is never resolved.

The poet hints that the contents of the tomb will remain unintelligible, too, even before they are disclosed to the reader:

> Wy3t werkemen with þat   wenten þertille;
> 70   Putten prises þerto;   pinchid one-under;
> Kaghten by þe corners   with crowes of yrne;
> And were þe lydde never so large,   þai laide hit by sone.
> Bot þen wos wonder to wale   on wehes þat stoden,
> That my3t not come to knowe   a quontyse strange. (69–74)

The cinematographic sleight-of-hand creates a sense of wonder that supersedes its very object. The syntactic reversal around "Bot" is pointed, suggesting as it does that the Londoners' hopes are raised only to be frustrated by the unknown. The poet uses *bot* in the same way at 52, 54, 101, 156, and 263.

Deprived of the tell-tale signs of decay, the onlookers are thrown into doubt about the age of the corpse:

> Þer was spedeles space   to spyr uch on oþer
> Quat body hit my3t be   þat buried wos ther;
> How longe had he þer layne,   his lere so unchaungit,
> And al his wede unwemmyd; –   þus ylka weghe askyd. (93–96)

In keeping with the historical prologue, the importance of the relic is its superdurability. Like baffled archaeologists, the bystanders do not wonder 'when' but "How longe" (cp. 147 and 187).[10] They can see that this is no illusion, that the man must have meant something to someone:

> Hit my3t not be bot suche a mon   in my(n)de stode longe;
> He has ben kynge of þis kithe,   as couthely hit semes
> He lyes dolven þus depe;   hit is a derfe wonder
> Bot summe segge couthe say   þat he hym sene hade. (97–100)

Even the man's (unknown) reputation is set on a large time-scale ("longe"). But neither memory nor written record can explain the discovery:

> Bot þat ilke note wos noght,   for nourne none couthe,
> Noþer by title, ne token,   ne by tale noþer,
> Þat ever wos brevyt in burghe,   ne in bok(e) notyde,
> Þat ever mynnyd suche a mo(n),   more ne lasse. (101–4)

And the answer matters. Messengers reporting to bishop Erkenwald tell of "troubulle in þe pepul" (109), and "pyne wos with þe grete prece" (141) who re-enter the tomb. The dean goes so far as to imply that one scrap of information about the John Doe would be worth the cathedral's entire necrology:

> Þer is no lede opon lyfe   of so longe age
> Þat may mene in his mynde   þat suche a mon regnyd,
> Ne noþer his nome ne his note   nourne of one speche;
> Queþer mony porer in þis place   is putte into grave
> Þat merkid is in oure martilage   his mynde for ever. (150–54)

The frustration is palpable. While the poem self-consciously aligns itself with the *Brut* tradition ("As ȝet in crafty cronecles | is kydde þe memorie," 44), it portrays a "mervayle" (43, 65, 114, etc.) that surpasses the limits of human knowledge. Somehow, the man has managed "To malte . . . out of memorie" (158). And yet there he lies. The "toumbe-wonder" stumps an entire library: "And we have our librarie laitid | þes longe seven dayes, / Bot one cronicle of þis kynge | con we never fynde" (155–56).

There is something uncomfortable about the apophaticism with which bishop Erkenwald attempts to reassure the populace:

> 160   Hit is mervaile to men,   þat mountes to litelle
> Towarde þe providens of þe Prince   þat Paradis weldes,
> Quen hym luste to unlouke   þe leste of his myȝtes.
> Bot quen matyd is monnes myȝt,   and his mynde passyde,
> And al his resons are torent,   and redeles he stondes,
> 165   Þen lettes hit hym ful litelle   to louse wyt a fynger
> Þat alle þe hondes under heven   halde myȝt never.
> Þere as creatures crafte   of counselle oute swarves,
> Þe comforthe of þe creatore   byhoves þe cure take.
> And so do we now oure dede,   devyne we no fyrre;
> 170   To seche þe sothe at oureselfe,   ȝee se þer no bote;
> Bot glow we alle opon Godde,   and his grace aske,
> Þat careles is of counselle   and comforthe to sende. (160–72)

Emphasis seems to fall as heavily on human ignorance, "quen matyd is monnes myȝt, | and his mynde passyde, / And al his resons are torent, | and redeles he stondes," as on divine omnipotence. Even as the unknowability of the pre-Christian past is folded into apophatic theology, the bishop's words underscore the Londoners' helplessness to explain the phenomena before them. If the onlookers can expect a divine answer to the questions that have been raised by the events of the poem so far, it is on pure faith.

The corpse might have been made to clear things up when he begins speaking. Instead, he declares his own antiquity to be unfathomable before launching into a supremely obscure reckoning:

> Þe lengthe of my lyinge here,   þat is a lewid date;
> Hit (is) to meche to any mon   to make of a nombre:
> After þat Brutus þis burghe   had buggid on fyrste
> Noȝt bot (aght) hundred ȝere   þer aghtene wontyd –
> Before þat kynned ȝour Criste   by Cristen acounte
> (Þre hundred) ȝere and þritty mo,   and ȝet threnen aght. (205–10)

Calculation fails. Christian chronology itself fails ("þat is a lewid date"), despite the modern editor's best efforts.[11] Like the letters carved into the lid of the tomb, the corpse proves an unreadable relic.

When the body speaks, the people are distressed:

> Quil he in spelunke þus spake,   þer sprange in þe pepulle
> In al þis worlde no worde,   ne wakenyd no noice,
> Bot al as stille as þe ston   stoden and listonde,
> With meche wonder forwrast,   and wepid ful mony. (217–20)

The reaction of the onlookers expresses not so much pity on a heathen soul as the unspeakable horror of reanimation. For all that the resurrection of the judge recalls typologically the Resurrection of Jesus, in the world of the poem it embodies the unaccountable. The verbs convey violent surprise (*sprange, forwrast*). After hearing the judge's story, Erkenwald responds "with bale at his hert" (257), another affective description that seems to slide away from pity toward terror. When Erkenwald looks "balefully" (311) and the townsfolk weep "for woo" (310), it is as though they share in a dark damnation they can scarcely imagine.

The sense of a doomed and inaccessible past is confirmed, not dissolved, by the judge's ad hoc baptism. The poet allots one line to the ascent to heaven, but labors over the disgusting residue:

> Bot sodenly his swete chere   swyndid and faylide,
> And alle the blee of his body   wos blakke as þe moldes,
> As roten as þe rottok   þat rises in powndere.
> 345   For as sone as þe soule   was sesyd in blisse,
> Corrupt was þat oþer crafte   þat covert þe bones. (342–46)

The mismatch is not altogether glossed over by the platitude that bodily decay heralds spiritual immortality (347–48). An unmistakable ambivalence rings through the final image of the poem:

Þen wos lovynge oure Lorde   with loves uphalden;
Meche mournynge and myrthe   was mellyd togeder;
Þai passyd forthe in procession,   and alle þe pepulle folowid,
And alle þe belles in þe burghe   beryd at ones. (349–52)

No tidy 'amen' can be appended. Are the bells ringing for a baptism or a funeral?[12] Are the people weeping for the death of a righteous man or the dreadful end of a mysterious episode? If the former, the Londoners recall the judge's contemporaries at his first death, who, he says, "Alle menyd my dethe, | þe more and the lasse" (247). Do the pagans resemble the Christians, or vice versa? The message of Christian consolation is there for any reader interested in extracting it, but it coexists with a vision of an irrepressible un-Christian past that haunts the foundations of the Christian present. *St. Erkenwald* begins and ends not in heaven but on earth, not in spiritual bliss but in postcolonial unease. The analogy to modern postcolonial contexts is approximate, of course, but it helps elucidate the historiographical and linguistic effects of the cyclical conquests of medieval England, which fire the historical imagination of *St. Erkenwald*.[13]

St. Erkenwald and the Idea of Alliterative Verse in Late Medieval England

If *St. Erkenwald* seems unusually sophisticated in its treatment of the distant past, one might ask how much the poet owes to the conventions of alliterative poetry specifically as opposed to romance generally. Alliterative poets' avoidance of reflexive statements about metrical form may disappoint modern expectations, but it also serves as a reminder that the alliterative meter remained available as an unselfconscious choice long after the ascendance of syllable-counted English meters.[14] One way of measuring the connotations of a verse form that has left behind no *ars poetica* is to read the moments when it interacts with adjacent literary traditions. After 1250, there seems to have been cachet in flaunting a familiarity with alliterative poetry and its supposed generic limitations. So for example the unique copy of an alliterative epitaph was made because a late thirteenth-century compiler invented "a leaden vessel [*quoddam vas plumbeum*]" on which the verses were supposed to have been engraved centuries earlier, then "rediscovered [*inueniebantur*]" beneath a chapel in Shrewsbury.[15] Fully six of the twelve short alliterative poems that survive from the period 1125–1325 are proverbs quoted in passing by authors or scribes writing in Latin, e.g., the one-line maxim prefaced by "whence a wise man said [*unde senex dixit*]" at the end of a Latin legal note in the margins of two copies of Henry de Bracton's *De legibus et consuetudinibus Angliæ* (*c.* 1235).[16] Like the Old English *Proverb from Winfrid's Time* (eighth century) and *Bede's Death Song* (eighth/ninth centuries), short gnomic poems that survive only indirectly, in Latin contexts, these twelfth- and thirteenth-century alliterative snippets showcase sententiousness and vernacularity. The appreciation of alliterative verse as a literary form was of little concern to these authors and scribes, who produce only enough homespun wisdom to prove their points.

By the fourteenth century, the alliterative meter has assumed a minor position in a newly diversified metrical landscape. The oft-quoted remark by Chaucer's Parson that he "kan nat geeste 'rum, ram, ruf,' by lettre" (*Canterbury Tales* X 43) is not primarily intended to denigrate alliterative verse but to characterize the Parson as one totally lacking in poetic skill. If alliterative meter is not supposed to rate highly for Chaucer's fashion-forward audience, it nevertheless makes the short-list of forms that lie beyond the Parson's abilities. That he rhymes "but litel bettre" (X 44) and is "nat textueel" (X 57) belies the Parson's excuse for foregoing alliterative meter ("I am a Southren man," X 42), and it is by no means certain that Chaucer is here endorsing the designation of alliterative verse as lowbrow, provincial, and generically typecast. The immediate meaning of the reference seems to be only that a bumbling southerner would be likely to disparage alliterative poetry in this way. Ultimately, the value of mentioning the "'rum, ram, ruf,' by lettre" may not be metropolitan snobbery so much as the implication that Chaucer himself was better informed about alliterative verse. Indeed, in two much-discussed battle sequences (*Canterbury Tales* I 2601–20 and *Legend of Good Women* 637–49), Chaucer adorns his pentameter with alliteration in an apparently unironic gesture toward alliterative chivalric romance.

Chaucer's other use of "geeste" (<OF) as a formal term, this time as a noun, does little to clarify his perceptions of the alliterative tradition. After he has interrupted the mock-romance *Sir Thopas*, the Host's injunction to Chaucer the pilgrim to "tellen aught in geeste" (VII 933) cannot refer to romance generally, yet it is unclear whether it can refer to alliterative romance specifically (as the note in the *Riverside Chaucer* guesses on the basis of X 43). *Geeste* is here explicitly opposed to either rhyming or versification generally ("ryme" [vb.], VII 932). Elsewhere in Chaucer, "geestes" are classical and/or lengthy (hi)stories (*Canterbury Tales* II 1126, III 642, and IV 2284; *House of Fame* 1515 and 1518; etc.). Moreover, both *Canterbury Tales* passages draw a primary formal distinction, not between alliterative and non-alliterative meters, but between (alliterative) romance and (didactic) prose ("telle in prose somwhat," VII 934, and "I wol yow telle

a myrie tale in prose," X 46). Chaucer expects his audience to recognize the alliterative tradition as one territory within this broader formal/generic division. The difficulty of mapping medieval testimonia about poetic form onto modern analytical categories illustrates the extent to which such testimonia emerge under pressure from other kinds of historical discourse, in this case discourses of class, literary genre, and regionalism.

Comparison between *St. Erkenwald* and these proverbs and one-liners begins to define a continuum of perception and practice within which the alliterative tradition operated in the late medieval centuries. A different kind of verbal showmanship might explain what four alliterative long lines are doing in the mouth of John Trevisa's clerk in the *Dialogus inter dominum et clericum*, which prefaces Trevisa's English translation (1387) of Ralph Higden's *Polychronicon* (quoted from Waldron, "Trevisa's Original Prefaces," p. 293):

DOMINUS: ... [Ich] wolde haue a skylfol translacion þat myȝt be knowe and vnderstonde.

CLERICUS: Wheþer ys ȝow leuere haue a translacion of þeuse cronyks in ryme oþer yn prose?

DOMINUS: Yn prose, vor comynlych prose ys more cleer þan ryme, more esy and more pleyn to knowe and vnderstonde.

CLERICUS: Þanne God graunte grace [greiþlyche] to gynne, <w>yt and wysdom wysly to wyrche, myȝt and muynde of ryȝt menyng to make translacion trysty <and> truwe, plesyng to þe Trynyte, þre persones and o god in maieste, þat euer was and euere schal be.

Asked by his patron to effect a translation "yn prose," the cheeky clerk produces four alliterative lines followed by three monorhyming lines in four-stress verse (lineation mine, and one addition to Waldron's text in square brackets):

> Þanne God graunte grace   greiþlyche to gynne,
> wyt and wysdom   wysly to wyrche,
> myȝt and muynde of ryȝt   menyng to make
> [to make þis] translacion   trysty and truwe
> 5 plesyng to þe Trynyte,
> þre persones and o god in maieste,
> þat euer was and euere schal be.[17]

The use of the 'God-grant-grace' prologue (see Ch. 4) solemnizes the sermon on Creation that follows the poem and concludes the *Dialogus*, and it even, perhaps, consecrates the translation as a whole. One might compare similarly worded invocations at the close of two fourteenth-century sermons in English and in the concluding lines of *Piers Plowman*

B 7, marking the end of the *Visio* and beginning of the *Vita de Dowel*.[18] Indeed, two manuscripts of the *Dialogus* (Waldron's S and G) end the preface with *Trynyte*, making the clerk's reply into a pithy metrical coda.

Yet there seems to be a joke in the clerk's spontaneous versifying, whether it is on the lord, the clerk, or alliterative meter itself. Perhaps alliterative verse, which Trevisa will approach with some circumspection in the St. Kenelm episode (see below), is ironically supposed to be even less "esy" and "pleyn to knowe and vnderstonde" than the "ryme" that the lord rejects. Perhaps, too, Trevisa has his clerk quibble on *ryme* 'verse' but also 'rhymed verse.' In any event, the appearance of alliterative verse in this context shows that alliterative meter still had some currency (but only as a punchline?) in the most educated southern circles in the last quarter of the fourteenth century. Certainly the composition bears no signs of ignorant imitation. The double poetic inversion in l. 3 (prose order *myȝt and muynde to make menyng of ryȝt*) is particularly idiomatic. The coincidence of alliterative verse with chronicle writing resonates with *St. Erkenwald*. As before, however, the contrast between an apparently lighthearted exchange and the high seriousness of our poem registers the extent to which the alliterative tradition had become conspicuously marked in literary culture by the end of the fourteenth century.

A vignette from *St. Kenelm* in the *South English Legendary* (late thirteenth century) provides the most intensive contemporary reaction to alliterative verse. It speaks volumes about the English literary scene on the eve of the fourteenth century that the reaction comes from a non-practitioner. Two lines of alliterative verse lie embalmed in the end-rhymed saint's life, standing in for mystery, sanctity, the manuscript page, and above all Englishness (quoted from *South English Legendary*, ed. D'Evelyn and Mill, 'De Sancto Kenelmi'; D'Evelyn and Mill's medial punctuation replaced with a tabbed space):

> Þo þis holy body nemoste beo   ikud in Engelonde
> 250 Oure Louerd þat wot alle þing   þerto sette is honde
> For as þe pope stod at Rome   and song is masse a day
> At seinte Petres weued in churche   as al þat folk ysay
> A coluore wittore þanne eni snou   com doun fram heuene fle[o]
> And leide upe þe weued a lite writ   & suþþe gan to heuene te[o]
> 255 And flei up aȝen anhei   as oure Louerd it wolde
> Þis writ [was] wiȝt & ssinde briȝte   þe lettres al of golde
> Þe pope þonkede Iesu Crist   and al þat folk also
> Þe pope nom þis holi writ   þo þe masse was ido
> He nuste wat it was to segge   ne in wit neccuþe iwite

260 For he ne couþe Engliss non   and an Engliss it was iwrite
     He let clupie ech maner men   of ech diuerse londe
     ȝif eny couþe of þis holy writ   eny þing vnderstonde
     Þo were þere men of Engelond   þat weste wat is sede
     And vnderstode wel þat writ   þo hi it hurde rede
265 Þe writ was iwrite pur Engliss   as me radde it þere
     And to telle it wiþoute rime   þis wordes riȝt it were
          In Clent Coubach   Kenelm kinges bern
          Liþ vnder a þorn   heued bireued
     Þis writ was wel nobliche   iwest and up ido
270 And iholde for grete relike   & ȝute it is also
     Þe nobloste relike it is   on þerof of al Rome
     As it aȝte wel wo so vnderstode   riȝt wel wanne it come
     For wanne it out of heuene com   & of oure Louerdes honde
     Wat noblore relike miȝte be[o]   i necan noȝt vnderstonde. (249–74)

As in the Latin *Vita Sancti Kenelmi* (1045–75), on which *St. Kenelm* is
based, the document leads to the rediscovery of the saint's body ("Hi lete
seche þis holy body | and fonde it oute iwis," 287). The poet sets in motion
many correspondences – between sacred text and sacred corpse, between
Rome and Canterbury, between human knowledge and divine dispensa-
tion. The poet's diffidence toward the vernacular is in line with the 'choice
of English' *topos* popular at the turn of the fourteenth century.[19] On the
one hand, English is an arcane skill that the Pope, naturally enough, does
not possess. On the other hand, English is God's language here. (The *South
English Legendary* goes on to narrate the 'Angle'/'angel' pun made by Pope
Gregory I, who did learn a little English.) The obscurity of English
authorizes its efficacy as "holy writ."

The alliterative snippet, of late eleventh- to early thirteenth-century
vintage, circulated on its own and as a gloss to the corresponding scene
in three manuscripts of the *Vita Kenelmi*.[20] Whereas the letter in the *Vita* is
a means to an end, in *St. Kenelm* the writ itself becomes "iholde for grete
relike" (270). The difference lies in the declining reputation of alliterative
verse. Alliterative meter was the only English meter in 1075, when the *Vita*
was written, but it becomes a marked choice in the context of the late
thirteenth-century vernacular legend. The *Kenelm* poet exploits the newly
antiquated feel of alliterative verse, turning the document itself into an
embodiment of the distant Anglo-Saxon past ("olde dawe," 19). Unlike the
late eleventh-century author of the *Vita*, the late thirteenth-century *Kenelm*
poet notes the salient feature of this verse form: it lacks rhyme ("wiþoute
rime," 266 – though a different plausible translation would be 'without
metrical form').

The *Kenelm* vignette summarizes the bounds assigned to alliterative poetry by writers who had long since moved on to newer forms. Alliterative verse becomes useful only when one wants something antiqued, sententious, and profoundly vernacular. The message delivered by the dove represents what every Englishman recognizes upon hearing it ("þo hi it hurde rede," 264), and yet its dramatic purpose is to be translated out of English, presumably into Latin, for the Pope. In some manuscripts of *St. Kenelm* the English snippet is glossed by the rhyming Latin couplet found in the *Vita*, while the earliest manuscripts of the *Vita* lack the English snippet altogether. To judge from the activities of scribes and readers, it is as though the anticlimactic translation of the divine instructions had occurred in reverse, Latin to English. The Pope's message for the Archbishop of Canterbury (278–84), presumably also in Latin, conveys in plain terms the location of Kenelm's body, without reference to the language or poetic form of the writ. The translation of the text makes possible the translation of the corpse. The alliterative poem, like the body it homes in on, has value not in itself but in what God imparts to it – in both cases, perfect purity ("wittore þanne eni snou," 253; "ssinde briȝte | þe lettres al of golde," 256; and "pur Engliss," 265) encased in perfect substantiality ("Þis writ [was] wiȝt," 256). This is how alliterative poetry should be treated: decode it when a saint's body is at stake, then enshrine it as a relic. In *St. Kenelm*, the alliterative snippet is little more than a curious impediment. There can be no doubt that the poet would have ignored alliterative verse altogether if his source had not contained two lines of it. Retelling the anecdote of the sacred letter in his English translation of the *Polychronicon*, Trevisa already felt the need to translate from alliterative verse to "Englisshe þat now is used."[21] Viewed from the outside, alliterative poetry seemed nearly as old-fangled in the thirteenth and fourteenth centuries as it does today. Who needs a Revival?

In a powerful reading of *St. Erkenwald*, Christine Chism argues that the tomb is an apt metaphor for the Alliterative Revival itself. For Chism the tomb represents "the break between a forgotten past and a barely incipient present" that symbolizes alliterative poets' "deliberate archaism" and "invention of a tradition."[22] Chism is surely correct to identify the tomb as a *mise en abîme*. It may be the most overt *mise en abîme* in the entire alliterative tradition. However, the previous chapters have argued that the alliterative long line was never reinvented from scratch. The condescension of some more progressive Middle English authors did not sum up all possible uses of alliterative verse. The Otho revision of the *Brut*, roughly coeval with the composition of *St. Kenelm* and the copying of the

Shrewsbury epitaph and the Bracton proverb, holds the capabilities of alliterative poetry in higher esteem. From the thirteenth to the fifteenth centuries, some poets continued to find the alliterative meter suitable for serious work. The deprecations foist upon alliterative verse by certain increasingly influential sectors of literary culture did not destroy it, but radicalized it.

The meaning of the tomb in *St. Erkenwald* can be revised in light of the verse history narrated in the previous chapters. Chism's book explores the presentist meaning of the tomb ('Of what use is it to us?') by carefully situating alliterative poetry in fourteenth-century politics and social history. Thus her chapter on *St. Erkenwald* reads the poem as a response to "the late [*sc.* fourteenth-]century social mobilities – physical, occupational, and class-jumping – that were recreating the London civic landscape."[23] The durability of the alliterative tradition directs attention instead to the historical meaning of the tomb ('From what sort of world does it come?'). The gratuitously perplexing details in the poem, the focus on wonder and terror rather than pity and joy, indicate which question our poet preferred to pursue. The fulfillment of the tomb's immediate purpose in the retroactive baptism seems little more than a pretext for the real motives of the poem. This is just the opposite of the Shrewsbury epitaph and the alliterative writ in *St. Kenelm*, which make better targets for Chism's arguments. Whereas the epitaph survives because of its retrojection into an antiquarian, Latinate, hagiographical scene, and the writ quickly yields up its secret and outlives its usefulness except as a 'ye olde' sign, the "roynyshe" writing lingers on past the end of *St. Erkenwald*, emblazoned on a now-empty tomb and still untranslated.

By way of conclusion, I would like to suggest a direct relationship between the two main strands of the argument thus far, the *Erkenwald* poet's sense of history and the idea of alliterative verse in late medieval England. *St. Erkenwald* not only instantiates the idea of alliterative verse; it also responds to that idea poetically, though in a different way, I believe, from the one proposed by Chism. Like the *Kenelm* episode, *St. Erkenwald* explores the limits of language, knowledge, and bodies. In *St. Erkenwald*, however, these stereotypical preoccupations of alliterative verse are modulated into a richer historical vision. Here I identify some points of contact between the historical imagination of *St. Erkenwald*, late medieval stereotypes about alliterative meter, and alliterative verse history as reconstructed in this book.

For a late medieval composition, *St. Erkenwald* is "full of oddly advanced notions."[24] Its achievement is not to redeem the past, but to traverse a *longue durée* so broad that it connects Christianity with what Christianity would repudiate. In the course of events every possible response to this conjunction is mooted, but none is endorsed. Like the squabbling clans of *Beowulf* in the wake of the hero's death, the Londoners of *St. Erkenwald* seem doomed to squander the legacy of the past. Construction grinds to a halt; the hoi polloi just gawk. After a week of research and prayer, the tomb is as inscrutable as ever. The tearful baptism is inadvertent and of debatable sacramental efficacy. An attentive late medieval reader would have wondered why God preserved the corpse in the first place, whether He therefore preserved others, what the inscription meant, how old the judge was, what sort of England he lived in, and whether pagan souls could, or should, be saved by baptism. Six hundred years have not made any of these questions easier to answer. The bishop's confrontation with the unknown is all the more striking for being unexpected. No one in *St. Erkenwald* goes in search of a tomb, or a judge, or a pagan past. Tomb, judge, and past simply materialize. The *Erkenwald* poet discerns doctrinal, linguistic, and sartorial hysteresis in cultural history, mirroring the metrical hysteresis that this book discerns in verse history.

The will to remain open to the unknown bespeaks a subtler historical sense than is typically imputed to medieval thinkers. Hints at the limits of historical perspective are thin on the ground in most of the genres inhabited by *St. Erkenwald* (chronicle, hagiography, *inventio*, romance). Langland's treatment of the Trajan legend (*Piers Plowman* B.11.140 ff.) is more overtly presentist. Centuries earlier, the *Beowulf* poet showed more interest in what could be learned and felt about the past than in its mysteries. These two *comparanda* indicate that the *Erkenwald* poet's sense of history is subtle even by the stringent standards of the alliterative tradition. Certainly the genre of the *inventio* gives little precedent for curiosity about heathen life. For example, when Matthew Paris's decrepit old man interprets the books found in the ruins of a large palace, Abbot Eadmar's response is totally uncompromising. The large book, an account of St. Alban "whose rubrics and titles glittered in golden letters [*quarum epigrammata et tituli aureis litteris fulserunt redimiti*]," Eadmar "deposited most lovingly in the vault [*in thesauro carissime reponebatur*]" and "had faithfully and diligently expounded, and more widely taught in public by preaching [*fecit fideliter ac diligenter exponi, et plenius in publico prædicando edoceri*]." The other books, containing "fabrications of the Devil [*commenta diaboli*]," including "invocations and rites [*invocationes et ritus*]" to "Mercury, called 'Woden' in English [*Mercurium, 'Woden' Anglice appellatum*]," he burned immediately ("*abjectis igitur et combustis libris*").[25]

The recognition in *St. Erkenwald* that the *antiqui* lived irrecoverable but possibly worthwhile lives seems exceptionally capacious. The poem's interest in and evident sympathy for pagan England troubles the modern assumption that the salvation of pagan ancestors remained a live issue for only a few centuries after conversion.[26] If the *Erkenwald* poet's sense of history corresponds to anything in our own time, it is the postmodern turn in historical studies, with its sensitivity to cultural difference and its resistance to totalizing narratives. Without a doubt, the *Erkenwald* poet took it on faith that pagans were damned to hellfire. But this only makes the ambivalence of the poem more remarkable. The human desire to know the past challenges the specifically Christian desire to convert it. The *moderni* in the poem wait anxiously for the past to explain itself, or as the bishop has it, "Sithen we wot not qwo þou art, | witere us þiselwen" (185). The impulse to ask questions first, even if you plan to shoot later, is extraordinary in any century. Within a poetic tradition increasingly dismissed as archaistic in late medieval English literary culture, the *Erkenwald* poet staged an ambitious historical investigation.

Like the dragon's hoard buried by the last survivor in *Beowulf*, the tomb in *St. Erkenwald* expresses the longevity of the alliterative verse form. To see history with the *Erkenwald* poet's eyes is not, as Chism would have it, to colonize the past, but to realize that one is colonized by it.[27] The familiar things of the present are undone, out of joint, forever altered by the long view. Undergirding this mode of historiography is an ethical imperative. Because the past cannot be cordoned off from the present, it must not be ignored. More than any other alliterative poem, *St. Erkenwald* dramatizes the necessary interrogation of the past, and the necessary failure of the interrogation. The *lacrimae rerum* of *St. Erkenwald* is the poignancy of a backward gaze conscious of its own futility. The plot may unfold along predictable religious lines, but the poet casts the Christian present far in the past as well. To apply the same historical method to Christian and pagan worlds is to imply, however faintly, that they belong to a progression greater than either. The sensation of belatedness, of being born after time or out of time, counterbalances the more familiar sensation of chosenness, raising an irresistible analogy between the Londoners and the pagan judge who knows himself "exilid fro þat soper so, | þat solempne fest" (303). Augustine's *regio dissimilitudinis* lives in this poem in time as well as space. The demise of the alliterative tradition itself in the sixteenth century, around the same time as the destruction of the tomb of the historical Erkenwald, renders *St. Erkenwald* more poignant than ever. More acutely even than *Beowulf*, because more explicitly, *St. Erkenwald* senses its own transience in the transience of the past it figures forth.

Authors, Styles, and the Search for a Middle English Canon

Of all the questions raised by *St. Erkenwald*, the question of authorship has provoked the most speculation, on the slimmest evidence. It is a question about which the compiler of British Library MS Harley 2250, a late fifteenth-century anthology of hagiography, must have cared little. *St. Erkenwald* is no more or less anonymous than most other alliterative poems. Its connection in modern criticism with the *Gawain* group is based upon aesthetic similarities and the conviction that one "gifted poet" can be extricated from his metrical tradition.[28] Middle English scholars, with good reason, have remained skeptical of the overstatements of oral-formulaic theory. Yet the ubiquity of formulas in alliterative poetry cannot be denied. Alliterative poetry may not be any more oral than other late medieval verse forms, but its formulaic style draws in its train all the difficulties of dating and attribution faced by Old English specialists.

Hard evidence for co-authorship of *St. Erkenwald* and the *Gawain* group, drawn from lexical, literary, and dialectal analysis, crumbles upon closer inspection.[29] To connect *St. Erkenwald* and *Gawain* on the basis of vocabulary (as though *nornen* and *gleuen* were an author's private property) is as optimistic as connecting them on the basis of literary value and surmised authorial dialect (as though the northwest Midlands were too small to contain two talented alliterative poets). Similarities between neighboring poems are to be expected. At any rate, so much manuscript evidence is missing that arguments from absence hold little weight. The handful of features unique to *St. Erkenwald* and the *Gawain* group, which some have found convincing, might dissolve if a dozen new alliterative poems came to light. The shared-words approach is an especially weak evaluative criterion as applied to a fragmentary corpus. It can be used, for example, to link *Beowulf* to conservative Old English poetry or late Old English prose.[30] To believe that poetic style can diagnose authorship is to misapprehend the status of tradition and innovation in late medieval literary culture, not to mention the possibility of direct literary influence. Moreover, if *St. Erkenwald* was composed as late as the 1450s or 1460s, then its author cannot possibly have written *Gawain* in the second half of the previous century.[31]

More fundamentally, fixation on the authorship of *St. Erkenwald* is of dubious historical value to begin with. The author-centric format of the Norton anthology sends up the Romantic fantasy of transcendental, original genius, anticipated to some degree in the fifteenth-century reception of Chaucer. It is largely inapplicable to other medieval English poetry.

(One might hasten to add that such ideology does not really fit the fifteenth-century reception of Chaucer either, or Romantic poets themselves, or perhaps, as suggested by recent poststructuralist critiques of the lyric, any poetry at all.) In my view, discussion of the corpora of anonymous authors co-opts the very features that might have pointed the way to a more fine-grained picture of literary communities. Affinities between *St. Erkenwald* and the *Gawain* group are matters of poetic style in the first instance. The identity of the author(s) is less important, except where it has traction as an organizational principle or a feature of reception in the Middle Ages. For the majority of alliterative poems, all such gestures toward an authorial canon remain the stuff of groundless speculation. Apart from Bede, Richard Rolle, and John Trevisa, who may or may not have composed one short alliterative poem apiece (*Bede's Death Song*, "Alle perisches and passes," and "Þanne God graunte grace," respectively), William Dunbar is the only alliterative poet with a verifiable biography. Like Bede, Rolle, and Trevisa, Dunbar's name survives on the strength of a large corpus of non-alliterative writings. The similarity in language, lexis, and style between *St. Erkenwald* and the *Gawain* group probably testifies to their close proximity in space and perhaps time. The primary value of these five poems from a literary-historical perspective is the way they symbolize a larger literary community now lost to history. Whether one, two, or five persons authored them seems much less important.

The irony of the co-authorship debate is that it has been unkind to *St. Erkenwald*, which figures in anthologies and criticism, if at all, as an optional addendum to an important foursome of poems – with which, again, not a single medieval reader, compiler, scribe, or author is known to have connected it. Like *Beowulf*, *St. Erkenwald* may have been stupendously unimportant, unread, unimitated, and quickly forgotten by contemporaries. Of course, modern scholars are under no obligation to take a medieval view of the poem's literary merits (I certainly do not); but, equally, the poem is under no obligation to yield intelligible answers to modern questions. *St. Erkenwald* deserves separate treatment in any case, not because it is a work of genius that transcends its tradition, but because it epitomizes its tradition. For it is in one way, at least, a more perfect poem than *Sir Gawain and the Green Knight*: it crystallizes the problem of history with none of the distractions of chivalric romance. It could be called a "philosophical poem," though that term fails to convey the vividness of the bishop's encounter with the distant past.[32]

Controversy over the dating and authorship of *St. Erkenwald* underscores the relative paucity of alliterative poems that may be assigned to the mid fifteenth century or later. The next chapter tracks the development of the alliterative meter and the alliterative tradition from the late fifteenth century into the sixteenth century. Resisting the temptation to imagine (or simply dismiss) this poorly attested period of alliterative verse history as decadent, the chapter traces the generic, codicological, textual, and cultural contexts for alliterative meter in the century before it disappeared from the active repertoire of verse forms. In doing so, the chapter lays the groundwork for a new literary history of the sixteenth century.

CHAPTER 6

The Alliterative Tradition in the Sixteenth Century

Alliterative meter after 1450 has received much less attention than its fourteenth-century ancestor.[1] As a result, basic questions about metrical phonology and metrical typology remain unanswered. Yet if the alliterative tradition exerted pressure on adjacent literary forms before 1450, as argued in Chapters 3, 4, and 5, then mapping the forms of post-1450 alliterative meter promises to sharpen understanding of post-1450 English literary culture as a whole.

This chapter traces the generic, codicological, textual, and cultural contexts for alliterative meter in the century before it disappeared from the active repertoire of verse forms. In doing so, this chapter lays the groundwork for a new literary history of the sixteenth century. After surveying the extant alliterative poems composed after 1450, I describe the systemic changes manifested in alliterative meter in this period, completing the formal evolution set out in Chapters 1, 3, and 4. The second section considers mid sixteenth- to mid seventeenth-century print and manuscript evidence for the reception of earlier alliterative meter, focusing on the two manuscript texts of *Scottish Field* (1515–47), the first of the three printings of Robert Crowley's edition of *Piers Plowman* (published in rapid succession in 1550), and Crowley's own poetry. I reconstruct scribes' and authors' perceptions of the alliterative meter in the period after the conclusion of active metrical practice but before the advent of modern metrical theory. I conclude by arguing that the contribution of the alliterative tradition to the so-called invention of modern literature has been underestimated by literary histories that enforce a division between 'medieval' and 'modern' periods of literary activity.

The Alliterative Tradition in its Tenth Century

In contrast to the relative abundance of alliterative poetry dating from the previous hundred years, only eight extant (unrhymed) alliterative poems are datable to after 1450: the *Ireland Prophecy* and the *Vision of William Banastre*, political prophecies containing coded references to the Wars of the Roses; the *Prophecie of Beid, Prophecie of Bertlington, Prophecie of Waldhaue,* and *Prophesie of Gildas* in the printed *Whole Prophesie of Scotland, &c.* (first published 1603), which allude to significant post-1450 dates or events (respectively, 1480: James III of Scotland goes to war against Edward IV of England; 1485: Battle of Bosworth; 1513: Battle of Flodden Field; and the first Act of Supremacy, 1534); William Dunbar's *Tretis of the Tua Mariit Wemen and the Wedo* (*c.* 1500), a synthesis of romance, satire, and didacticism; and *Scottish Field*, a victory composition.[2] It is easy now to take a teleological view and categorize these eight poems as remainders of a tradition that had already produced its geniuses and suffered its death-blow. But the poets themselves were unburdened by either hindsight or foreknowledge. By the middle of the fifteenth century Hoccleve, Lydgate, Caxton, and other taste-makers had succeeded in canonizing 'Maister Chaucer.' When in 1485 Caxton printed Malory's *Morte Darthur* (1469–70), he appears to have extensively bowdlerized the alliterative lexis found in "The Noble Tale betwixt Kyng Arthure and Lucius the Emperour of Rome," for which Malory's primary source had been the alliterative *Morte Arthure* (late fourteenth/early fifteenth centuries).[3] Over the course of the fifteenth century, the rhythms of alliterative poetry were increasingly transposed to the thirteen-line rhyming stanza, as in the *Awntyrs off Arthure* (late fourteenth/early fifteenth centuries). The combination of semi-syncopated rhythms with end rhyme proved enticing, and the unrhymed long line could have perished on the spot. But such is the momentum of a tradition lumbering toward its second millennium that some poets continued to make serious use of the older meter.

The choice to employ the alliterative meter in the late fifteenth and early sixteenth centuries was far from a nationalistic gesture. Chaucer's penta-meter had been unmistakably anointed as the prestige vernacular verse form. Nor, however, was it an act of desperation. None of the eight post-1450 poems gives the impression that the alliterative meter was felt to be in need of defense or rehabilitation. None of them apologizes for the choice, any more than Lawman had three centuries prior. Each belongs to a genre of alliterative verse that had gone before, whether prophecy, the *Piers Plowman* tradition of didactic and topical compositions, or battle poetry like that in the Anglo-Saxon Chronicle. Alliterative verse fared better after 1450 than tail rhyme had by the end of the previous century, when Chaucer could parody it so offhandedly. To judge from surviving evidence, there never was a *Tale of Sir Thopas* to mock an obsolescent alliterative tradition.

Only Dunbar's *Tretis* could be described as a parody: the expectations of ornate alliterative romance are raised in the opening of the poem, including a 'May-morning' prologue (see Ch. 4), only to be undercut by the women's bawdy discourse on marriage. Yet the joke is on marriage as much as on the exploded genre conventions, and Dunbar's handling of alliterative meter and lexis is more dexterous than derogatory.[4] The ambivalence between parody and skilful homage is characteristic of this poet. The alliterative meter remained a viable choice for poets writing in English after 1450.

All the same, the eight surviving poems testify to the increasing marginalization of alliterative poetry in literary culture. The perceived capacities of the alliterative form must have undergone severe restriction after 1450. Fully six of the eight poems are political prophecies; all eight have connections to Scotland, whether thematic, geographical, or codicological. All eight are recorded in northern dialect forms in manuscript and early print, though certainty about authorial dialect can only be attained in the case of Dunbar's poem and *Scottish Field*. (The latter, ll. 416–18, claims to have been composed by a native of Baguley, Cheshire.) The long-mooted idea "that alliterative poetry retreated northwards under pressure from London English and the Chaucerian tradition," which Derek Pearsall in an important essay found "difficult to resist," describes a late medieval cultural stereotype about alliterative meter as much as it describes an actual historical process.[5] The feedback loop between poets, printers, compilers, scribes, and an incipient reading public colored the alliterative tradition northern after 1450, completing a process of prosodic typecasting that had begun at least a century earlier.

In order to assess the historical significance of the last phase of the alliterative tradition, it is necessary to determine how the alliterative meter evolved after 1450. Though eight compositions are scant enough evidence to go on, they nonetheless permit some provisional conclusions about metrical change. The following account of the evolution of alliterative meter, 1450–1550, is based on a 400-line sample corpus, being ll. 1–200 of Dunbar's *Tretis* (in the text of *Poems*, ed. Bawcutt) and ll. 1–199 of *Scottish Field* (in the text of *Scotish Ffeilde*, ed. Oakden; including l. 110a for a total of 200 lines). I choose these two poems for several reasons. They are the longest of the eight post-1450 alliterative poems; the most firmly datable to after 1450, on biographical and historical grounds, respectively; the most firmly localizable on external and internal evidence, respectively; and, apart from the *Ireland Prophecy* and *Vision of William Banastre*, which I have edited and whose meter I have discussed elsewhere, the only ones to appear in modern critical editions.

I shall begin with metrical phonology, moving on to meter itself once the metrical status of historical -*e* becomes clearer. The most pressing reason to believe in the metrical reality of -*e* in post-1450 alliterative poetry is the historical one. The pervasive use of -*e* in alliterative poetry before 1450 establishes an expectation that the same phantom syllables will be used in the same way in alliterative poetry after 1450. Such -*e*'s had ceased to correspond to spoken usage by the middle of the fourteenth century at latest. There was no intrinsic reason (certainly no linguistic reason) they could not have continued in use in meter. The concept of metrical hysteresis provides a reason to expect metrical features to endure in tradition and helps to expose the formal processes by which they do so. The survival of metrically expedient -*e*'s from the fourteenth to the sixteenth centuries would be a non-event and a non-problem in verse history; only their desuetude would call for comment.

Nevertheless, it should be possible to demonstrate the metrical significance of historical -*e* in a synchronic perspective. In most of the b-verses in the sample corpus, the presence or absence of -*e* from the count makes no metrical difference, either because no words with -*e* happen to occur in them or because a word with -*e* happens to occur before an already long dip. In many cases, however, -*e* would make a short dip into a long dip, or it would form the final short dip. Here I focus on four metrical patterns whose distribution is clearcut. First, in seven cases the omission of -*e* from the metrical count gives the pattern xSxSx where counting -*e* would produce the ubiquitous Type 1 pattern, e.g., *Tretis* 4b *with hawthorne treis* (xS(x)xSx; *haw-* <OE *hagu*; no -*e* -*thorne* <OE *þorn* (m.); or perhaps pl. -*e* with *hawthorne* parsed as an adjective).[6] The pattern xSxSx never occurs in the sample corpus where -*e* is not at issue metrically. That is, there occur no b-verses like *with cedre treis* (xSxSx; *cedre* <OF). This distribution strongly suggests that -*e* counts in these seven verses. Second, of twelve b-verses with two long dips among the scansions dependent on -*e*, all twelve end in a short dip if -*e* is counted, e.g., *Scottish Field* 85b *with the leaue of our Lord* (xxSxxSx; *Lord* <OE *hlaford*).[7] That there occur no b-verses in the sample corpus like *with the leaue of our Chief* (xxSxxS; *Chief* <OF) argues in favor of counting -*e* at line end in these poems. Third, the pattern Sx . . . xS never occurs in the sample corpus independent of -*e*, but it occurs fifteen times if -*e* is discounted, e.g., *Scottish Field* 1b *grant me this time* (SxxS(x); *time* <OE *tima*).[8] Like the evanescent patterns xSxSx and x . . . xSx . . . xS, the pattern Sx . . . xS occurs in the sample corpus only when -*e* is discounted. That is, there occur no b-verses like *grant me this day* (SxxS; *day* <OE *dæg*). To summarize, the exclusive appearance of

xSxSx, x . . . xSx . . . xS, and Sx . . . xS under the assumption of discounted -*e* suggests that this is the wrong assumption.

The fourth argument in favor of scanning historical -*e* in these poems is another kind of absence: -*e* never occupies a final long dip in the sample corpus. A separate word occupies the final short dip in two instances: *Tretis* 129b ʒ*eilde for he gane* is (SxxxSx) and 197b *myght ane say amang thaim* (xxSxSx; *say* 'attempt' (noun) <OF *assai: Poems*, ed. Bawcutt, n. to 197b). However, there occur no b-verses like **myght ane say amidde thaim* (xxSxS(x)x; *amidde* <OE *onmiddan*). The absence of b-verses ending in a long dip in the sample corpus also implies that the post-1450 poets avoided placing proparoxytones at line end, including plural and/or weak trochaic adjectives and plural preterite verbs descended from Old English weak verbs of Class I.[9] Proparoxytones with -*e* form a tiny minority of the poetic lexicon. However, if -*e* did not count, one would expect them to appear at line end at least a few times in 400 b-verses.

These four arguments in favor of counting historical -*e* should be especially persuasive, insofar as they do not depend on any predefined metrical rules. Note the variety of words with -*e* picked out here (above and nn. 6–8): nouns with historical -*e* (e.g., *realme*), other etymologically disyllabic nouns (*lord*), petrified datives (*to the ground*), and genitives of proper names in -*s* (*Venus*); weak and/or plural adjectives; adverbs with -*e* (*bricht*) and -*es* (*needs*); singular finite verbs (*heete*), plural finite verbs (*pleis*), subjunctive finite verbs (*speede*), and infinitives (*witt*). On the basis of this evidence it is safe to conclude that post-1450 alliterative poets manipulated most of the kinds of metrically significant -*e* known to their fourteenth- and early fifteenth-century predecessors. At the same time, -*e* makes a metrical difference in a very small proportion of verses in the sample corpus. I have adduced only twenty-eight such verses: fifteen to make the final short dip of Type 3, seven to make the long dip of Type 1, and six to make the final short dip of the pattern x . . . xSx . . . xSx. Perhaps post-1450 alliterative poets had begun to doubt whether audiences would expect -*e* and chose to use this metrical entity more sparingly than their predecessors.

Evidence of the loss of metrically significant historical -*e* in the sample corpus is limited and may be outlined briefly. In two cases, -*e* would make a final long dip: *Scottish Field* 40b *many told thousands* (xxSxSx(x); final long dip or no -*e thousands*; pl. adj. *told*) and *Tretis* 67b *quhen thai lak curage* (xxSxSx(x); final long dip or no -*e curage* <OF *corage*; pl. *lak*). Stress shift in *thousands* and *curage* would create a metrically difficult second long dip, or at least a non-schwa medial dip if plural *told* and plural *lak* have no

metrically significant inflection. Such scansions are within the realm of possibility, but in both verses discounting -*e* in the final word seems to me the simpler solution. In two cases, I scan plural auxiliary *were* as a monosyllable: *Scottish Field* 72b <u>*were*</u> *seene on their masts* (xSxxSx) and 188b <u>*were*</u> *put to their ransome* (xSxxSx; *ransome* <OF *ransoun*). This innovative scansion was already available to fourteenth-century alliterative poets.[10] In five other cases, words with -*e* pose a choice between Type 2 with loss of -*e* and patterns with two long dips, e.g., *Scottish Field* 6b *that was alwayes noble* (xxSx(x)Sx; *alwayes* <ME *alwei(e)s*).[11] Patterns with two long dips are rare but authentic in all phases of the alliterative tradition, yet most of the -*e*'s in this group are uncommon or obscure and so easily discounted in perception of meter.

Seven verses in the sample corpus pose a choice between stress shift or syncope on the one hand and loss of historical -*e* on the other, e.g., *Scottish Field* 113b *to goe on his message* (xSxxSx with no -*e* *message* <OF; or xSxxxSx with stress shift *message*).[12] In each case, the metrical pattern remains the same under either interpretation. Therefore, the question of the metrical value of -*e* need not arise as such in this context. A phenomenological conception of meter, as practiced throughout this book, enables us to see that the status of -*e* does not actually come to issue here. Some readers will count -*e* and assume stress shift or syncope, while others will discount -*e*, but every well-versed reader will project the same metrical patterns onto the verses. Intriguingly, six of these seven doubtful -*e*'s occur in *Scottish Field*. The more innovative metrical phonology of that poem as compared with the *Tretis* and earlier alliterative verse may reflect its later date, changing audience expectations of -*e*, a less formal style, and/or scribal revision.

Before turning from metrical phonology to meter, a word on Dunbar's phonologies. If most kinds of historical -*e* remained available to post-1450 alliterative poets, it becomes possible to notice that Dunbar uses a much more conservative phonology for the *Tretis* than for the 83 non-alliterative poems in his extant corpus. As exemplified by *Tydingis fra the Sessioun* (Bawcutt's no. 2), Dunbar's non-alliterative poems differ from the *Tretis* in metrical treatment of nouns with historical -*e*, plural nouns, plural adjectives, weak adjectives, adverbs with -*e*, preterite verbs, singular finite verbs, plural finite verbs, and infinitive verbs.[13] Dunbar's divergent treatment of -*e* in divergent metrical contexts constitutes more evidence of the significance of -*e* in post-1450 alliterative poems but not (or not to the same extent) in contemporary rhymed poetry. More generally, Dunbar's treatment of -*e* demonstrates that the availability of metrical -*e* is specific to individual metrical traditions but not necessarily to individual dialect areas, particular centuries, or even individual poets. Metrical -*e* bears no necessary relationship to the -*e* reconstructed by linguists.

Having established the metrical significance of historical -*e* in post-1450 alliterative verse, we are now in a position to assess the development of the alliterative meter in this period. Counting all -*e*'s except those excluded earlier, the frequency of patterns found in the 400 b-verses in the sample corpus is as follows:

Type 1 (xSx … xSx)	180x
Type 2 (x … xSxSx)	87x
Type 3 (Sx … xSx)	36x
Type 5 (x … xSSx)	35x
three lifts	26x
Type 1 – final (xSx … xS)	15x
x … xSx … xSx	10x
Type 4 (x … xSxS)	7x
Type 5 – final (x … xSS)	4x

The post-1450 poems attest to a transitional moment in verse history, in which the fourteenth-century requirement of a final short dip has begun to be eroded but still applies in most cases. The absence of Sx … xS and the rarity of x … xSS suggest that the four-position minimum remained fully in force after 1450. The fourteenth-century requirement of exactly one long dip still applies, with the asystematic pattern x … xSx … xSx found in a small minority of b-verses, as in earlier alliterative meter. As in fourteenth-century alliterative verse, the a-verse is considerably less constrained than the b-verse. However, a-verse/b-verse symmetry has increased as a result of the expansion of the b-verse repertoire to include patterns with no final dip. Fully 110 of the 400 a-verses in the sample corpus (28%) have a pattern found in the b-verse, excluding patterns with three lifts or two long dips and counting historical -*e* where possible, as against 65% for Early Middle English alliterative poetry and 5% for fourteenth- and early fifteenth-century alliterative poetry with the same qualifications. These figures show how alteration of one metrical feature can interrupt an adjacent developmental process in verse history.

Though I treated the two categories separately as an analytical convenience, the preceding account illustrates the interdependence of metrical phonology and meter in verse history. Most kinds of historical -*e* turned out to be metrically necessary in a few b-verses in the sample corpus, yet the vast majority of possible *-e*'s were perceptually irrelevant. A post-1450 b-verse like *Scottish Field* 2b *thy seluen to please* might plausibly be scanned xSxxSx (Type 1), counting *-e* in infinitive *please*, or xSxxS, discounting *-e* in *please*. Only the former scansion was possible in alliterative meter before 1450. After 1450, occasional b-verses with no final dip, e.g., *Tretis* 13b *so hard I inthrang* (xSxxS; *inthrang* <OE *in-* + *prang*), erode the expectation of *-e* at line end. Conversely, discounting possible *-e*'s at line end erodes the expectation of final short dips in the b-verse. The interdependence of meter and metrical phonology can guide the modern recovery of alliterative meter, but it also must have been an important aspect of the experience of versification and scansion for alliterative poets and their first audiences. This consideration, in turn, helps explain why the availability of metrical *-e* is historically linked to the development of individual metrical traditions. Even within the alliterative tradition, metrical/metrical-phonological reinter-pretation followed different trajectories in different metrical contexts. While the connection between line-end final *-e* and final short dips began to be disrupted after 1450, other aspects of the meter/phonology interface endured. For example, the sample corpus contains no secure instance of a b-verse with no long dip and no indication that *-e* may be discounted when it would make a long dip.

The foregoing exposition of post-1450 alliterative meter lends further formal specificity and historical depth to Kristin Lynn Cole's claim that the *Destruction of Troy* (?late fourteenth/early sixteenth centuries) is metrically unique within the alliterative tradition. The b-verse patterns found in the sample corpus are similar to the ones Cole identified in *Destruction*, apart from the pattern Sx ... xS, which is found in *Destruction* but not in the sample corpus.[14] However, the high degree of a-verse/b-verse symmetry in *Destruction* (*c.* 50 percent) cannot be paralleled in any other post-1250 alliterative poem. The *Destruction* poet (or an enterprising scribe) severely subordinated the organizing principle of differentiation of a-verse and b-verse patterns. The idiosyncrasies of the *Destruction* meter cannot all be referred to a late date.

Comparison of post-1450 alliterative meter with its earlier and better-documented manifestations affords one last opportunity to reconsider the relationship between metrical form and linguistic form. On the basis of the arguments advanced so far, I find it difficult to concur with Hoyt Duggan that "Dunbar and the *Destruction of Troy*-poet ... provide evidence for the revision of metrical rules to adapt to language which had changed."[15] I would argue instead that the two poems provide evidence of two different processes in verse history, neither of which depended in any straightforward way on language change. The *Tretis* shows some reinterpretation of meter and metrical phonology at line end, the metrical position most vulnerable to such reinterpretation. *Destruction* shows a more radical reintepretation of metrical principles by someone either unaware or unconcerned that such a reinterpretation places the poem far outside the metrical mainstream. Both reinterpretations of metrical form were doubtless amplified by innovative scansions of words with historical -*e*, but the experience of spoken Middle English or Middle Scots had no determinative effect on such scansions. If it had, the *Tretis* meter would have emerged three centuries earlier, at the time of the loss of spoken -*e* in northern dialects.

Moreover, it may be premature to assume that metrical-phonological innovations would necessarily precede and induce metrical ones. I noted earlier how metrical phonology and the expectations that poets and scribes bring to metrical phonology cannot be separated experientially from meter and the expectations that poets and scribes bring to meter. The erosion of the expectation of historical -*e* in the alliterative tradition was not a reduction of verse history to language history ("to adapt to language which had changed") but was itself a complex verse-historical process. Duggan's proposition that metrical phonology mirrors linguistic phonology makes sense from the perspective of Saussurean synchronic analysis, but it does not turn out to hold for any phase of the alliterative tradition, Old to Middle English. The generalizable conclusion is that researchers must combine synchronic and diachronic formal analysis in order to achieve a richly historical perspective onto metrical systems.

This section has reconceptualized the relationship of meter to language in a more fundamental way, as well. If consideration of Henry of Huntingdon's Latin translation of the *Battle of Brunanburh* (Ch. 4 and Appendix C) has not already, the inclusion of a Scottish writer in the pantheon of English alliterative poets must indicate the inadequacy of imagining alliterative poetry as a geographically or linguistically monolithic tradition. Always in theory, and sometimes in practice, the alliterative tradition exceeded linguistic and proto-national boundaries. Both Henry's alliterative Latin translation and Dunbar's choice to compose in the alliterative meter signal the prestige and portability of the idea of alliterative verse. The two poems constitute the *ultima Thule* of the 'diversity' trend in alliterative verse discussed in Chapters 3 and 4. By categorizing Henry's translation and Dunbar's *Tretis* as 'English' poems, I mean to dislodge the narrowly national and linguistic associations that term will inevitably convey to modern readers. This book has been predicated upon an account of the evolution of a specific meter; and inasmuch as meter occurs as an idea or mental event, rather than a heard sound or a seen spelling, it may migrate and metamorphose like any other idea. If the English alliterative tradition can be made the basis of English literary history, it must be in full knowledge that English literary history has always been multilingual and transnational.

Unmodernity: The Idea of Alliterative Verse in the Sixteenth Century

In addition to charting the development of alliterative meter after 1450, the previous section noted three sources of direct and indirect evidence for recovering the cultural meanings of alliterative verse in the sixteenth century: Caxton's treatment of alliterative lexis in Malory's *Morte Darthur*, the Scottish coloring of the extant post-1450 alliterative poems, and Dunbar's unique choice of the alliterative meter for his longest poem. In what follows, I trace the late reception of alliterative meter through three more sources of evidence: the two extant manuscript texts of *Scottish Field*; the preface of Robert Crowley's edition of *Piers Plowman*; and the meter of Crowley's *One and Thyrtie Epigrammes* (1550), an original poetic composition exactly contemporary with his *Piers Plowman* edition. A future study could go on to coordinate and synthesize all six of these sources of evidence, and others, to achieve a broader view of the connotations and habits of alliterative composition, 1450–1600.

Scottish Field is extant in two manuscripts: Manchester, John Rylands Library Lyme Hall (late sixteenth century) and British Library MS Additional 27879 ('Percy Folio') (mid seventeenth century).[16] The Lyme Hall manuscript consists of six long, thin strips of vellum containing an acephalous text of *Scottish Field* (25b–252b and 276b–422b in Oakden's lineation) followed by "The names of the lordes and gentilmen of Scotland that were slaine in deede attis late battail vpon brankston more [=Battle of Flodden]." The Percy Folio is a large, eclectic anthology of Middle English poetry compiled in the middle of the seventeenth century. The existence of two manuscript witnesses affords a rare opportunity to isolate locations of scribal intervention in the textual transmission of an alliterative poem. However, in what follows I remain circumspect about attributing individual readings to author or scribe on a metrical basis.

There are 80 substantial textual variants in 71 b-verses between the two texts of *Scottish Field*. Of the 142 b-verse texts in question, 127 (89%) are metrically conformant, counting patterns with two long dips or three lifts as unmetrical and discounting some historical -*e*'s as discussed below. Of the 71 variant b-verses, 8 (11%) show 2 different acceptable metrical patterns.[17] There is thus a strong *prima facie* case for scribal understanding of alliterative meter between these 2 textual states. One or more scribes in the textual history of *Scottish Field* made numerous alterations to the received text, mostly producing metrical b-verses and occasionally revising a b-verse from one metrically conformant pattern to another.

Most of the 80 variants show addition or substitution of metrically unstressed function words, e.g., Lyme *his* at 62b where Oakden prints the Percy Folio reading *our*, or substitution of metrically equivalent content words, e.g., Lyme *hilles* at 175b where Oakden prints the Percy Folio reading *feilds*. Among the remaining variants, many seem to have been partly motivated by considerations of meter and poetic style. Several involve b-verse patterns with two long dips, e.g.:

$$x \quad S \quad x \quad x \quad x \quad S \quad x$$
25b (L)   that <u>dred</u> was sone after   (1; *sone* <OE *sona*)

$$x \quad x \quad S \quad x \quad x \quad S \quad x$$
25b (PF)   that <u>adread</u> was thereafter.[18]   (two long dips)

Metrically significant variants are underlined, and Yakovlev scansions accompany the verse with one long dip. The Lyme reading has plainer meter, but more difficult sense, 'so that there was danger soon after' (*MED* Online, 'drēde,' 5a) beside 'who was fearful after that' (*MED* Online, 'adrēden,' 3a) in the Percy Folio. The variant thus either shows a reviser actively systematizing the meter or one willing to introduce metrical complications in order to clarify the sense. Another group of variants suggests divergent perceptions of historical -*e* in plural nouns at line end, e.g.:

$$x \quad S \quad x \quad x \quad x \quad S \quad x$$
59b (L)   the saddest of all <u>others</u>   (1)

$$x \quad S \quad x \quad x \quad x \quad S \quad x$$
59b (PF)   the saddest of all <u>other</u>.[19] (1)

Here the Lyme reading shows either syncope of -*er*- or loss of plural -*e* in *others*. Perhaps a reviser substituted *other* for *others* in order to avoid an unmetrical final long dip or metrical ambiguity. Alternately, a reviser may have substituted for *other* the metrically and linguistically more innovative *others*. A third set of variants involve syntactical rearrangements, e.g.:

```
           x    S   x   x  S  x
112b (L)   that doughtie was euer        (1)

           x    x   S   x S  x
112b (PF)  that was doughtye euer.²⁰     (2)
```

Here the Lyme reading shows poetic inversion of *doughtie* and *was* where the Percy Folio reading follows prose syntax. Both readings are metrically conformant.

The three types of alteration discussed so far, involving patterns with two long dips, historical *-e*, and poetic syntax, come together in an especially complex variant:

```
           x    S    x   x  x   S x
156b (L)   that knowen was full wide    (1)

           x    x   S  (x)  x   S x
156b (PF)  that was knowne full wide.   (two long dips or Type 2;
                                         knowne <OE cnawen)
```

The Percy Folio reading, preferred by Oakden, poses a choice between a pattern with two long dips and innovative loss of *-e* in participial *knowne*. The Lyme reading not only circumvents this choice but retains (or adds) poetic inversion of *knowen* and *was*. If metrical systematicity and poetic ornament be valid editorial criteria, Oakden ought to have selected the Lyme reading. Yet the direction of revision here may be less significant than the fact of it. Someone encountered one of the readings and, for one reason or another, revised it.

Three variants involve one of the poetic words for 'man' used in Middle English alliterative verse, e.g.:

```
           S   x   x   S   x
222b (L)   rinckes ten thousand         (3)

           S   x   x   S   x
222b (PF)  knights ten thousand.²¹      (3)
```

Like the similar variants in the text of Lawman's *Brut* (*c.* 1200) discussed in Chapter 3, and like the cases of prosified poetic syntax just cited, these alterations probably point to lexical modernization by one or more forward-thinking scribes. Three centuries after the alliterative tradition was decisively demoted within the English literary field, the alliterative synonyms for 'man' could still provoke stringent aesthetic reactions.

For at least a few late sixteenth- and/or mid seventeenth-century scribes, then, the idea of alliterative verse was still a familiar idea that could be put into practice in formally precise ways. Taken together, the textual variants in the manuscripts of *Scottish Field* paint a picture of multiple post-1550 revisers competent in the alliterative style and eager to interpose their own tastes between the received text and their projected audience. Given the paucity of manuscript or print copies of alliterative poems after 1550, the two texts of *Scottish Field* can be understood to stand in for a much larger continuum of scribal attitudes, now lost. The stark contrast with the extensively corrupt text of the alliterative *Death and Liffe* (?fourteenth/ sixteenth centuries), also found in the Percy Folio, raises questions about the metrical competence of the Percy Folio scribe.[22] Possibly this scribe was unfamiliar with alliterative meter, and the competent changes to the Percy Folio text of *Scottish Field* are due to an earlier scribe; or the Percy Folio scribe was responsible for some of the metrically conformant variants in the text of *Scottish Field* but already faced a hopelessly corrupt text of *Death and Liffe*; or the scribe was a *literatim* copier who happened to have access to a relatively good text of *Scottish Field* and a relatively bad text of *Death and Liffe*. In the last case, the Percy Folio would provide no evidence one way or the other about its scribe's understanding of alliterative meter. Without more manuscript evidence it may be impossible to decide between these alternatives. Nevertheless, the metrical competence implicit in the variants surveyed above must be attributable in part to some number of sixteenth- and/or seventeenth-century scribes, unless one could believe in the existence of multiple authorial recensions of *Scottish Field*.

A less direct but more historically prominent source of evidence for sixteenth-century perceptions of alliterative meter is Robert Crowley's 1550 edition of *Piers Plowman* (STC 19906).[23] Crowley's brief preface, "The Printer to the Reader," is a monument in the history of textual criticism. It features, inter alia, remarks on the authorship of the poem ("I haue learned that the Autour was named Roberte langelande," ii^r) and its dating ("we may iustly co*n*iect therfore, y^t it was firste written about two hundred yeres paste," ii^r), notice of alliteration ("the nature of hys miter is, to haue thre wordes at the leaste in euery verse whiche beginne with some one letter," ii^r), and acknowledgment of language change ("The Englishe is according to the time it was written in, and the sence somewhat darcke," ii^v) and textual variance ("diuerse copies haue it diuerslye," ii^v). Especially significant in the present context is Crowley's perception that alliterative meter is old-fashioned: "He [Langland] wrote altogyther in miter: but not after ye maner of our rimers that write nowe adayes (for his verses ende not alike)" (ii^r). This remark implies that Crowley did not regard alliterative meter as a live option in 1550 (with *rimers* 'poets' as well as 'poets who compose in rhyme'). It also implies Crowley's expectation that his readers might not recognize the metrical form of *Piers Plowman*. Nevertheless, Crowley trusts that his prefatory remarks on verse form will enable readers to enjoy the meter of *Piers Plowman* ("This thinge [i.e., alliteration] noted, the miter shal be very pleasaunt to read," ii^v).

Crowley's edition occupies a middle ground in the history of changing attitudes toward alliterative meter. Crowley does not show formal *savoir faire*, like the *Scottish Field* scribes and many earlier readers and practitioners of alliterative verse. Nor does he show total ignorance, which George Puttenham had achieved toward the end of the century, when, in his *Arte of English Poesie* (1589), he could describe the form of *Piers Plowman* as "but loose meetre" without further comment (STC 20519, 50). Already in 1575 George Gascoigne, in a tract entitled *Certayne Notes of Instruction Concerning the Making of Verse or Ryme in English*, had quoted Chaucer's Parson offhandedly in a list of superficial poetic effects: "[I]t is not inough to roll in pleasant woordes, nor yet to thunder in *Rym, Ram, Ruff,* by letter (quoth my master *Chaucer*), nor yet to abounde in apt vocables, or epythetes, vnlesse the Inuention haue in it also *aliquid salis*" (STC 11637, 291). Scholars usually infer that Gascoigne has missed Chaucer's allusion to alliterative romance, but this is not entirely clear. Perhaps the intended contrast is between alliteration as a clichéd ornament and "some fine inuention" (291), irrespective of metrical form. Certainly the alliterative meter was not on Gascoigne's prosodic radar in 1575.

Despite the different contexts of their remarks, in a significant respect Crowley's and Puttenham's preconceptions about alliterative verse coincide. In his preface Crowley takes pains to dispute the authenticity and interpretation of two passages in *Piers Plowman* that might be construed as political prophecies ("And that which foloweth and geueth it the face of a prophecye is lyke to be a thinge added of some other man than the fyrste autour" and "Loke not vpon this boke therfore, to talke of wonders paste or to come," ii^v). These are the 'two monks' heads' and 'Abbot of Abingdon' set-pieces (*Piers Plowman* B.6.321–31 and B.10.322–35).[24] In the second printing of his edition, Crowley added a marginal note to the 'Abbot of Abingdon' passage for good measure: "This is no prophecy but a pronostication" (STC 19907a, xxxvi^r). Significantly, Crowley titled his edition *The Vision of Pierce Plowman*, and later commentators would read the poem in this form as well as continuing to read manuscript copies. Crowley's desire to foreclose a political-apocalyptic interpretation of *Piers Plowman* may have partly motivated him to produce his edition. In his passing mention of *Piers Plowman*, Puttenham likewise dubs Langland "a very true Prophet" of the Reformation (50). In his *Scriptorum illustrium maioris Bryttanie* (1557–59), John Bale noted that Langland "foretold many (things) prophetically, which we have seen fulfilled in our days [*propheticè plura prędixit, quę nostris diebus impleri uidimus*]" (STC 1296a, 474). The unnamed author of the *Petition directed to Her Most Excellent Maiestie* (1591), sometimes identified as the pamphleteer Job Throckmorton, cites *Piers Plowman* as political prophecy: "*Piers Plowman* likewise wrote against the state of Bishops, and prophecied their fall in these wordes," quoting B.15.553–56a (STC 1522a, 34). The alliterating poem *Dauy Dycars Dreame*, printed probably in the late 1540s, echoes the 'two monks' heads' and 'Abbot of Abingdon' passages.[25] And Gascoigne's *Steele Glas* (1576) houses Davy the Diker in a long sequence of prophetic hypotheticals ("when Dauie Diker diggs, and dallies not," STC 11645, H.iii^v). These notices and responses join the evidence of the eight extant post-1450 alliterative poems in suggesting the extent to which alliterative meter and political prophecy overlapped in perception and practice after 1450.

Alongside this print evidence of a prophetic *Piers Plowman* and a prophetic alliterative tradition in the sixteenth century is a variety of contemporary manuscript evidence. The manuscript evidence remains less visible than the print evidence in modern scholarship but is in fact more extensive. Early in the century, *Piers Plowman* B appeared in Cambridge University Library MS Gg.4.31 as "The Prophecies of Piers Plowman," complete with glosses and table of contents, including annotations and cross-references for, among others, the 'two monks' heads' and 'Abbot of Abingdon' passages.[26] British Library MS Sloane 2578 (mid sixteenth century) contains a combined freestanding excerpt of both of the same two passages, while British Library MS Additional 60577 contains a freestanding excerpt of the 'two monks' heads' passage in an early sixteenth-century hand, followed by the tag "Quod piers plowman."[27] Two heretofore unrecognized combined texts of the 'two monks' heads' and 'Abbot of Abingdon' passages occur among other prophecies in Oxford Bodleian MS Rawlinson C.813 (mid sixteenth century).[28] The second Rawlinson *Piers Plowman* excerpt is immediately followed by one of the two surviving texts of the late alliterative prophecy the *Vision of William Banastre*. Later in the same manuscript there occurs an English rhyming prophecy, found in at least five copies in four manuscripts, which reworks both prophetic *Piers Plowman* passages.[29] A late hand in Oxford Bodleian MS Bodley 814 annotated the 'two monks' heads' passage with "Prouesie."[30] A late hand in Cambridge University Library MS Ll.4.14 annotated the 'Abbot of Abingdon' passage with "A prophecy agaynste ye Relygyouse."[31] Several other manuscripts of *Piers Plowman* B show late annotations at 6.321–31 and 10.322–35.[32] A copy of the C text, British Library MS Additional 35157, shows Sir Edward Ayscough's late sixteenth-century annotation "A prophecye.trulye fulfilled by Kinge henrye.the.viij.th," referring to the revised version of the 'Abbot of Abingdon' passage (C.5.168–79).[33] Another annotator of a C manuscript added B.6.327–29 in the margin for insertion in the revised version of the 'two monks' heads' passage (C.8.341–52).[34] The sixteenth-century antiquarian Stephan Batman added the 'two monks' heads' passage to one of his copies of *Piers Plowman*.[35] A sixteenth-century annotator marked the 'two monks' heads' passage as "pearcys Profacye" and noticed the 'Abbot of Abingdon' passage as "an other profycye of desoluyng of abayes" in British Library C.122.d.9, a copy of the second printing of Crowley's edition of *Piers Plowman*.[36] The appearance, reappearance, and recombination of these two *Piers Plowman* 'prophecies' is typical of the ways in which vernacular prophecies circulated and proliferated in late manuscript and early print culture. The manuscript evidence for a prophetic *Piers Plowman*, earlier overall than the print evidence, helps illuminate the metrical-cultural milieu in which Crowley's edition could appear as an intervention.

The generic coloring that attached to the alliterative meter in the sixteenth century explains the comments of Crowley, Bale, Puttenham, and the author of the *Petition*, as well as the presentation and excerpting of *Piers Plowman* in sixteenth-century manuscripts. It also explains the practice of the poets responsible for the six post-1450 alliterative prophecies. Finally, it explains the preservation of these poems. Four of them survive because of their inclusion in the printed *Whole Prophesie of Scotland, &c.*, issued to celebrate the accession of a Scottish king to the English throne (James VI/I), a key prediction of medieval English political prophecies. The other two, the *Ireland Prophecy* and the *Vision of William Banastre*, appear in large late fifteenth- and sixteenth-century manuscript anthologies of prophecies and political writings. *Scottish Field*, a late alliterative non-prophecy, shows that poets who chose the alliterative meter after 1450 were not automatically beholden to the genre of political prophecy; but the non-prophetic content of this alliterative poem must have constituted a heavily marked choice by 1515, the earliest possible date for the poem.

And then, the topic of the poem plays squarely into another stereotype about alliterative poetry, that it is northern. Taken together, the composition, copying, presentation, excerpting, printing, editing, and interpretation of alliterative poetry register the same intensifying typecasting in literary culture.

To judge by his own poetry, Crowley heard more than alliteration and prophetic-sounding language in *Piers Plowman*. John N. King has argued that the meter of Crowley's *One and Thyrtie Epigrammes*, published in the same year as the edition of Langland's poem (1550), was influenced by the metrical form of *Piers Plowman*. King, writing in 1982, posited the "four-beat accentual rhythm" of the *Epigrammes* as an effect of Crowley's "juncture of the indigenous alliterative tradition with the imported tradition of rhymed couplets."[37] More recent scholarship, as elaborated in this book, has shown that the regularity of alliterative meter lies as much in the dips as in the lifts, while problematizing the dichotomy between "indigenous" and "imported" metrical traditions. Nonetheless, I believe King was correct to discern influence from Middle English alliterative meter in Crowley's versification. The date of the *Epigrammes*, their subject matter (religious invective and social satire), and the ostentatious use of alliteration in the openings of nine individual sections all invite the comparison.[38] Yet it is the differences, not the similarities, that seem to me most significant in this case. Crowley uses a roughly anapestic tetrameter, graphically and syntactically broken into two short lines (quoted from STC 6088, iii[r]; for ease of comparison I replace the line break between short lines with a tabbed space representing the caesura of the long line):

```
x S    x  x S      x   S   x   x S
If bokes may be bolde   to blame and reproue
x   S   x x  S       x   S   x   S
The faultes of al menne   boeth hyghe and lowe:
x   x   S  x(x) S      x   x   S x  x   S
As the Prophetes dyd   whom Gods spirite did moue
x    S   x   x   S x   x  S    x x   S
Than blame not myne Autor   for right well I knowe.
```

This meter conceivably reflects a reading of *Piers Plowman* attuned to half-line structure, the most common disposition of lifts (two per half-line), and the most common kind of long dip (two syllables), but not to a-verse/b-verse asymmetry, the requirement of a final short dip in the b-verse, three-lift half-lines, inductive scansion, or, probably, most kinds of metrically significant *-e*. If so, Crowley joins a long line of poets who transposed alliteration and alliterative meter into a deductive verse form. One could compare not only alliterating, stanzaic poems like the *Awntyrs off Arthure* but also the Harley Lyrics (late thirteenth/early fourteenth centuries) and much medieval English drama. In Crowley's lifetime, Edmund Spenser's *Shepheardes Calendar* (1579) alludes to *Piers Plowman* and gestures toward alliterative rhythms for antiquarian effect within an aggressively deductive iambic metrical practice.[39]

From the perspective of alliterative verse history, Crowley's *Epigrammes* may be most valuable as a representation of what a mid sixteenth-century reader could perceive in the rhythms of *Piers Plowman*. Crowley's meter implies a scansion of *Piers Plowman* that has itself become a historical curiosity, since it occurred outside the context of a living metrical tradition or an explicit theory of meter. The differences between fourteenth-century alliterative meter and the *Epigrammes* meter illustrate how incomplete perceptions of metrical form can be productive rather than destructive – and, indeed, can count as historical knowledge in the fullest sense.

It is worth pausing to notice the extent to which the last chapter of alliterative verse history fails to intersect the first chapter of the study of medieval English poetry. In the second half of the sixteenth century, Crowley, Bale, Gascoigne, Puttenham, Spenser, and the author of the *Petition* were situated in an interregnum between medieval practice and modern theory. The sixteenth century witnessed the inauguration of medieval studies as a field of historical inquiry. However, the focus of the earliest publications was on Old English prose. Individual manuscript codices of medieval English verse, such as the Junius MS and the Percy Folio, would not be mobilized as historical evidence until the seventeenth and eighteenth centuries. Crowley's edition of *Piers Plowman* (reissued by Owen Rogers in 1561) is an aberration in many ways, and the experiment was not repeated until Thomas Whitaker's edition of 1813. Crowley's and Puttenham's brief comments on Middle English alliterative meter bear little resemblance to the increasingly sophisticated field of alliterative metrics in the eighteenth century and later, when this meter was recognized first as quantitative, then as an arrangement of identical initial sounds ('alliterative,' a term borrowed from humanist rhetorical theory), and finally and most enduringly as accentual.[40] Within the interregnum between practice and theory, the experience of alliterative meter was to a large extent an experience of *Piers Plowman*. Accordingly, the more we learn about the uses and perception of *Piers Plowman* in the sixteenth century, the more we will learn about the final phase of the alliterative tradition and the literary-cultural atmosphere of the sixteenth century more generally.

The gap of a century and more between the end of verse history and the advent of disciplinary history suggests one general conclusion. Alliterative meter was not a topic of intrinsic historical interest even for its latest practitioners, including nearly all the scribes responsible for the surviving records. With this realization, an initially attractive explanation for metrical death – a shift from practical to historical knowledge in step with the early modern invention of the Middle Ages – is removed. In the sixteenth century, alliterative poems were not pinned to the lepidopterist's board so much as quietly forgotten. In order to understand why alliterative poetry was composed, transmitted, preserved, and even edited between 1450 and 1600, scholars would be well advised to look backward, to the history of practice, before looking forward, to the history of theory.

The title of this section introduces the neologism 'unmodernity,' a term that seeks to avoid the teleological connotations of 'early modern,' 'medieval,' and 'premodern' without promising an easy escape from the problem of seeing an early metrical tradition through modern eyes. Such a neologism seemed especially apt to describe the largely non-practical but also largely non-theoretical uses to which alliterative meter was put in the sixteenth century. The textual transmission of *Scottish Field*, Crowley's preface to *Piers Plowman*, the meter of Crowley's *Epigrammes*, and the compilation of the *Whole Prophesie of Scotland, &c.*, offer other ways of understanding poetic tradition than the ones that would come to define English literature in later centuries. The concept of unmodernity is one of the least prejudicial ways I can think of to measure this difference. At the same time, the concept of unmodernity has historical traction within the sixteenth century, insofar as it can serve to index the widening metrical and cultural gap between the alliterative tradition and newer literary forms. That is, 'unmodernity' not only describes a characteristic literary-cultural atmosphere, but it also helps isolate the formal and cultural processes by which that atmosphere endured, evolved, and ultimately gave way to something else. None of the poets, scribes, editors, or prosodists discussed in this chapter would have understood themselves to be active at a transitional moment in literary history: such a judgment is entirely ours, and entirely retrospective. Under the rubric of verse history, the concept of unmodernity can help recapture the historical meaning of alliterative verse in the decades between the conclusion of metrical evolution and the introduction of recognizably modern linguistic and metrical science.

This chapter clears the ground for a future study that would coordinate the last phase of the alliterative tradition with the other metrical options on the sixteenth-century literary scene. This work would complement and complicate O. B. Hardison's survey of "Crosscurrents in English Sixteenth-Century Prosody" and Martin Duffell's chapter on "The Emergence of English Metrical Canons" in his *New History of English Metre*, neither of which takes account of the alliterative tradition in the sixteenth century.[41] By comparing contemporaneous metrical traditions, it should be possible to notice ruptures and continuities in verse history not already prophesied by cultural, linguistic, political, or textual history. Such a study could map the interrelations of the late manuscript and early print media and reconsider the segmentation of literary history into 'medieval' and 'modern' periods. The sixteenth century in English literary history may look very different indeed when the influence of a millennium-old verse tradition can be appreciated.

Conclusion: Whose Tradition?

In the opening of his *Introduction to English Poetry* (2002), James Fenton excludes Old English poetry from consideration on the grounds that "[i]t is somebody else's poetry." Fenton confides, "I can't accept that there is any continuity between the traditions of Anglo-Saxon poetry and those established in English poetry by the time of, say, Shakespeare."[1] He goes on to reject Middle English poetry as well, though "[w]ith Chaucer we are much nearer home."[2] Predictably, Fenton's chronological dividing line between "somebody else's poetry" and its unstated opposite, 'our poetry,' coincides with the English Reformation. Such schematic periodization takes literary history back to the brave new world of George Puttenham, who opined in his *Arte of English Poesie* (1589) that "beyond that time [i.e., the reigns of Edward III and Richard II] there is litle or nothing worth commendation to be founde written in this arte [i.e., verse]" (STC 20519, 48).

For Puttenham, the reasons for the irrelevance of pre-1327 English poetry were (explicitly) political, intellectual, legal, linguistic, and (implicitly) racial. He writes of "the late Normane conquest, which had brought into this Realme much alteration both of our langage and lawes, and there withall a certain martiall barbarousnes, whereby the study of all good learning was so much decayd, as long time after no man or very few entended to write in any laudable science" (48). In 1589 this was a powerful new insight into the shape of English literary history. Indeed, Puttenham's is one of the earliest attempts to constitute English literary history as a discrete field of inquiry. He describes the goal of his investigation this way:

> that their [i.e., English poets'] names should not be defrauded of such honour as seemeth due to them for hauing by their thankefull studies so much beautified our English tong (as at this day it will be found our nation is in nothing inferiour to the French or Italian for copie of language, subtiltie of deuice, good method and proportion in any forme of poeme,

but that they may compare with the most, and perchance passe a great many of them. (48)

By 2002 Fenton could activate the same discourses of nation, language, and race without identifying them as such, except to remark that "English poetry begins whenever we decide to say the modern English language begins."[3] Moreover, Puttenham's own milieu has become for Fenton the decisive watershed, further aligning the putatively spasmodic history of English poetry with the consolidation of the discourses on which that history rests.

For most of English literary history, of course, "somebody else's poetry" was everybody's poetry. The present-day configuration of ideologies about Poetry with a capital 'P' makes a poor starting point for historical investigation. The same is true, for that matter, of English with a capital 'E.' Students of early English literature must inquire on what basis (or, indeed, whether) a Fentonian dividing line was drawn historically. By devoting the present study to "somebody else's poetry," I have sought to recapture the cultural meaning of poetic forms and styles that were new many centuries ago. One implication of the verse history narrated in the foregoing chapters is that pre-Shakespearean literary history was not an inevitable progression from mumbo-jumbo to the modern. Instead, it was the result of stylistic choices by writers working in specific contexts, as well as long historical processes whose shape and significance would become apparent only in retrospect. Fenton's tacit modern 'us' is not some transhistorical *donnée* in the history of letters; it had to be constructed through serial practices of versification and scansion.

If the rationale for Fenton's periodization of English poetry is explicitly linguistic, it is also implicitly metrical: he favorably compares Chaucer's *Troilus and Criseyde* ("much nearer home, both linguistically and in terms of poetic practice") to *Sir Gawain and the Green Knight* ("baffling and comprehensible in turns").[4] Fenton's presentism here echoes the Old Historicist view of alliterative poetry as a backwater tradition, drowning in the welter of new literary forms in the Age of Chaucer. As this book has endeavored to demonstrate, the alliterative tradition itself transcends such stereotypes. Around 1250 alliterative meter lost its position as the default English verse form. But this meter endured, and the poets who continued to use it produced some of the most memorable poetry of the medieval centuries, not, in all likelihood, for king or for court – certainly not for country – but because of the cultural momentum that accrues to a poetic tradition over time, or what I have called metrical hysteresis.

Cursory as they are, Fenton's remarks illustrate how the discipline of literary study, including prosody, can retrospectively simplify literary history and obscure the cultural stakes of poetic forms. Like Puttenham, Fenton compartmentalizes the poetic past into binaries: native and continental, local and cosmopolitan, popular and literary, anachronistic and historicizing, medieval and modern. Insistence on such dichotomies has ceased to be a feature of literary-critical discourse, yet their force continues to be felt in the way research fields are organized and individual texts or authors are judged. Chaucer, to take the *egregium exemplum*, continues to occupy a central position in English studies precisely because he is (perceived to be) the most continental, cosmopolitan, literary, historicist – in a word, modern – medieval author writing in English. But, of course, Chaucer inaugurates a modern literary or linguistic tradition only from the retrospect of later centuries.[5] Scholars must beware retrojecting the consolidation of modern nations, modern literary traditions, and modern conceptions of authority into a variegated medieval literary landscape in which incipient consolidations of nation, tradition, and authority stood at one end of a different continuum of practice and theory. This is not to say that modernity and modernization are simply foreign subjects for the student of medieval literature – as though there could ever have been a Middle Ages without two somethings to be in the middle of! Rather, study of medieval literature and culture must continually strive to unthink the inevitability of modern categories while retracing, in many cases, the very histories that created those categories. In this sense, the alliterative tradition poses the problem of modernity acutely. I have tried to show that the rewards of historicism are proportional to the risk of presentism.

One way to resist the inevitability of the received narrative of English literary history is to situate it in an unorthodox perspective. The definition of alliterative meter developed in this book raises the question of interaction between the alliterative tradition and adjacent literary forms with new urgency and enables researchers to address the question with new precision. The appropriation of alliterative style in non-alliterative contexts, as in the Kenelm episode discussed in Chapter 5, serves as another reminder that the old view of "a final (and doomed) struggle of native verse techniques in the face of Norman and Latin domination" fails to capture the intricacies of late medieval English literary culture.[6] The alliterative tradition and other medieval English metrical traditions were not propagated by armies of loyal ideologues, but by poets making stylistic choices. Poets could make more than one choice, as witness the mix of alliterative and non-alliterative poems in the corpora of the *Gawain* poet and William

Dunbar. In order to write alliterative verse history, I have been primarily concerned to trace the development of the alliterative meter in the context of adjacent metrical traditions in English and other languages. This comparison can be reversed, however, yielding a defamiliarizing perspective onto the early metrical traditions that would become most emblematic of the English literary field for later practitioners and commentators.

The influence exerted by the alliterative tradition on the development of English poetry as a whole has yet to be calculated. The borrowing of alliteration and other aspects of alliterative style in template meter, stanzaic poetry, and cycle drama is well known. These verse forms and genres, conflated with the alliterative tradition in some prior studies, typify the "penumbra shading off on every side into other forms of writing" of which Derek Pearsall has written.[7] Works such as the Harley Lyrics (late thirteenth to early fourteenth centuries), the *Awntyrs off Arthure* (late fourteenth/early fifteenth centuries), and the *N-Town Plays* (late fifteenth century) are the corpus of first recourse for a broader account of the literary-cultural impact of the alliterative tradition.

This book, self-consciously renovating the biological metaphors favored by some earlier scholars, has described the evolution and death of a literary tradition. However, traditions can also have afterlives, which stand in roughly the same relation to their lifespans as do the genetically engineered dinosaurs in Michael Crichton's *Jurassic Park* to dinosaurs of the Cretaceous period. I have resisted the application of terms like 'afterlife' and 'antiquarian' to late phases of the alliterative tradition, but these words are certainly appropriate for some of the uses to which alliterative meter was put after metrical death *c.* 1550. The afterlife of the alliterative tradition is a book-length study in need of writing. Chris Jones has pioneered this research field, producing a monograph and a series of articles and essays on the use of Old English poetry by modern and contemporary British and American poets.[8]

Jones's contributions could be enriched by future research in at least three ways: first, by comparing the use of Old English poetry to the use of Middle English alliterative poetry by the same modern authors, and so charting the divergent or convergent lines of literary influence descending from the two halves of the alliterative tradition; second, by comparing medievalism in modern-language poetry to post-medieval poetry composed directly in medieval English language; and third, by incorporating new results in the study of alliterative meter while historicizing the theories of medieval meter available to nineteenth- and twentieth-century medievalizing poets.[9] Some relatively neglected sources of evidence that can serve these priorities for future study are N. F. S. Grundtvig's *cento* in Old English, prefacing his early edition of *Beowulf* (*Beowulfes Beorh eller Bjovulfs-Drapen*, Copenhagen, 1861); Gerard Manley Hopkins's negative assessment of *Piers Plowman* and its meter ("degraded and doggrel," the poem "not worth reading") beside his admiration for Old English ("a vastly superior thing to what we have now"), expressed in letters of 1882 to the poet and prosodist Robert Bridges;[10] Francis Gummere's treatment of Old and Middle English alliterative meter in *Handbook of Poetics for Students of English Verse* (first published 1885), a work largely forgotten today but influential for generations of writers; Ezra Pound's use of Middle English vocabulary as part of the virtuoso multilingual interfaces of his modernist poetic, which also include medieval Latin and Old English; C. S. Lewis's essay "The Alliterative Metre" (1939), directed at an audience of aspiring neo-Saxonist poets but quite theoretically perceptive in its own right; and J. R. R. Tolkien's unfinished *Fall of Arthur* (first published posthumously in 2013), composed in imitation of Old English meter but positioned as a prequel to Middle English Arthurian romance. As this preliminary list already suggests, the afterlife of the alliterative tradition is intimately bound up with the modern recovery of alliterative verse and modern theorization of the alliterative meter.

In closing, it is worth reiterating just why the teleologies lingering behind much prior research on alliterative meter need to be suspended, where possible, in the writing of verse history. Teleologically charged metaphors of decay and renaissance informed both the early-century scholars who posited continuity between Old English and Middle English alliterative meter and the late-century scholars who doubted continuity. Specifically, interwar revivalism and later reactions against it shared the assumption that the development of poetic traditions points toward or away from landmarks in cultural history, such as the Norman Conquest and the English Reformation. Where the revivalists affirmed that the alliterative tradition resisted political centralization and cultural internationalization, the skeptics sought to understand fourteenth- and fifteenth-century alliterative verse as a novel expression of centralization and internationalization. For the revivalists, formal continuity established the continued presence of an aboriginal counterculture in English history. For the skeptics, the rejection of continuity seemed the best available means by which to deny the existence of such a counterculture.

This book has reaffirmed the continuity of the alliterative tradition without reactivating the teleological metaphors associated with the twentieth-century debate about a so-called Alliterative Revival. The rejection of points of origin and the rejection of points of culmination in this book are attempts to accomplish the same essential task: to put flesh on old bones, or (to reverse the metaphor) to strip away the layers of mediation that preinterpret a culturally remote literary tradition.

The story of alliterative poetry is neither one of decay and neglect nor of the inevitable triumph of a language or a culture. That this story unfolded without the help of a movement or a school or a theory, political, intellectual, or literary, suggests the inadequacy of some traditional literary-historical terms of engagement. Reversing a familiar encounter, the alliterative tradition, now understood in its synchronic variety and diachronic non-directedness, reveals the historical specificity and non-inevitability of modernity itself.

Note to the Appendices

In all Appendices Sievers and Yakovlev scansions accompany the b-verses, or SSSS-type scansions where Sievers scansions would ignore lifts. 'P' before or after a scansion indicates an omitted prefix before the first or second lift, respectively; 'r' before or after a Sievers or Yakovlev scansion indicates resolution of the first or second lift, respectively, while 'r' in an SSSS-type scansion indicates resolution of the preceding lift; and 'three' indicates a three-lift b-verse. Texts are from the indicated sources, with any editorial punctuation removed, capitalization reserved for proper names, and caesura represented by a tabbed space.

In many cases, e.g., *Accession* 4b *ond Godes lage lufode*, the b-verse either contains three lifts (*ond Gódes láge lúfode*) or two with metrical demotion of a content word (*ond Godes láge lúfode* or possibly *ond Gódes lage lúfode*). The difference between these scansions has to do with the competing morphological and accentual aspects of the alliterative meter. Ambiguity between two- and three-lift interpretations of verses like *Accession* 4b may be one key to the transition between the morphological and accentual phases of the alliterative tradition (Chs. 1 and 3). In all Appendices I prefer two-lift scansions where possible.

During the period covered by the Appendices, metrical resolution was in the process of ceding ground to other principles of metrical organization (Chs. 1 and 3). In Appendix A, I assume the operation of resolution only where lack of resolution would violate the dynamically evolving principles of alliterative meter described in Chapters 1 and 3. Likewise, I note lack of resolution only where resolution would violate these dynamically evolving principles. In Appendix B, I do not assume the operation of resolution.

Fifteen Late Old English Poems Omitted from ASPR

Below is a diplomatic edition of fifteen late Old English poems not printed in *ASPR* 6. The texts of **nos.** 1–8 are from the *ASCCE* vol. for the earliest MS witness, with variants from other Chronicle MSS where applicable; the text of **no. 9** is from Robinson, "Old English Literature," p. 24; of **no. 10,** a–c, from Bliss, "Some Unnoticed" (I do not include Bliss's fourth 'line,' *her he gesyndrode wæter and eorðan*, because it does not alliterate, nor his fifth line, *Seth wæs sæli*, because it lacks a b-verse); of **no. 11**, from Okasha, *Hand-list*, item 114; of **no. 12**, from Pulsiano, "Prefatory Matter," p. 99; of **no. 13**, from Ker, *Catalogue*, item 229; of **no. 14**, from Wilson, *Lost Literature*, p. 15, with Wilson's short-line layout converted to long-line layout for purposes of like-to-like comparison; and of **no. 15**, from Ker, *Catalogue*, item 131. The Tironian note is silently expanded to *ond*. A few editorial line boundaries have been silently moved for metrical reasons.

(1) *The Accession of Edgar the Peaceful* (959D) (975–1051)

	on his dagum hit godode georne ond God him geuðe	(1)
	þæt he wunode on sibbe þa hwile þe he leofode	(1r)
	ond he dyde swa him þearf wæs earnode þæs georne	(3)
	he arærde Godes lof wide ond Godes lage lufode	(1r5r)
5	ond folces frið bette swyþost þara cyninga	(3r)
	þe ær him gewurde be manna gemynde	(1)
	ond God him eac fylste þæt cyningas ond eorlas	(1r)
	georne him to bugan ond wurdon underþeodde	(2)
	to þam ðe he wolde ond butan gefeohte	(1)
10	eall he gewilde þæt he sylf wolde	(5)
	he wearð wide geond þeodland swyðe geweorða[d]	(3)
	for þam ðe he weorðode Godes naman georne	(1r3)
	ond Godes lage smeade oft ond gelome	(3)
	ond Godes lof rærde wide ond side	(3)

15	ond wislice rædde oftost a symble	(3)
	for Gode ond for weorulde ealre his þeode	(3)
	ane misdæde he dyde þeah to swyðe	(r1)
	þæt he elðeodige unsida lufode	(SSrSrx)
	ond heþene þeawas innan þysan lande gebrohte to fæste	(1)
20	ond utlændisce hider in tihte	(SrSSx)
	ond deriende leoda bespeon to þysan earde	(1)
	ac God him geunne þæt his goddæda	(5)
	swyðran weorðan þonne misdæda	(5)
	his sawle to gescyldnysse on langsuman siðe	(1)

11 geweorðad E] geweorðað D
22 goddæda] gode dæda E, *Type 2*

(2) *The Second Death of Edgar* (975DE) (975–1051)

	her Eadgar gefor Angla reccend	(A)
	Westseaxena wine ond Myrcna mundbora	(three)
	cuð wæs þæt wide geond feola þeoda	(rC)
	þæt afaren Eadmundes ofer ganetes beð	(r4)
5	cynegas hyne wide wurðodon swiðe	(3)
	bugon to þam cyninge swa him wæs gecynde	(1)
	næs se flota swa rang ne se here swa strang	(r4)
	þæt on Angelcynne æs him gefætte	(3)
	þa hwile þe se æþela cyning cynestol gerehte	(r3)

6 swa him wæs] swa wæs him E, *Type 5 not counting* ge-

(3) *The Young Edward the Martyr* (975D) (978–1051)

	on his dagum for his iugoðe	(5)[1]
	Godes wiþærsacan Godes lage bræcon	(r3)
	Ælfere ealdorman ond oþre manega	(xSxSrx)
	ond munucregol myrdon ond mynstra tostæncton	(1)
5	ond munecas todræfdon ond Godes þeowas fesedon	(r1)[2]
	þe Eadgar kyning het ær þone halgan biscop	(2)
	Aþælwold gestalian ond wydewan bestryptan	(r1)
	oft ond gelome ond fela unrihta	(5)
	ond yfelra unlaga arysan up siððan	(5)
10	ond aa æfter þam hit yfelode swiðe	(r1)

ond on þam timan wæs eac   Oslac se mæra   (3)
eorl geutod   of Angelcynne   (xSxSx)

(4) *Sweyn Forkbeard Razes Wilton* (1003CDE) (1003–45)[3]

þa sceolde se ealdorman Ælfric   lædan þa fyrde   (3)
ac he teah ða forð   his ealdan wrencas   (xSxSx)
sona swa hi wæron   swa gehende   (A)
þæt ægðer here   on [oðer] hawede   (three)[4]
5 þa gebræd he hine seocne   ond ongan hine brecan to   (three)
   spiwenne
ond cwæð þæt he gesicled wære   ond swa þæt folc becyrde   (5p)
þæt he lædan sceolde   swa hit gecweden ys   (4)[5]
þonne se heretoga wacað   þonne bið eall se here   (4r)
swiðe gehindrad   þa Swegen geseah   (B)
10 þæt hi anræde næron   ond þæt hi ealle toforan   (2p)
   þa lædde he his here   into Wiltune   (5)
   ond hi þa buruh   geheregodon ond forbærndon   (r1)
   ond eode him þa to Searbyrig   ond þanone eft to sæ   (4)
   ferde þær he wiste   his yðhengestas   (three)

4 oðer DE] oþerne C, *unmetrical*
6 swa] swa þeah D
6 becyrde] beswac E, *Type 4 counting* be-
10 þæt hi²] *om.* DE, *Type 1 counting* to-

(5) *The Return of Edward the Exile* (1057D) (1057–61)

her com Eadweard æþeling   to Englalande   (xSxSx)
se wæs Eadweardes   broðorsunu kynges   (3)
Eadmund Irensid wæs geclypod   for his snellscipe   (5)[6]

(6) *The Chastity of St. Margaret* (1067D, *recte* 1070) (1070–71)

Margaretan   ac he ond his men ealle   (5)
lange wiðcwædon   ond eac heo sylf wiðsoc   (4)
ond cwæð þæt heo hine ne nanne   habban wolde   (A)
gyf hire seo uplice arfæstnys   geunnan wolde   (xSxSx)
5 þæt heo on mægðhade   mihtigan Drihtne   (3)
   mid lichomlicre heortan   on þisan life sceortan   (2)
   on clænre forhæfednysse   cweman mihte   (A)

(7) Rhyming line on the marriage of Emma and Ralph (1076D/75E)
(late eleventh century)

þær wæs þæt brydealo   þæt wæs manegra manna bealo   (three)

1 þæt wæs manegra manna bealo] mannum to beala E, *Type 3 with lack of resolution of* beala

(8) *The Death of William the Conqueror* (1086E, *recte* 1087) (1087–1121)

castelas he let wyrcean   ond earme men swiðe swencean   (three)[7]
se cyng wæs swa swiðe stearc ond benam   of his underþeoddan (4)
                                                                        [man
manig marc goldes   ond ma hundred punda seolfres   (three)
ðet he nam be wihte   ond mid mycelan unrihte   (?)[8]
5 of his landleode   for littelre neode   (1)
he wæs on gitsunge befeallan   ond grædinæsse he lufode mid ealle (three)
he sætte mycel deorfrið   ond he lægde laga þærwið   (three)
þet swa hwa swa sloge heort oððe hinde   þet hine man sceolde (ri)
                                                                        [blendian
he forbead þa heortas   swylce eac þa baras   (2)
10 swa swiðe he lufode þa headeor   swilce he wære heora fæder   (3)
eac he sætte be þam haran   þet hi mosten freo faran   (5)
his rice men hit mændon   ond þa earme men hit beceorodan (three)
ac he wæs swa stið   þet he ne rohte heora eallra nið   (three)
ac hi moston mid ealle   þes cynges wille folgian   (1)[9]
15 gif hi woldon libban   oððe land habban   (5)
land oððe eahta   oððe wel his sehta   (2)
walawa þet ænig man sceolde modigan swa   (three)
hine sylf up ahebban   ond ofer ealle men tellan   (three)

(9) Poetic gloss to the Lindisfarne Gospels (late tenth century: Ker, *Catalogue*, item 165)

ðvs Beda ðe broema   boecere cuęð   (E)

(10) Captions to illustrations in the Junius MS (copied late tenth century: Ker, *Catalogue*, item 334, and Lockett, "An Integrated Re-examination")
    (a)
    hu se engyl ongon   ofermod wesan   (rSSSx)
    (b)
    her se hælend gesceop   helle heom to wite   (3)
    (c)
    her he todælde   dæg wið nihte   (A)

(11) The Sutton brooch inscription (late tenth / early eleventh centuries: Okasha, *Hand-list*, item 114)

Ædvpen me ag   age hyo Drihten   (3)
Drihten hine aperie   ðe me hire ætferie (1r)
bvton hyo me selle   hire agenes pilles   (2)[10]

(12) Cryptogram in British Library MS Cotton Vitellius E.xviii (*c.* 1031: Pulsiano, "Prefatory Matter," p. 100)

Ælfuuine me uurat   ræde ðu ðe cenne (3)

(13) Scribble in British Library MS Harley 208 (tenth/eleventh century: Ker, *Catalogue*, item 229)

hwæt ic eall feala   ealde sæge (A)[11]

(14) Excerpt of a lost poem on Wade (tenth/twelfth centuries) in Peterhouse College Cambridge MS 255 (twelfth century: James, *Descriptive Catalogue: Peterhouse*, p. 314)

summe sende ylues   and summe sende nadderes (1)[12]
summe sende nikeres   the bi den watere wunien (r2r)[13]
nister man nenne   bute Ildebrand onne   (1)[14]

(15) Scribble in British Library MS Additional 40000 (eleventh/twelfth centuries: Ker, *Catalogue*, item 131)

Eglaf *comes*   ond his broðer Vlf (4)

Six Early Middle English Alliterative Poems

Below are the texts of six Early Middle English alliterative poems. The texts of **no. 1, a–c,** are from *Gerald of Wales*, tr. Thorpe, p. 241; of **no. 2, a–c,** from *Digital Index of Middle English Verse* (*DIMEV*) 2486 (= *NIMEV* 1477.5), sources 1–3; of **no. 2, d–f,** from *Three Eleventh-Century*, ed. Love, p. 66 (glosses in Love's MSS G, H, and J); of **no. 2, g,** from *Chronicle*, ed. Vaughan, p. 15; of **no. 2, h,** from *Chronica*, ed. Coxe, vol. 1, p. 274; of **no. 2, i,** from *Mattæi Parisiensis*, ed. Luard, vol. 1, p. 373; of **no. 2, j,** from *Polychronicon*, ed. Lumby, vol. 6, p. 306; of **no. 2, k–l,** from *Polychronicon*, ed. Lumby, vol. 6, p. 307; of **no. 2, m,** from *Early South-English Legendary*, ed. Horstmann, 'Vita sancti Kenelmi. Regis,' l. 261; of **no. 2, n,** from *South English Legendary*, ed. D'Evelyn and Mill, 'De Sancto Kenelmo,' ll. 267–68; of **no. 3,** from Pickering, "Early Middle English," p. 412; of **no. 4,** from Wilson, *Lost Literature*, p. 38; of **no. 5,** from Breeze, "New Texts," pp. 284–85, source b (British Library MS Additional 11579), with metrically significant variants from the other sources, using Breeze's designations; and of **no. 6,** from a facsimile of Lambeth Palace Library MS 93, fol. 60a, checked against James, *Descriptive Catalogue: Lambeth*, p. 153. Note: only **no. 2, b,** the oldest text of **no. 2,** is included in the b-verse counts in Ch. 3.

(1) English proverbs in Gerald of Wales, *Descriptio Kambriæ* (before *c.* 1194)

(a)
God is togedere   gamen and wisdom   (3)
(b)
Ne halt nocht al sor isaid   ne al sorghe atwite   (2p)
(c)
Betere is red thene rap   and liste thene lither streingthe   (three)

(2) Two lines on St. Kenelm (?late eleventh / early thirteenth centuries)

DIMEV 2486

(a)

| In cleu under thorncat ku beche | (?) |
| lith kenelmus kunebri heued bireued | (3) |

(b)

| In clench qu becche under ane þorne | (3) |
| liet kenelm kinebern heued bereued | (3) |

(c)

| in clent cowbachi kennellme kyngysbyrth | (three) |
| lyth vndyre thoryne beheddyd | (?) |

Vita Sancti Kenelmi

(d)

| In Klent Koubeche Kenelm kunebearn | (three) |
| liy under yorne heaved bereved | (3) |

(e)

| Ine clent cubeche Kenelm kine bern | (three) |
| lid under thorne hefdes bireaved | (3) |

(f)

| Kenelm kinebern inne clenc dene | (5) |
| under þa þorne lið hefd bereved | (3)[1] |

'Wallingford' chronicle

(g)

| In Cleng Cubeche under ane þorne | (3) |
| lith Kenelm kenebern eweð beireuueð | (3) |

Roger of Wendover's chronicle

(h)

| In clento cou bathe Kenelm kynebearn | (three) |
| lith under thorne hæuedes bereaued | (3) |

Matthew Paris, *Chronica Majora*

(i)

| In clenc cu beche Kenelm cunebearn | (three) |
| lith under thorne hauedes bereafed | (3) |

Ralph Higden, *Polychronicon*

(j)

| At Clenc in Coubache Kenelme kyneberne | (three) |
| lith under thorn hevyd bywevet | (3) |

John Trevisa, *Polychronicon*

(k)

| At Clent in Cowbache Kenelin kynebern | (three) |
| lith under þorn heved byweved | (3) |

Anonymous Englished *Polychronicon* in British Library MS Harley 2261

(l)

| At Clente Conbache | Kenelm kynbern | (three) |
| liþ under a þorne | heved bewevyd | (3) |

South English Legendary life of Kenelm

(m)

| In klent covbache | kenelm kyngues sone | (three) |
| lijth onder ane þorne | is heued him bi-reued | (1) |

(n)

| In Clent Coubach | Kenelm kinges bern | (three) |
| Liþ vnder a þorn | heued bireued | (3) |

(3) The Shrewsbury epitaph (?twelfth/thirteenth centuries: Pickering, "Early Middle English," pp. 413–14)

Her lis arfaxat	fader brandan	(A)
ant kolmkilne	ant cowhel þer halewe	(1)[2]
ant dame coroune	moder þeyre halewe	(3)
þat komen in to bretene	sautes to seke	(3)

(4) Two lines on the sons of Ragnar Lodbrok (mid twelfth / early thirteenth centuries)[3]

| Ynguar and Ubbe | Beorn wæs þe þridde | (3) |
| Loþebrokes sunes | loþe weren criste | (3) |

(5) English proverb in Odo of Cheriton, *Liber parabolarum* (before *c.* 1219)

Þey þou þe vulf hore	hode to preste	(3)
Þey þou him to skole sette	salmes to lerne	(3)
Heuere bet hise geres	to þe grove grene	(2)

1 hode to preste] vnto a preest worthe cj (a] þe j), *Type 5*
2 salmes to lerne] and psalmes him leren di (and] an i), *Type 1*; and salmes lere ef, *xSxSx*
3 grove grene] wodewar(d) cdfij, groveward ae, *Type 4*

(6) English proverb in a marginal note in two MSS (late thirteenth/early fourteenth centuries) of Henry de Bracton's *De legibus et consuetudinibus Angliæ* (*c.* 1235)

| ofte owene dom | at[4] owene durre charret[5] | (2) |

An Early Middle English Alliterative
Poem in Latin

Below is a diplomatic edition of Henry of Huntingdon's Latin verse translation of the *Battle of Brunanburh*, contained in his *Historia Anglorum* (*c.* 1125–40). The text is from Rigg, "Henry of Huntingdon," pp. 69–70, except that some half-line boundaries have been moved to improve the syntax and the correspondence to the original. Punctuation and accentuation are my own. Numbers in parentheses collate the translation with the text of *Brunanburh* from *ASPR* 6.

To describe Henry's poem in the terms of twelfth-century English alliterative meter requires certain assumptions. Unlike Rigg, I assume that the prosodic hierarchy of English alliterative meter applies. Function words do not receive metrical stress, e.g., *Sic namque iis ingénitum fúerat*, not *Síc námque*, etc., except by metrical promotion, e.g., *Néc enim páucos*, as in alliterative meter. Content words take exactly one metrical stress, on the classically accented syllable irrespective of quantity, e.g., *dúcum, splendéntes, cecidérunt,* including English proper names by analogy, e.g., *West-séxe* not *Wést-sèxe, Brittónes* not *Bríttones*. One word (33b *déperiítque*) shows compound stress: the additional stress falls on the nearest (in this case the only) quantitatively long syllable. One could compare *Phoenix* 678b *méruéri* (Sievers Type A).

I hypothesize that resolution applies to a short, stressed syllable followed by any syllable, as in alliterative meter. In alliterative meter and Latin quantitative meters alike, 'short' syllables are quantitatively short, open syllables. The equivalence of two consecutive short syllables to one long is a feature of classical Latin meters, of course, but the evident requirement that the first syllable be stressed conforms to English alliterative practice. That is, there are no instances in which the ictus must fall on two consecutive short *unstressed* syllables. That resolution is a feature of Henry's poem is strongly suggested by the distribution of proparoxytones. Of seventeen line-final proparoxytones, sixteen have a short antepenult, while just over half (eighteen of thirty-five) of proparoxytones elsewhere in the poem have a short antepenult. Some of these probably also show metrical resolution, e.g., 7b *ingénitum* (xSx), avoiding two long dips, and 28a *grémio* (Sx), avoiding a final long dip. Like other late Old English and Early Middle English alliterative poets, Henry treated resolution as an attractive option rather than a binding requirement, thus 1b *décus* (Sx). In many instances, English-style resolution and classical synaeresis explain the scansion equally well, e.g., 10b *xénia*, where one may syllabify *xén-i-a*, with resolution (Sx), or *xén-ia*, with synaeresis (Sx). Henry may have enacted an analogy between the two accommodation principles, in a kind of metrical macaronics. But because there are only two scansions that must be explained by synaeresis and cannot be explained by resolution (9b *pátriae*, Sx, and 41b *appáruit*, xSx) as against six that must be explained by resolution and cannot be explained by synaeresis (7b *ingénitum*, xSx; 14b *laetíficans*, xSx; 32b *número*, Sx; 42b *pópuli*, Sx; 49b *praestíterint*, xSx; and 56b *ánimo*, Sx), and because of the suggestive distribution of syllable quantity in Henry's proparoxytones, I assume resolution in the ambiguous cases as well. One scansion seems to require both classical synaeresis and English-style resolution (51b *concílio*, xS, but see n. 5 for an alternative). If Henry did employ metrical resolution in the way I have assumed, then his translation furnishes a striking and surprising example of translingual prosody.

Henry claims to have rendered the poem "word for word [*de verbo in verbum*]."[1] A slight rearrangement of Rigg's text vindicates Henry's description. The translation is line for line, with a few transpositions and other licenses that do not affect the count, except that Henry expands *Brunanburh* 24 into two lines and omits to translate, or condenses by a full line, *Brunanburh* 54b and 55b, 57b and 58a, 68a and 68b, and 69a and 70b.

	Rex Adelstan décus dúcum	(A)
	nobilibus torquium dator et fráter eius Edmúndus	(1)
	longa stirpis série splendéntes	(3)
	percusserunt in bello ácie gládii	(3r)
5	apud Brunesburh scutórum múros fidérunt	(three)[2]
	nobiles ceciderunt doMésticae relíquiae	(1r)
	defuncti Edwardi. Sic namque iis ingénitum fúerat	(r2r)
	a genibus cognationum ut béllis frequéntibus	(?)[3]
	ab infestis nationibus defénderent pátriae	(1)[4]
10	thesauros et domos pecúnias et xénia.	(1r)
	Gens vero Hibernensium et púppium habitatóres	(1)

	fatales corruerunt cólles resonuérunt	(3)
	sudaverunt armati ex quo sól máne	(5)
	prodiit micans hiláriter laetíficans	(1r)
15	profunda Dei luminare fáx Creatóris	(3)
	usque quo idem nobilis ductor occásu se occúluit	(1r)
	ibi viri jacuérunt múlti	(2)
	a Dacia oriundi télis perforáti	(3)
	sub scutis lanceati símul et Scótti	(3)
20	bello fatigati. Géns vero West-séxe	(3)
	tota simul die príus elécti	(3)
	post indefessi invísae géntis	(xSxSx)
	globos straverunt víri elegántes	(3)
	hastas caedebant víri Mercénses	(3)
25	acuta jacula mittébant dúro	(xSxSx)
(25)	manus ludo. Sánitas ibi núlla	(3)
	his qui cum Anlavo trans máris cámpos	(rC)
	in ligni gremio térram petiérunt	(3)
	Marte morituri quínque occubuérunt	(3)
30	in loco belli réges júvenes	(Ar)
(30)	gladiis percussi ducésque séptem	(xSxSx)
	regis Anlavi ábsque número	(Ar)
	ceciderunt Scotti déperiítque	(3)
	Normannorum tumor. Néc enim páucos	(3)
35	ad litem belli dúxerant sécum.	(3)
	Cum paucis vero in mátris flúctus	(xSxSx)
(35)	rex navi provectus intrínsecus gemébat	(1)
(37)	simul et Froda dúctor Normánnus	(3)
	cumque suis notis dúx Constantínus	(3)
40	de Martis congressu jactáre nequiérunt	(1)
(40)	ubi cognationis suae frágmen appáruit	(3)
	ubi amici sui corruerant in statióne pópuli	(2r)
	bello prostrati et fílium súum	(1)
	in loco proelii vulnéribus demolítum	(1)
45	carum reliquit. Nec Gúde Dácus	(xSxSx)
(45)	declamare potuit licet vérbis blándus	(2)
	et mente vetustus nec Ánlaf ípse	(xSxSx)
	cum reliquiis suis mentíri pótuit	(xSxSrx)
	quod ad hoc negotium súi praestíterint	(rAr)
50	in campo belli íctuum immanitáte	(3)
(50)	telorum transforatione in concílio probórum.	(r2)[5]

Matres vero et nurus   planxérunt súos   (Br)
belli alea cum Edwardi   fíliis lusísse.   (3)
Cum Normanni   návibus clavátis   (3)
55 et Anlaf tabefactus   ultra profúndum flúmen   (2)
(56) terras suas   móesto ánimo   (Ar)
(57) repetissent postea   fráter utérque   (3)
(59) rediit Westsexe   bélli relíquias   (3r)
(60) post se deserentes   cárnes virórum   (3)
60 in escam paratas.   Ergo córvus níger   (4r)
ore cornutus   et búffo lívens   (xSxSx)
aquila cum milvo   cánis lupúsque   (rA)
mixtus colore   híi sunt delíciis   (3r)
(65) diu recreati.   Nón fuit béllum   (3)
65 hac in tellure   május patrátum   (3)
nec caedes tanta   praecéssit ístam   (xSxSx)
(69) postquam huc venerunt   trans máre látum   (rC)
Saxones et Angli   Brittónes pulsúri   (1)
(72) clari Martis fabri   Walénses vicérunt   (1)
70 reges fugaverunt   régna suscepérunt.   (3)

Glossary of Technical Terms

ACCENTUAL: A descriptive term for metrical systems, emphasizing a functional connection between metrical stress assignment and word accent. Cp. *morphological, quantitative.*

ALLITERATING: Denotes a text that employs alliteration, regardless of metrical form. Cp. *alliterative.*

ALLITERATION SHIFT: Shift of the alliteration from a metrically stressed syllable to a nearby metrically unstressed syllable.

ALLITERATIVE: Denotes the unrhymed, inductive English meter whose historical development this book narrates. Cp. *alliterating.*

ALLITERATIVE LONG LINE: An a-verse plus a b-verse.

ANACRUSIS: A special case of the prefix license, whereby a verbal prefix or the negative particle *ne* is discounted before a half-line-initial lift.

ASYSTEMATIC: See *systematic.*

A-VERSE: The first, metrically self-contained half of the alliterative long line.

A-VERSE/B-VERSE SYMMETRY: The extent to which the set of acceptable metrical patterns in the a-verse overlaps the set of acceptable metrical patterns in the b-verse at a given point in verse history.

B-VERSE: The second, metrically self-contained half of the alliterative long line.

CAESURA: The metrical boundary between the a-verse and the b-verse.

COMPOUND STRESS: The assignment of two or more metrical stresses to a single word.

CONTENT WORD: A noun, adjective, infinitive verb, or other content-bearing word. Cp. *function word.*

DEDUCTIVE: A descriptive term for metrical systems, emphasizing the concatenation of perceptually similar metrical units. Cp. *inductive.*

DIP: In the alliterative meter, one or more consecutive metrically unstressed syllables. Cp. *lift.*

FUNCTION WORD: An article, preposition, pronoun, or other non-content-bearing word. Cp. *content word.*

HALF-LINE: An a-verse or a b-verse.

ICTUS: See *metrical stress.*

INDUCTIVE: A descriptive term for metrical systems, emphasizing the concatenation of perceptually dissimilar metrical units. Cp. *deductive.*

LIFT: In the alliterative meter, a metrically stressed syllable or its equivalent by metrical resolution. Cp. *dip.*

LONG DIP: A dip of two or more syllables. Cp. *short dip.*

METRICAL BEAT: Metrical stress in deductive meter.

METRICAL DEMOTION: Lack of metrical stress on a content word. Cp. *metrical promotion.*

METRICAL HYSTERESIS: The tendency of metrical systems to accrue momentum, resist complete systematization, and lag developments in adjacent cultural domains. A cause of asystematic metrical patterns.

METRICAL PATTERN: In the alliterative meter, a metrically licit sequence of lifts and dips constituting a half-line.

METRICAL PHONOLOGY: The set of metrically significant, historically justified linguistic forms available to a poetic tradition or an individual poem at a given point in verse history.

METRICAL POSITION: A lift or a dip.

METRICAL PROMOTION: Metrical stress on a function word. Cp. *metrical demotion.*

METRICAL RESOLUTION: A feature of alliterative meter before *c.* 1250, whereby a metrically stressed long syllable is equivalent to a metrically stressed short syllable plus the following syllable. 'Long' syllables are those with etymologically long vowels and/or one or more postvocalic consonants; other syllables are 'short.'

METRICAL STRESS: A metrical quality projected or not projected onto metrical positions in accordance with a prosodic hierarchy. Also *ictus.*

METRICAL TYPOLOGY: The set of metrical patterns available in a poetic tradition or an individual poem at a given point in verse history.

MORPHOLOGICAL: A descriptive term for metrical systems, emphasizing a functional connection between metrical stress assignment and the category membership of individual morphemes regardless of their position within the word. Cp. *accentual, quantitative.*

NON-ALLITERATIVE: See *alliterative.*

PREFIX LICENSE: A feature of the alliterative meter before *c.* 1250, whereby verbal prefixes and the negative particle *ne* may count or be discounted as unstressed syllables for metrical purposes.

PROSODIC HIERARCHY: In the alliterative meter, a hierarchy of grammatical class membership used to select words for metrical stress within the half-line. Content words outrank function words.

PROSODIC WEIGHT: The position of a word or class of words in the prosodic hierarchy.

QUANTITATIVE: A descriptive term for metrical systems, emphasizing a functional connection between metrical stress assignment and syllabic quantity ('long' or 'short'). Cp. *accentual, morphological.*

REANALYSIS: See *regularization.*

REGULARIZATION: A common type of systematization in verse history, whereby asystematic metrical patterns and/or incidental features of systematic metrical patterns are reanalyzed as expressions of the metrical system. Also *reanalysis.*

SHORT DIP: A dip of exactly one syllable. Cp. *long dip.*

STRESS SHIFT: Shift of metrical stress from the root syllable to another non-schwa syllable (usually a later syllable) within the same word.

SUSPENSION OF RESOLUTION: Lack of metrical resolution of a pair of resolveable syllables. In the alliterative meter before *c.* 1100, suspension of metrical resolution is quasi-obligatory immediately after a metrically stressed syllable.

SYSTEMATIC: Describes those metrical patterns generated by synchronic metrical principles, as opposed to rare but authentic metrical patterns generated by diachronic historical processes (*asystematic*).

SYSTEMATIZATION: The historical process whereby metrical features and metrical principles crystallize within metrical traditions; also, the perceptual process whereby asystematic metrical patterns are revised to conform to the synchronic metrical system.

Notes

Introduction: The Durable Alliterative Tradition

1. Jarvis, "For a Poetics," p. 933. Influential work in the field, e.g., Prins, "Historical Poetics," and Martin, *Rise and Fall*, historicizes the metadiscourse of prosody while avoiding descriptive scansion. On the need to measure theory against practice see Glaser, [Review of Martin, *Rise and Fall*]; Jarvis, "What is Historical Poetics?"; and Weiskott, "Before Prosody."

2. Myklebust, "Misreading," pp. 233–37, outlines "A New Notion of Metricality" along these lines.

3. Hanna, "Defining," p. 59 (first quotation) and pp. 59 and 60 (second quotation, twice). For 'homomorphic,' see below, n. 4.

4. Cole, "Rum, Ram, Ruf, and Rym," pp. 21–27. A roughly equivalent distinction is homomorphic/heteromorphic, first applied to medieval English meter by McIntosh, "Early Middle English," pp. 21–22. I have preferred Cole's terminology because it highlights what the mind does with meter rather than the form the meter takes in the abstract.

5. Yakovlev, "Development," pp. 23–24: "The defining properties of any verse are those that determine the *commensurability* of poetic lines … In contrast to that, end-rhyme or alliteration only determine the *correlation* of poetic lines. They are ornamental, rather than structural devices." Cp. Cable, *English Alliterative Tradition*, pp. 132–33; Hanna, "Defining," pp. 50–51; and Yakovlev, "Development," p. 77.

6. Turville-Petre, *Alliterative Revival*; Hanna, "Defining" and "Alliterative Poetry"; *Middle English Alliterative Poetry*, ed. Lawton, pp. 155–57 ('formal' and 'informal' corpus), and Lawton, "Unity," pp. 72–73 n. 5; and Oakden, *Alliterative Poetry*.

7. Except, rarely and for historical reasons, Sx(x …)S: Weiskott, "Three-Position Verses."

8. Cable, "Foreign Influence." To the following discussion cp. Cole, "Rum, Ram, Ruf," pp. 145–55, and "Chaucer's Metrical Landscape," pp. 103–4.

9. Duggan, "Notes toward a Theory" (in contrast to his later opinions, e.g., "End of the Line," p. 68 n. 5); Barney, "Langland's Prosody," pp. 82–85, and "Revised Edition," pp. 277–88; Cole, "Rum, Ram, Ruf," pp. 29–73; Cable,

"Progress," pp. 247–48; Burrow, "Endings"; Cornelius, *Reconstructing*, ch. 4; and Weiskott, "*Piers Plowman*."

10. Alliteration shift is the shift of the alliteration from a metrically stressed syllable to a nearby metrically unstressed syllable, as in *Cleanness* 105b *þat me renáyed hábbe*. Cp. Skeat, "Essay," pp. xvii–xviii; Borroff, "*Sir Gawain and the Green Knight*", pp. 170–71; and Kane, *Chaucer and Langland*, pp. 83–84 ('modulation').

11. For more detailed and historicized discussion of prior research in alliterative metrics and literary history, see Weiskott, "Alliterative Meter and English Literary History."

12. Simpson, [Review of Scattergood, *Lost Tradition*], p. 110.

13. Blake, "Rhythmical Alliteration" and "Middle English Alliterative Revivals"; Matonis, "Middle English Alliterative Poetry"; McIntosh, "Early Middle English," p. 23; Bennett, "Survival and Revivals"; Salter, *English and International*, pp. 170–79; Hanna, "Defining" and "Alliterative Poetry"; and Schiff, *Revivalist*.

14. Gollancz, "The Middle Ages," Oakden, *Alliterative Poetry*, and Chambers, *On the Continuity*, pp. lxv–lxviii; later, Wilson, *Lost Literature*, Everett, *Essays*, pp. 46–49, Wrenn, "On the Continuity," and Moorman, "Origins."

15. Chism, *Alliterative Revivals*, p. 16.

16. Hanna, "Alliterative Poetry," pp. 488–89.

1 *Beowulf* and Verse History

1. Cable, *English Alliterative Tradition*, p. 38: "For Sievers' Five Types the question comes down to whether those patterns are the paradigm itself or the epiphenomenal results of a simpler paradigm." For more detailed and historicized discussion of Yakovlev's non-accentual theory of OE meter, see Cornelius, "Accentual Paradigm."

2. Yakovlev, "Development," p. 82: "the accentual principle . . . is present in the background of the [OE] metrical system." Note that many OE metrists scan verses like *Beowulf* 22a as one-lift, without promotion of a function word, thereby violating the four-position principle that Yakovlev places at the center of the OE metrical system.

3. Both quotations since the previous note from Yakovlev, "Development," p. 69.

4. The adv. ending *-lice* (later *-li(ch)(e)*) was disyllabic in OE verse, but variably disyllabic or monosyllabic in ME alliterative verse. The pattern x . . . xSxxpS (x), in which *-lic(h)e* forms the second apparently long dip before a verbal prefix, is well attested in Lawman: Yakovlev, "Development," pp. 223–25. Perhaps suffixes, like prefixes, had a special license.

5. The remaining scansions of *Alfred* are: 16b Type 1 without final syllable (xSx . . . xS occurs in the *Brut*, but rarely: Yakovlev, "Development," p. 244, finds 3 examples in 200 b-verses), 17b Type 1, 18b Type 5, 19b Type 1, 20b Type 3, 21b Type 1, 22b Type 5, 23b Type 4, and 24b and 25b Type 1.

6. Fulk, *History*, §304. The other verses picked out by Fulk are 8b (Type A, -*ge*-omitted by the prefix license: Yakovlev, "Development," p. 199, argues that -*i*- in *uni*- is subject to the prefix license in the *Brut*; alternately, Type D*), 12a (three lifts), 15a (ditto), 16b (C), and 17b (three lifts).

7. Fulk, *History*, §§303 and 304. The other verses picked out by Fulk are *Durham* 12b (xSxSx), 15b (ditto), and 16a (three lifts). Cp. *Beowulf* 9b (xxSSSx, but *para* deleted *metri causa* by most editors), 107a (xSxSx), 1549a (Type 1), 1563a (xSxSS, *ge*- omitted by the prefix license), 1987a (Type 1), 2093a (ditto), 2297a (Type 2; regarded as a lone hypermetric verse by most editors, unknown elsewhere), and 2651a (Type 2; usually regarded as Type A3, but *micel* is always stressed elsewhere).

8. Recent metrical arguments for a very early *Beowulf* are Russom, "Dating Criteria"; Fulk, "Old English Meter" and "*Beowulf* and Language History"; Hartman, "Limits"; and Bredehoft, "Date of Composition." For doubts about the validity of linguistic-metrical testing see esp. Whitelock, "Anglo-Saxon Poetry," esp. p. 81, and *Audience*, pp. 26–28; Sisam, *Studies*, pp. 6–7; Blake, "Dating"; Amos, *Linguistic Means*; Niles, *Beowulf*, pp. 96–101; Busse, *Altenglische*, pp. 40–68; Liuzza, "On the Dating"; and Frank, "Scandal."

9. Fulk, *History*, §279, finds that only *Beowulf* 1904b has the *i*-stem gpl. in -*a*. Cp. Fulk, "*Beowulf* and Language History," p. 26. Fulk would scan 1a, 242a, 253b, 668a (non-parasiting on *aldor*), and 1769a as Type C with resolved second lift, but this pattern appears only twice in *Beowulf*, both b-verses (Russom, "Constraints on Resolution," pp. 151–52 and n. 26). Fulk would also scan 392a, 427a, 609a, 616a, 1044a, 1069a, and 1319a as Type D with resolution of the third lift, but this pattern never appears in *Beowulf* (Russom, "Constraints on Resolution," p. 152 and n. 29).

10. Campbell, *Old English Grammar*, §170, and Hogg, "Old English Palatalization." The alternative timeline offered by Minkova, "Velars and Palatals," is based on the evidence of OE alliteration itself.

11. Fulk, *History*, §95, and "Old English Meter," p. 321; and *Klaeber's Beowulf*, ed. Fulk, Bjork, and Niles, pp. 326–27. Likewise *Beowulf* 913a *eþel* (or Type D*), 998b *iren*-, 1675a and 1871a *þeoden* (or Type D*), 1918a *oncer*-, 1968a and 2475a *Ongen*- (*Klaeber's Beowulf*, ed. Fulk, Bjork, and Niles, pp. 327–28, posits a short vowel on -*þeow*-, but 2387b *Ongen*- shows faux non-parasiting, and resolution of -*þeow*- in 1968a and 2475a would produce otherwise unknown contours), 2020b *dohtor* (or Type D*), 2387b *Ongen*-, 2440a *broðor* (or Type D*), and 2728a *dogor*- (Fulk, "Old English Meter," p. 312 n. 16).

12. Fulk, *History*, §36 and §42. Cp. Fulk and Cain, *History*, pp. 29–30 and 302.

13. Fulk, *History*, §36.

14. Cp. above, n. 11, to Fulk, *History*, §§93 and 95. *Waldere A* 18a *furðor* may be a ninth instance outside of *Beowulf*, or Type 2. *Widsith* 18b and 88a *Eorman*-, the former adduced by *Klaeber's Beowulf*, ed. Fulk, Bjork, and Niles, p. 328, are uncertain in light of the unusual metrical treatment of proper names in *Widsith*. The prototheme *Eorman*- cannot show faux non-parasiting at *Widsith* 8b.

15. All quotations since the previous note from *Klaeber's Beowulf*, ed. Fulk, Bjork, and Niles, p. clxv. Fulk, "Old English Meter," p. 321, wonders how Kaluza's law could have survived the leveling of circumflex intonation. Weiskott, "Semantic Replacement," gives a specific answer, and Weiskott, "Phantom Syllables," a general answer. Fulk, "*Beowulf* and Language History," p. 30 n. 28, responds but does not address the general answer, the comparison in both cases to ME alliterative verse, or my analytical distinction between meter and language.

16. Datably pre-850 are *Bede's Death Song* (five lines), *Cædmon's Hymn* (nine lines), the Franks Casket inscription (five lines), and *Proverb from Winfrid's Time* (two lines). The Ruthwell Cross inscription may postdate the eighth-century cross: Page, *Introduction*, p. 150; Meyvaert, "Apocalypse Panel," pp. 23–26; Stanley, *Collection*, pp. 384–99; and Conner, "Ruthwell Monument." Contrast Ó Carragáin, "Who Then Read" and "Sources or Analogues?" and Meyvaert, "Necessity" (contra his earlier opinion). The manuscript text of the *Leiden Riddle* may date from the tenth century: Parkes, "Manuscript," disputed by Gerritsen, "Leiden Revisited." Fulk, *History*, §72, dates the *Leiden Riddle* between the eighth century and "the middle of the ninth" (cp. Fulk, *History*, pp. 404–5) on linguistic and orthographical grounds. A recently discovered silver object from Lincolnshire is inscribed in runes with a few fragmentary lines of OE verse, dated to the eighth century on linguistic and orthographical grounds by Hines, "*Benedicite* Canticle."

17. Russom, "Dating Criteria," pp. 251 (first quotation), 252 (second quotation), and 253 (third quotation).

18. Both quotations since the previous note from Russom, "Dating Criteria," p. 250.

19. Russom, "Dating Criteria," p. 250, and Cable, "Metrical Style," p. 80.

20. An idea mooted repeatedly by Fulk, *History*, §§11 (dialect), 21 ("dialect, style, and scribal interference"), 24 (dialect), 33 ("scribal modernization"), 35–43 (style and genre), 56 (dialect), and 333 (style and genre).

21. *Ibid.*, §14.

22. *Ibid.*, §61.

23. Stanley, *Collection*, pp. 115–38; Busse, *Altenglische*, pp. 12–13 and 22–26; and Orchard, "Old English and Latin," pp. 65–68. Daniel Paul O'Donnell, "Manuscript Variation," distinguishes scribal treatment of "fixed context poems" like *Cædmon's Hymn* from "anthologised and excerpted poems" like *Beowulf* in the strongest terms.

24. Thornbury, *Becoming a Poet*, p. 209. Thornbury builds on the work of Tyler, *Old English Poetics*, pp. 1–8 and 157–72, who argues for the need to historicize conservative poetic styles, and Trilling, *Aesthetics*, who proposes to do so by attending to modes of historical consciousness.

25. Thornbury, *Becoming a Poet*, p. 237.

26. For example, Suzuki, *Metrical Organization*, p. 223, criticizes Fulk's formulation of Kaluza's law for its reliance on the evanescent notion of

'foot.' Cp. Fulk, *History*, §175 n. 12. Yakovlev, "Development," pp. 70–82, gives reasons to dispense with feet in metrical theory, specifically noting (p. 76 n. 49) that the metrical phenomenon described by Kaluza's law occurs across putative foot boundaries.

27. Cp. 106a, 283a, 567b, 656a, 901a, 1148a, 1198b, 1206a, 1261b, 1453b, 1947b, 1949b, 2051b, 2064b, 2201b, 2207a, 2351b, 2356a, 2388b, 2395b, 2437a, 2474b, 2501a, 2806b, 2888b, 2911b, 2914b and 2920b, and 3002a. Bately, "Linguistic Evidence," pp. 421–31, considers the poet's use of *syððan* distinctive. *Longues durées* not introduced by *syððan* are 1–2, 15–16a, 31, 104b–105, 113b–14a, 151b–52a, 1354–55a, 1748, 1863b–65, 1915–16, 2130, 2158–59, 2183b, 2208b–209a, 2233–35, 2391–93a, and 2779–80a.

28. Cronan, "Poetic Words," p. 41. See now also Neidorf, "Lexical Evidence," and Hartman, "Limits," pp. 89–94.

29. Both quotations since the previous note from Cronan, "Poetic Words," p. 47.

30. Cronan, "Poetic Words," pp. 24 (first quotation) and 39 (second quotation). Cp. Neidorf, "Lexical Evidence," pp. 11–14 and 26–27. Frank, "Sharing Words," pp. 11–15, building on Frank, "Three 'Cups,'" considers words and collocations appearing only in *Beowulf* and (late) prose sources.

31. All quotations since the previous note from Neidorf, "*VII Æthelred*," p. 134. Busse and Holtei, "*Beowulf*," make similar inferences about the reception of the poem *c.* 1000 but remain agnostic about its ulterior origins. For *Beowulf* as Wallace Stevens's "jar in Tennessee," see Liuzza, "On the Dating," p. 284.

32. Neidorf, "Scribal Errors," p. 251, picked up by Shippey, "Names in *Beowulf*," p. 59. Cp. Neidorf, "*VII Æthelred*," pp. 133–34, and "Dating of *Widsið*," pp. 168–69. Contrast Busse, *Altenglische*, pp. 18–22.

33. The 'errors' in 18a and 53b *Beowulf* may have been the poet's. Type D* occurs in the b-verse in *Beowulf*, e.g., 1323b, 1525b (the editors of *Klaeber's Beowulf* assume elision of *-de* in *ðolode*, a dubious concept), 1663b (emended *metri causa*), 1932b, 1997b, etc. MS *sigemunde* at 875a is not an error (Weiskott, "Three *Beowulf* Cruces," pp. 6–7), and even if it were, no misrecognition of the name would be involved. MS *eotenum* at 902b and 1145a is either an acceptable by-form of *Eotum* 'Jutes' (dat. pl.) or an allusion to 'giants': *Klaeber's Beowulf*, ed. Fulk, Bjork, and Niles, n. to 902b–904a. For a more uncompromising view, see Neidorf, "Cain, Cam," pp. 616–23. No editor elects to emend MS *garmundes* at 1962a to *Wærmundes* as Neidorf, "Scribal Errors," p. 257, recommends.

34. Sisam, *Studies*, p. 37.

35. Neidorf, "Cain, Cam," pp. 601–15, argues that the uncorrected reading in the first passage (*Cames*) is authorial. If so, the scribe has still blundered: in that case, by hypercorrecting the poet's conflation of Cain and Ham.

36. Neidorf, "Dating of *Widsið*," p. 169.

37. MS *wala* for presumptive *Hwala* at 14a, MS *holm rycum* for presumptive *Holmrygum* at 21a, and MS *henden* for presumptive *Heoden* at 21b. Neidorf, "Dating of *Widsið*," p. 168, adds 62b *Sweordwerum* and 81a *hæðnum* and *hælepum*.

38. The MS of the *Chronicon* is Ker, *Catalogue*, item 170, burnt beyond recognition but datable on the basis of fragments bound with Ker, *Catalogue*, item 171. The MS of Asser is Ker, *Catalogue*, item 172; Tiberius B.v is Ker, *Catalogue*, item 193, and the 'Textus Roffensis' is Ker, *Catalogue*, item 373. In the MS of Asser, Scef is replaced by a second 'Seth.'

39. For knowledge of the Merovingians throughout the OE centuries, see Goffart, "The Name 'Merovingian,'" responding to Shippey, "Mero(vich) ingian." See now also Shippey, "Names in *Beowulf*," pp. 74–75.

40. Wormald, *Times of Bede*, pp. 71–105.

41. Neidorf, "*VII Æthelred*," p. 134 (quotation), "Dating of *Widsið*," p. 171, and "Scribal Errors," pp. 260–61.

42. Neidorf suggests that MS *Beulfus* could represent Beaduwulf (private communication). This is unlikely, for OE *d* is regularly retained between vowels in Domesday: Feilitzen, *Pre-Conquest*, §§102–104. The spellings *e* for OE *eo* and *u* for OE *wu* are the expected ones for this scribe. Reaney, "Notes," p. 86, includes the Domesday form under 'Beowulf.' At any rate, the name Beowulf occurs five more times in eleventh- and twelfth-century historical records: Reaney and Wilson, *Dictionary*, p. xl.

43. Wormald, *Times of Bede*, p. 76. Wormald erroneously lists Garmund and Hrothulf as "recorded only poetically": these names appear in the *Durham Liber Vitae*, once and three times respectively. Wormald, *Times of Bede*, p. 74, notes Garmund in the *Durham Liber Vitae*, in self-contradiction.

44. Neidorf, "Dating of *Widsið*," p. 179 (quotation). Contrast Weiskott, "Meter of *Widsith*."

45. Tolkien, "Beowulf," p. 248.

46. *Ibid.*, p. 245.

2 Prologues to Old English Poetry

1. Eighteen OE poems exceed 100 lines but do not begin with prologues (Fig. 3). Conversely, twelve poems have fewer than 100 lines but begin with prologues: *Cædmon's Hymn* (but Cædmon's future compositions are the 'text': see below), *Husband's Message, Kentish Hymn, Meters of Boethius* 1 and 13, *Paris Psalter* 65, *Partridge, Riddle 67, Vainglory, Wife's Lament, Whale*, and the couplet appearing as a gloss in the Regius Psalter (but the psalms of David are the 'text': see below). To the arguments of this chapter cp. Battles, "Toward a Theory," who proceeds by a similar method but discerns three types of prologue.

2. Orton, "Deixis"; Frantzen, "Form and Function" (who, however, treats what I call prefaces and prologues together); and Godden, "Prologues and Epilogues."

3. Hunt, "Introductions"; and Minnis, "Influence," and *Medieval Theory of Authorship*, esp. pp. 9–72.

4. To the following discussion cp. Parks, "Traditional Narrator."

5. Quoted from Bergman, "Supplement," p. 13. See further Gretsch, *Intellectual Foundations*, pp. 78–79 and 309–10, and Bredehoft, *Authors, Audiences*, pp. 114–15.
6. For the date see *ASPR* 6, pp. lxv–lxvi.
7. The Latin text is quoted directly from Bibliothèque Nationale MS latin 8824, fols. 76r (first quotation) and 77r (second quotation), including manuscript punctuation.
8. Liuzza, "Old English *Christ* and *Guthlac*," sees *Guthlac A* 1–29 as a hinge passage connecting *Christ III* and *Guthlac*. Liuzza, "Old English *Christ* and *Guthlac*," pp. 8–9, discusses *Guthlac A* 30 ff. as a prologue.
9. Hunt, "Introductions," p. 93.
10. Conner, "On Dating Cynewulf," disputed by McCulloh, "Did Cynewulf Use."
11. Fulk and Cain, *History*, p. 45.
12. *Seasons* survives only in an early modern transcript. Richards, "Old Wine," argues for a very late date of composition; Thornbury, *Becoming a Poet*, p. 226, includes *Seasons* in the late 'Southern mode.'
13. Thornbury, *Becoming a Poet*, pp. 224 (first quotation) and 232 (second quotation).
14. Hines, "*Benedicite* Canticle." The fragmentary inscription corresponds to *Azarias* 73–75 / *Daniel* 362–64.
15. Holding *Beowulf* to one side, the most proximal past conjured up by an OE 'days-of-yore' prologue is *Meters of Boethius* 1 (Boethius, *fl.* early sixth century; poem no earlier than *c.* 890=*c.* 375 years).
16. For the earliest date see Fulk, *History*, §419. The poet's form 'Hygelac' is closer to the form in the *LHF* (*Chochilaicus* in the A text, *Chochilagus* in the B text) than the one in Gregory of Tours, where the name begins *Chlo-* or *(C) hro-* in all MSS.
17. I note, however, the poetic gloss to the Lindisfarne Gospels (late tenth century) (Appendix A, no. 9), invoking Bede in a primarily Latinate prose context.
18. Frank, "*Beowulf* Poet's Sense," pp. 53–54.

3 Lawman, the Last Old English Poet and the First Middle English Poet

1. Blake, "Rhythmical Alliteration," pp. 121–22; Turville-Petre, *Alliterative Revival*, pp. 9 ("fluid and imprecise") and 11; Friedlander, "Early Middle English," p. 220; Brehe, "'Rhythmical Alliteration,'" p. 65, and "Rhyme and the Alliterative Standard," p. 11; Kooper, "Laȝamon," p. 118, and "Laȝamon's Prosody," p. 435; and Stanley, "Scansion," p. 186 ("mismetred").
2. Georgianna, "Periodization and Politics"; Morrison, "Vernacular Literary Activity"; Treharne, "Categorization, Periodization" and *Living through Conquest*; and Faulkner, "Rewriting."

3. Bredehoft, "Ælfric and Late Old English," *Early English Metre*, pp. 81–90, and *Authors, Audiences*, pp. 146–70.
4. Yakovlev, "Development," p. 292 n. 19. Cp. Russom, "Evolution," p. 297, and Yakovlev, "Metre and Punctuation," pp. 261–63.
5. Yakovlev, "Development," p. 219: "[W]hile strong final dips were prohibited in Layamon, resolution was functional in the final lift of the [b-verse]," and p. 249: "Polysyllabic final dips do not occur in either two- or three-lift a-verses."
6. Alliteration, word boundary, and 'secondary stress' aside, virtually all metrical patterns in OE appear in either half-line. The main exceptions are the asystematic five-position patterns Types A* and D*, which mostly occur in the a-verse.
7. *Eugenia* 1b, 4b, 6b, 12b, 13b, and 15b; *Basil* 4b, 6b, 7b, 11b, 12b, 14b, 15b, 16b, and 17b; *Julian* 7b, 8b, 10b, 11b, and 12b; *Sebastian* 6b, 7b, 9b, 12b, 15b, 16b, and 19b; *Maur* 9b, 12b, 17b, 18b, and 20b; and *Agnes*, 2b, 5b, and 15b.
8. I assume disyllabic subjunctive *scyle*, a metrically determined choice. Cp. 1b *were*, 2b *come*, and 4b *were*.
9. I assume monosyllabic *þire* (cp. ME *þi*). Forms of *þi(ne)* scan as monosyllables in the roughly contemporary *Soul's Address*. Yakovlev, "Development," p. 244, finds the rare b-verse pattern xSx ... xS three times in a 200-line sample from the *Brut*. The remaining scansions of the *Grave* are: 11b and 12b Type 3, 13b–17b Type 1, 18b Type 4, 19b Type 2, 20b Type 1, 21b Type 2, 22b Type 1, 23b and 24b Type 3, and 25b Type A.
10. I reject as unnecessary Hall's 7b *[fif]* bec. I omit Hall's 2b and 23b, because corrupt in MS. I take Hall's ll. 8 and 11–14 to be prose lists and Hall's 20b–21b to be a prose quotation in Latin, and so I omit these b-verses, relineating accordingly.
11. Throughout the poem I assume monosyllabic *ure* (cp. ME *our*).
12. The remaining scansions of the *First Worcester Fragment* are: 11b Type 2, 12b Type 1 without final syllable, 13b Type 4, and 14b Type 1.
13. For the dates of the short poems not included in Appendices A and B, see Fig. 1.

    I count 323 b-verses in *Maldon*: those of the 325 lines of the poem in *ASPR* 6, minus 2 missing or incomplete (1b and 172b).

    I count 250 b-verses in *Proverbs of Alfred*: the even-numbered lines of *Proverbs*, ed. Arngart, minus 4 in deductive meter (4.24, 6.14, 23.12, and 23.16). Arngart prints the alliterative long line as 2 short lines and provides no lineation; Arngart's reproduction of the *punctus elevatus* normally represents the caesura. I ignore as extrametrical the speech tag "Þus cwað Alfred" at the beginning of sections 4–29 as well as the proverb "Wis child is fader blisse" in section 14; I impose lineation on all remaining short lines.

    I count 313 b-verses in *Soul's Address*: those of the 348 total lines of *Soul's Address*, ed. Moffat, minus 35 missing or corrupt (A 1b and 19b; B 10b; C 50b; D 7b and 47b; E 2b, 23b, and 25b; F 1b; and G 32b, 36b, 41b, and 49b), in Latin (B 31b; C 21b; E 41b, 46b, and 50b; F 2b, 44b, and 49b; and G 20b, 35b, and 56b), or in deductive meter (A 29b, 41b, and 43b; C 4b; D 37b, 38b, and 39b; E 39b; F 4b; and G 25b).

I count 147 b-verses in the *Physiologus*: those of ll. 1–26, 93–175, 261–81, 313–34, and 391–406 of *Physiologus*, ed. Wirtjes, minus 21 missing or corrupt (23b, 129b, and 132b) or in deductive meter (19b, 20b, 21b, 22b, 124b, 133b, 135b, 136b, 137b, 144b, 152b, 158b, 159b, 161b, 265b, 268b, 327b, and 406b).

In these scansions as in those discussed elsewhere in this chapter and displayed in the appendices, I posit metrical resolution, the prefix license, compound stress, stress shift, and linguistically innovative verbal endings (e.g., *mak(i)en* 'make (inf.)' Sx) where possible to avoid two long dips and final long dips. For purposes of like-to-like comparison in the scansions summarized in this n. and paragraph, I disregard possible metrical resolution and applications of the prefix license when these accommodations are not metrically determinative but would shorten an expandable dip. Thus *Maldon* 6b *yrhðo geþolian*, interpretable as SxSx with omission of *ge-* by the prefix license (and resolution of -*þoli*-), counts as Type 3 here.

14. Two long dips: *Coronation of Edgar* 13b; *Death of William* 4b; *Maldon* 21b, 34b, and 179b; *Physiologus* 11b; *Proverbs of Alfred* 1.8, 5.6, 11.6, 13.10, 15.16, 17.14, 18.2, 18.12, 22.8, 24.2, and 27.18; and *Soul's Address* C 31b and G 19b, 27b, and 31b. Final long dip: *Proverbs of Alfred* 1.4 (syncope -*lerede?*).

15. *Physiologus* 126a; *Proverbs of Alfred* 1.3 (stress shift or compound stress *biscopes?*), 8.5 (loss of -*e-* *ʒuʒeþe*? <OE *geogoþ* (f. + analogical -*e*: Cable, *English Alliterative Tradition*, p. 78)), 8.13 (ditto), and 18.15 (syncope *mameleþ?*); *Soul's Address* C 12a, E 9a and 20a (syncope *beræfedest?*), and G 12a (ditto); and *Young Edward* 7a. Yakovlev, "Development," p. 249, is unequivocal: "Polysyllabic final dips do not occur in either two- or three-lift a-verses," of Lawman. In scanning a-verses I posit metrical resolution, compound stress, stress shift, linguistically innovative verbal endings, and verse-final promotion of function words where possible to avoid final long dips.

16. Two long dips: OE: cp. *Beowulf* 83b, 455b, 487b, etc.; ME: Cable, *English Alliterative Meter*, p. 90, finds 7 possible instances of x . . . xSx . . . xS(x) in the b-verse in a 900-line sample from *Cleanness*. Yakovlev, "Development," p. 244, finds 7 possible instances of x . . . xSx . . . xS(x) in the b-verse in a 200-line sample from the *Brut*. Final long dips: in OE, the prohibition against long dips in the penultimate and final metrical positions ensured that final long dips did not occur (Introduction and Ch. 1); in ME, the requirement of a final unstressed syllable in the b-verse had the same effect (Ch. 4).

17. Yakovlev, "Development," pp. 163–67.

18. Stanley, "Date of Laʒamon's *Brut*," p. 85; Le Saux, *Layamon's 'Brut'*, pp. 1–13; and Perry, "Origins and Originality," pp. 69–71.

19. In opposition to previous consensus, Cartlidge, "Date," and Fletcher, "Genesis," date the *Owl and the Nightingale* to the late thirteenth century. The accentual-syllabic Bridekirk font inscription cannot be dated more precisely than 'twelfth century': R. I. Page, *Introduction*, pp. 195–96. The

three hymns of St. Godric (d. 1170) might predate *Poema* and *Ormulum*: Christopher Page, "Catalogue," pp. 69–71; but the earliest secular lyrics probably do not: Brown, *English Lyrics*, pp. xi–xiv. "Cnut's Song" in the *Liber Eliensis* (completed *c.* 1175) predates *Poema* and *Ormulum* by a decade at most. The rhyming soul-and-body poem in Trinity College Cambridge MS B.14.52 (late twelfth century) may predate *Poema* and *Ormulum* as well: Wymer, "Poetic Fragment."

20. Of a random selection of 1000 French loanwords in the *OED*, Baugh, "Chronology," found that only 11 (1.1 percent) were attested by 1200; for Mossé, "On the Chronology," the figure is 8 of 1807 (0.44 percent). A search for French-derived words attested by 1200 in the *OED* Online yields 198 results, including some quasi-integrated vocabulary discussed and defined in late OE grammars and some items probably rather from Latin.

21. Pearsall, *Old English and Middle English*, p. 85. On the international and multilingual contexts for English literature in the twelfth and thirteenth centuries, see also Salter, *English and International*, pp. 4–74 (48–70 on the *Brut*).

22. Rosamund Allen, "'Nv seið mid loft-songe,'" p. 253; Tiller, "Romancing History"; and Galloway, "Laȝamon's Gift," pp. 719–22. Mancho, "Is *Orrmulum*'s Introduction," reads the prologue to the *Ormulum* as an Aristotelian preface; cp. McMullen, "*Forr þeȝȝre sawle need*." To the following discussion cp. Jonathan Watson, "Minim-istic Imagination," and Bryan, "Laȝamon's *Brut*," pp. 678–84.

23. 981, 1021, 2073, 2122b, 2397, 2997–97[a], 2998b, 3119b, 3129b, 3147, 3450, 3453a, 3458, 3524, 3533a, 3533b, 3940, 4129, 4471, 4491, 4559a, 4804, 5102, 5573, 6317–18, 6853, 7071, 7187–88, 8175, 8432, 8589b, 9228, 9380, 9384, 9390, 9406, 9407, 9417, 10797b, 11874a, 11985, 12374, 12545–46, 13188, 13530, 13964b, 14200, 14288, 14295, 14406, 14644, 14814, 15016, 15796, 15799, 15802, 15877, 15883, 15947, 15963, 15964, and 16020b.

24. Bryan, "Two Manuscripts," p. 89.

25. Stanley, "Laȝamon's Un-Anglo-Saxon Syntax," p. 47; and Yakovlev, "Development," pp. 204–7, and "Metre and Punctuation," pp. 266–67.

26. Scholars initially dated *King Horn c.* 1225, but Allen, "Date and Provenance," dates the poem to the late thirteenth century.

27. One earlier exception may be a lost copy of the OE *Riming Poem*: Abram, "Errors." Yakovlev, "Metre and Punctuation," p. 275, argues from punctuation that two or more direct ancestor texts of the Caligula Lawman were laid out as prose.

28. These fragments were copied in "the middle or the second quarter of the fourteenth century": Doyle, "The Manuscripts," p. 91. By specifying 'free-standing' I mean to exclude short alliterative poems embedded in Latin or non-alliterative ME verse texts.

29. See further Edwards, "Editing and Manuscript Form."

30. Stanley, "Laȝamon's Antiquarian Sentiments."

31. Cannon, "Style and Authorship," pp. 201–2.

32. *Fæie-sið* appears nowhere else. *Gras-bæd* (OE *gærsbed*) appears four times in OE and ME, all in alliterative poems and always as a kenning for a site of bodily death (a battlefield or a grave): *Paris Psalter* 102.15.1b, *Brut* 11723b and 11970a, and *Wit and Will* E 1b.
33. Cannon, "Style and Authorship," pp. 201–4.
34. Cable, *English Alliterative Tradition*, p. 61, counts 102 four-syllable verses in Caligula (0.3% of all verses), but this excludes the transitional pattern xSxSx and includes patterns with more than two lifts. Yakovlev, "Development," p. 244, finds three two-lift b-verses with no long dip in a 200-line sample (1.5% of b-verses).
35. Sauer, "Knowledge," p. 792: "What is clear, at least from the evidence we have, is that there was only interest in [*sc.* OE] prose works during the ME period and not in poetry; the latter was probably too difficult, anyway." Cp. Faulkner, "Rewriting," p. 277. Note also the emphasis on prose in Cameron, "Middle English" (p. 218, of poetry: "the OE words may be garbled"); *Rewriting*, ed. Swan and Treharne; and Treharne, "Reading from the Margins."
36. Yakovlev, "Development," p. 283.
37. Donoghue, "Laȝamon's Ambivalence," p. 537.
38. Pollock, *Language of the Gods*, p. 23.
39. *Ibid.*, p. 26.
40. *Ibid.*, p. 25.
41. Hanna, [Review of Cannon, *Grounds*], p. 283, and Lawton, [Review of Cannon, *Grounds*].

4 Prologues to Middle English Alliterative Poetry

1. To this section cp. Cornelius, *Reconstructing*, ch. 3.
2. Borroff, "*Sir Gawain and the Green Knight*", pp. 155–58.
3. OE: Kendall, *Metrical Grammar*, Cable, *English Alliterative Tradition*, pp. 21–22, and Momma, *Composition*; ME: Duggan, "Stress Assignment," and Cable, *English Alliterative Tradition*, p. 80; comparison: Russom, "Some Unnoticed Constraints."
4. Yakovlev, "Metre and Punctuation," argues that the Caligula and Otho scribes had extensive knowledge of EME alliterative meter.
5. I assume an analogical -*e* on the historically feminine suffixes -*nes* (<OE) in 2a *wrechednes* and -*yng* (<OE -*ung*) in 4a *payntyng* and 8a *sorowyng*, as well as in *hell* <OE (f.) at 10b: Cable, *English Alliterative Tradition*, p. 78. The second root vowel in 5a *drewryse* <OF *drüerie* is historically justified and counts in the meter, while -*o*-² in 8a *sorowyng* <OE *sorgung* and -*e* in 9b *Criste* <OE *Crist* are not historically justified and do not count in the meter.
6. ME *dale* 'vale' <OE *dæl* (neuter) + ON *dalr* (m.) ought to scan S, despite the scribal -*e*. Has the word crossed over to the feminine (as if <OE **dalu*) by influence of L *vallis* and/or analogy to ME *bale* 'evil' <OE *bealo*, *tale* <OE

talu, etc.? Langland evidently counts an -*e* in sg. *dale* at *Piers Plowman* B.1.1b (Type 2?), and Chaucer clearly does so at *Canterbury Tales* VII 837 (rhyming pl. *smale*) and 2823 (rhyming *tale*). Cp. *Gawain* 2162b (Type 3?).

7. Doyle, "The Manuscripts," p. 91. To the following discussion cp. *Conflict of Wit and Will*, ed. Dickins, pp. 5–14 and nn. to B 34 and D 2 and 11.

8. Turville-Petre, *Alliterative Revival*, p. 17. To the following discussion cp. Yakovlev, "Development," pp. 285–87, concluding, p. 287: "[T]he changes in the alliterative metre between Old English and late Middle English can be explained by specific references to events in the history of English and do not need a recourse to creative efforts of an individual antiquarian."

9. To the following discussion cp. Tiller, "Anglo-Norman Historiography."

10. Rigg, "Henry of Huntingdon," p. 65. Translation mine.

11. These are *Piers Plowman* (over fifty complete, substantial, or fragmentary MSS; freestanding excerpts in three MSS; and four early printings); *Second Scottish Prophecy* (*c.* sixteen MSS, excluding copies certainly or probably containing only rhyming lines); *ABC of Aristotle* (fifteen MSS); *Siege of Jerusalem* (nine MSS); "Alle perishes and passes" (eight MSS); *First Scottish Prophecy* (*c.* six MSS, excluding copies certainly or probably containing only rhyming lines); "Þanne God graunte grace..." (six MSS); the *Ireland Prophecy* (six MSS: see Weiskott, "*Ireland Prophecy*"); and *Pierce the Ploughman's Crede* (three MSS and two early printings).

12. To this section cp. Cornelius, *Reconstructing*, ch. 5.

13. Three especially valuable studies are Turville-Petre, "'Summer Sunday'"; Fein, "Form and Continuity"; and *Three Alliterative*, ed. Kennedy.

14. *Awntyrs*: 73b (*I*), 74a (*I*), 99b (*euer*), 112b (*neuer*), 135b (*wheþer*), 171b (*while*), 173b (*while*), 191a (*Y*), 202a (*þou*), 250b (*þes*), 263b (*withouten*), 267a (*he*), and 280b (*you*); *Gawain*: 25a (*alle*), 90a (*also*), and 130a (*I*). Quotations of *Awntyrs* are from *Awntyrs*, ed. Hanna. The 200 lines from *Awntyrs* are ll. 1–289 in Hanna's text, minus 22 four-line wheels and the missing l. 48. The 200 lines from *Sir Gawain and the Green Knight* are ll. 1–255 in *Poems of the Pearl Manuscript*, ed. Andrew and Waldron, minus 11 five-line bobs and wheels.

15. *Awntyrs*: 16, 18, 20, 31, 43, 47 56 (rejecting Hanna's choice of the minority reading *þai werray þe wilde*), 59, 60, 121, 122, 124, 126, 159, 176, 183, 209, 222, 228, 238, 241, and 264; *Gawain*: 2, 8, 9, 10, 13, 21, 39, 40, 46, 60, 61, 64, 65, 67, 69, 73, 75, 76, 77, 87, 89, 98, 108, 109, 110, 111, 112, 113, 115, 116, 118, 119, 121, 123, 131, 135, 136, 140, 152, 153, 154, 155, 157, 159, 167, 181, 185, 187, 192, 193, 209, 210, 211, 212, 214, 217, 219, 220, 221, 222, 224, 226, 235, 236, 239, 250, and 254.

16. For partial report of percentages across the corpus, see Cable, *English Alliterative Tradition*, pp. 87–89 (esp. p. 89, "a frequency between 20 percent and 55 percent," summarizing his findings), and Duggan, "Extended A-Verses," pp. 65–71. My own percentages and procedures seem closer to Cable's than to Duggan's.

17. *King James VI and I*, ed. Rhodes, Richards, and Marshall, p. 33.

18. *Awntyrs*, ed. Hanna, pp. 14–15, and Putter, "Adventures," pp. 160–61.

19. Lawton, "Larger Patterns," pp. 611–12.
20. Pearsall, "Alliterative Revival," p. 37.
21. Liu, "Middle English Romance," pp. 342–44. Cp. Furrow, "Radial Categories."
22. An analogous though broader typology of Middle English prologues, one inclusive of prose texts, is Galloway, "Middle English Prologues."
23. To the following discussion cp. Sandison, *"Chanson D'Aventure"*, pp. 25–45; Middleton, "Audience and Public," pp. 111–15 and nn. 34–35; Weldon, "Structure of Dream Visions," pp. 258–70; and Galloway, *Penn Commentary*, pp. 21–26 and 34–35.
24. On the idea of a '*Piers Plowman* tradition,' see Pearsall, *Old English and Middle English*, p. 153; Lawton, "Unity," pp. 76–81; *Piers Plowman Tradition*, ed. Barr, pp. 5–8 and n. 14, and Barr, *Signes and Sothe*, pp. 1–22; and Scase, "Latin Composition Lessons."
25. *Wynnere and Wastoure*, ed. Trigg, pp. xxii–xxvii; but see Turville-Petre, "*Wynnere and Wastoure*," restating the early dating. On possible literary borrowings between *Piers Plowman* and *Wynnere and Wastoure* in either direction see Galloway, *Penn Commentary*, p. 10 (with references to prior scholarship), and Burrow, "Winning and Wasting."
26. To the following discussion cp. Turville-Petre, "Afterword," and Mueller, *Translating Troy*, pp. 172–80 and 202–5.
27. Everett, *Essays*, p. 50. To the following discussion cp. Turville-Petre, "Prologue of *Wynnere and Wastoure*."
28. Cooper, "Langland's and Chaucer's Prologues," p. 77.
29. Butterfield, *Familiar Enemy*, esp. pp. 55–65, prefers the broader term 'Anglo-French' as better able to comprehend the interconnected varieties of French in use by English speakers on both sides of the Channel. Butterfield is surely right to query "a single story of isolated and gradually degenerating French" (p. 65) in England, but 'Anglo-Norman' may still be useful for suggesting historical difference (literary and/or linguistic) between insular and continental varieties of French. To the following discussion cp. Rosalind Field, "Anglo-Norman Background."
30. *History*, ed. Wright, pp. vi–viii.
31. *History*, ed. Wright, pp. viii–x. Cp. *Fouke*, ed. Hathaway et al., pp. xxxv and liii–cxvi.
32. Malory, *Morte Darthur*, ed. P. J. C. Field, vol. 1, pp. 841 and 870. Norris, *Malory's Library*, pp. 131–36 and 169–72, discusses sources and analogues for the first passage. Cp. Field, "Malory's Sir Phelot," pp. 346–48, and *Morte Darthur*, ed. Field, vol. 2, p. 737.
33. Zeeman, "Tales of Piers and Perceval." Cp. Clifton, "Romance Convention," who sets English non-alliterative and French romance sources and analogues side by side.
34. Barron, "Alliterative Romance," p. 70.
35. Evans, "Afterword," p. 371.
36. All quotations since the previous note from Evans, "Afterword," p. 372.

5 The *Erkenwald* Poet's Sense of History

1. Frank, "*Beowulf* Poet's Sense," p. 56, of *Beowulf*. To the arguments of this chapter cp. Camp, "Spatial Memory," and Schustereder, "Coming to Terms."

2. Cp. *St. Erkenwald*, ed. Savage, n. to 5–6 (three dedications); *St. Erkenwald*, ed. Morse, p. 34 (two); and Scattergood, *Lost Tradition*, pp. 181–82 (one).

3. Otter, "'New Werke,'" p. 414.

4. Burrow, "*Saint Erkenwald* Line 1."

5. Donoghue, "Laȝamon's Ambivalence," p. 537.

6. Frank, "*Beowulf* Poet's Sense," p. 55, of *Beowulf* 2024–69. On the significance of the vestments see *St. Erkenwald*, ed. Savage, nn. to 81 and 83.

7. Rhodes, *Poetry Does*, pp. 146–67, and Sisk, "Uneasy Orthodoxy."

8. To *MED* Online, 'rēnish(e' and 'rūnish,' cp. *St. Erkenwald*, ed. Savage, n. to 52; Hoffman, "'Renischsche Renkes'"; and Scattergood, *Lost Tradition*, pp. 193–94 n. 30.

9. *Gesta*, ed. Riley, vol. 1, p. 26. Here and below, translations of the *Gesta* are mine. The Matthew Paris narrative is compared with *St. Erkenwald* by Otter, "'New Werke,'" pp. 403–4, and Scattergood, *Lost Tradition*, pp. 186–88.

10. Otter, "'New Werke,'" pp. 407–8: "*inventiones* – like *St. Erkenwald* – actually demonstrate an understanding of two basic archaeological notions: first, the correlation between the age of a find and the depth at which it is buried; and second, what has been called the metonymic aspect of archaeology, the idea that one object stands for a larger 'past era' and can, if suitably interrogated, yield information that goes far beyond itself."

11. *MED* Online, 'leued,' 1f, suggests '?unknown, ?forgotten,' but elsewhere the word always means 'uneducated; unhallowed; secular.' *St. Erkenwald*, ed. Savage, n. to 205, glosses 'unlettered' hence 'difficult.' The MS reads *fife* for *aght* and *a þousande* for *þre hundred*. The emendations are meant to produce a date of 1136 BCE for Brutus' arrival, the figure reckoned in *St. Erkenwald*, ed. Gollancz, pp. xxx–xxxiv, by an elaborate comparison of medieval authorities. Verse 210a thus becomes an a-verse with five content words, an extremely uncommon pattern. Four-lift verses already form a tiny minority: Duggan, "Extended A-Verses," pp. 54–55 and 74.

12. Cp. *Chevalere Assigne* 272 "Alle þe bellys of þe close | rongen at ones," at a baptism, and *William of Palerne* 5334–36 "þe prelates on procession | prestili out comen, / & alle þe belles in burw | busili were runge, / for ioye," before a coronation; but *Morte Arthure* 4332–33 "Throly belles thay rynge, | and *Requiem* syngys, / Dosse messes and matyns | with mournande notes," at Arthur's funeral.

13. Howe, *Writing the Map*, pp. 75–100, sensitively applies the term 'postcolonial' to Anglo-Saxon England, and Warren, *History on the Edge*, to Anglo-Norman Britain.

14. For three passages in ME alliterative poetry often taken as reflexive statements on meter but better interpreted otherwise, see Pearsall, *Old English and*

Middle English, pp. 153–54. For a fourth, see Cornelius, "Alliterative Revival," pp. 270–71.

15. Pickering, "Early Middle English," p. 412. Translation mine.

16. *Bracton,* ed. Woodbine, vol. 1, pp. 82–83; James, *Descriptive Catalogue: Lambeth,* p. 153; Bennett, "Survival and Revivals," p. 32; and Appendix B, no. 6. The others are Appendix A, no. 14, and Appendix B, nos. 1 (three in all) and 5. For resonances between the alliterative meter, legal traditionalism, and sententiousness, see Yeager, *From Lawmen to Plowmen.*

17. Cp. McIntosh, "Early Middle English," n. 12, and, on the poem as a whole, Mueller, *Translating Troy,* pp. 210–18. Line 3 means, with double poetic syntactical inversion, "power and memory to tell about what is right" (*MED Online,* 'mēning(e (ger.(1)),' 4b). A second *to make* appears to have been lost by haplography after the inversion. Verse 4a *þis* is added in another hand in Waldron's base MS and is present in all other MSS.

18. *Lollard Sermons,* ed. Cigman, pp. 92 ("God ... grante vs þoru his grace to wirche so wiseli") and 194 ("graunt vs þat grace þat [*sic*] ... to worche so wisely"), and *Piers Plowman* B.7.203–4 ("That god gyue vs grace | er we go hennes / Swiche werkes to werche, | while we ben here").

19. Nicholas Watson, "Politics," pp. 331–39.

20. See further *Three Eleventh-Century,* ed. Love, pp. cxvii–cxix and cxxxvi–cxxxix, and Appendix B, no. 2. To the following discussion cp. Pearsall, "Origins," pp. 11–12; Salter, *English and International,* pp. 172–73; Morgan, "'Lite bokes,'" pp. 153–56; Wogan-Browne, "Locating," pp. 258–59; and Yeager, *From Lawmen to Plowmen,* p. 159.

21. *Polychronicon,* ed. Lumby, vol. 6, p. 307.

22. Chism, *Alliterative Revivals,* pp. 15 (first quotation) and 16 (second and third quotations). Cp. Grady, "*Piers Plowman, St. Erkenwald,*" p. 85: "The 'roynyshe' figures are never deciphered or translated in the poem ... because they are a figure for the poem itself"; and Otter, "'New Werke,'" p. 413: "the marvelous tomb ... functions as a *mise en abîme,* ... an artifact that represents within the poem the intellectual operations of the poem."

23. Chism, *Alliterative Revivals,* p. 42. Cp. *ibid.,* p. 7: "To write the past is always to address the past's uses for the present."

24. Frank, "*Beowulf* Poet's Sense," p. 57, of *Beowulf.*

25. *Gesta,* ed. Riley, vol. 1, pp. 26 (first quotation) and 27 (second, third, fourth, fifth, sixth, and seventh quotations).

26. As in Hill, "*Beowulf* and Conversion History."

27. Chism, *Alliterative Revivals,* pp. 6 ("These poems are ... anxious to assimilate or overwrite the unfamiliar, to make the past theirs") and 66 ("The past we encounter in *St. Erkenwald* is, however inconclusively, already colonized").

28. Borroff, "Narrative Artistry," p. 46.

29. Benson, "Authorship," and *St. Erkenwald,* ed. Morse, pp. 45–48.

30. Contrast Cronan, "Poetic Words," with Frank, "Sharing Words."

31. For skepticism about a fourteenth-century date for *St. Erkenwald*, see Lawton, "Literary History," and Hanna, "Alliterative Poetry," p. 496.
32. Otter, "'New Werke,'" p. 404.

6 The Alliterative Tradition in the Sixteenth Century

1. To this chapter cp. Cornelius, *Reconstructing*, ch. 5.
2. On the *Vision of William Banastre* and the *Ireland Prophecy* see Weiskott, "Alliterative Meter after 1450" and "*Ireland Prophecy*." On alliterating stanzaic verse in the sixteenth century, see esp. Edwards, "The Blage Manuscript."
3. Stinson, "The Rise of English Printing," esp. pp. 190–94, noting, however, that alliterative lexis is often preserved by Caxton but not in the textual state attested by the Winchester MS. On Malory's treatment of the text more generally see also Hanna and Turville-Petre, "The Text of the Alliterative *Morte Arthure*," pp. 140–55.
4. See further Singh, "Alliterative Ancestry"; Bawcutt, *Dunbar*, pp. 370–79, and *Poems*, ed. Bawcutt, pp. 284–85; and MacDonald, "Alliterative Poetry."
5. Pearsall, "Alliterative Revival," p. 38.
6. Also *Scottish Field* 75b (inf. *witt*), 128b (pl. *sundry*) and 137b (*nyne* <OE *nigon*; *score* <OE *scoru*); and *Tretis* 12b (pl. *hautand*), 127b (gen. sg. *Venus*), and 183b (ditto). Throughout this chapter, I assume the continued metrical significance of the pl. inflection in nouns, regardless of scribal spelling.
7. Also *Scottish Field* 6b (*alwayes* <ME *alwei(e)s*), 34b (*more* <OE *mara*), 62b (*realme* <OF *reaume*), 92b (*about* <OE *onbutan*), 100b (inf. *know*), 141b (weak adj. *best*), 156b (*knowne* <OE *cnawen*; *wide* <OE), 168b (trisyllabic pret. pl. *raked*), 171b (*needs* <OE *nedes*), 173b (stress shift *enemyes*), and 184b (*truly* <OE *treowlice*). The two b-verses with two long dips among the scansions not dependent on *-e* both end in a short dip: *Scottish Field* 117b and *Tretis* 185b.
8. Also *Scottish Field* 86b (1st sg. *heete*), 96b (*seege* <OF *sege*), 104b (*wise* <OE *wisa*), 115b (petr. dat. *to the ground* <OE *to grunde*), 127b (inf. *know*), 135b (*hand* <OE (f.) + analogical *-e*: Cable, *English Alliterative Tradition*, p. 78), 166b (subjunctive sg. *speede*), 180b (inf. *shoote*), and 197b (weak adj. *sooth*); and *Tretis* 22b (*bricht* <OE *beorhte*), 33b (*smell* origin unknown), 61b (*maik* <OE *gemaca*), 63b (pl. *pleis*), and 100b (*about* <OE *onbutan*).
9. Cable, *English Alliterative Tradition*, p. 78.
10. Cp. *Piers Plowman* B.Prol.62b *mowe* and B.19.74b *come* and *Gawain* 144b *were* and 1590b *were*.
11. Also *Scottish Field* 100b, 156b, 168b, and 184b (see above, n. 7).
12. Also *Scottish Field* 144b (syncope or no *-e happened*), 145b (syncope or no *-e waters*), 178b (syncope or no *-e weapons*), 191b (stress shift or no *-e mountaines*), and 192b (stress shift or no *-e tydings*); and *Tretis* 40b (syncope or no *-e matiris*).

13. I assume alternating stress patterns where possible in *Tydingis* and a long dip and final short dip where possible in b-verses of the *Tretis*. Nouns with historical -*e*: 2.22 (monosyllabic *law* <OE *lagu*) and *Tretis* 4b (disyllabic *haw*- <OE *hagu*); pl. nouns: 2.14 (disyllabic *tythandis*) and *Tretis* 295b (disyllabic *handis*); pl. adjs.: 2.43 (disyllabic *dyuers*) and *Tretis* 12b (trisyllabic *hautand*); weak adjs.: 2.52 (monosyllabic *proud*) and *Tretis* 363b (disyllabic *fair*); advs.: 2.30 (disyllabic *besyd* <OE *be sidan*; or elision of -*e* in -*syd and*) and *Tretis* 213b (trisyllabic *about* <OE *onbutan*); pret. vbs.: 2.9 (disyllabic *ansuerit*) and *Tretis* 10b (disyllabic *dynnit*); sg. finite vbs.: 2.5 (monosyllabic *tell*) and *Tretis* 438b (disyllabic *wetis*); pl. finite vbs.: 2.46 (monosyllabic *Cwmis*) and *Tretis* 63b (disyllabic *pleis*); and inf. vbs.: 2.46 (monosyllabic *get*) and *Tretis* 79b (disyllabic *draw*).

14. Cole, "*The Destruction of Troy*'s Different Rules."

15. Duggan, "End of the Line," p. 78.

16. See further *Scotish Ffeilde*, ed. Oakden, pp. v–vi.

17. 57b *at his biddinge wyll* Lyme (L) (2; stress shift weak *biddinge*; *wyll* <OE *willa*)] *their free will* Percy Folio (PF) (5), 66b *that doughtie hath bene ever* L (1)] *he hath beene doughtie* PF (2), 70b *wrought as they lyked* L (3)] *& . . . them liiked* PF (1), 112b *that doughtie was euer* L (1)] *was doughtye* PF (2), 127b *full sone shold it know* L (1)] om. *full* PF (3), 156b (see below), 157b *that bolde hath bene ever* L (1)] *hath beene bolde* PF (2), and 212b *he caused a man to ride* L (2)] om. *to* PF (5).

18. Also 79b *both with Emperor and other* L (two long dips)] om. *both* PF (1), 92b *on sides all aboute* L (1; *about* <OE *onbutan*)] *all sides* PF (two long dips), 116b *as ye bid me woulde* L (two long dips; infinitive *bid*; *wold* <OE *wolde*)] *me bidd* PF (2), 171b *that byde must they neden* L (1)] *abyde* PF (two long dips), 223b *then he come beliue* L (2; sg. *come* <OE *cwom*)] *the comen* PF (two long dips), 240b *full well knowne in their contry* L (two long dips)] om. *full* PF (1), 306b *soe deere god it ordeyned* L (two long dips)] om. *it* PF (1 or three), 395b *to their blessed Kinge* L (two long dips; weak *blessed*)] *blithe* PF (2), and 396b *for the space of two yeeres* L (two long dips)] om. *for* PF (1).

19. Also 40b *many tolde thowsand* L] *thousands* PF, 67b *the saddest of all others* L] *other* PF, 178b *bowneth him to his weapon* L] *weapons* PF, 188b *were put to their ransomes* L] *ransome* PF, 217b *bowneth forth his standart* L] *standards* PF, and 249b *or he could clymbe the mountains* L] *mountaine* PF.

20. Also 92b (see above, n. 18), 112b (see above, n. 17), 116b (see above, n. 18), 156b (see below), and 157b (see above, n. 17).

21. Also 58b *lorde* L] *leede* PF and 143b *knightes* L] *rinckes* (MS *riggs*) PF.

22. See Hanford and Steadman, "*Death and Liffe*," and Jefferson and Putter, "Alliterative Metre."

23. To the following discussion cp. Stinson, "The Rise of English Printing," pp. 178–81.

24. References to *Piers Plowman* B are to *Piers Plowman*, ed. Kane and Donaldson.

25. Scase, "*Dauy Dycars Dreame.*"
26. Davis, "Prophecies." See *ibid.*, pp. 20 ('two monks' heads') and 29 ('Abbot of Abingdon').
27. Jansen, "Politics, Protest," and Warner, *Myth*, pp. 72–75.
28. See Weiskott, "Prophetic *Piers Plowman.*"
29. Warner, *Myth*, pp. 80–81 and n. 40.
30. Benson and Blanchfield, *Manuscripts*, p. 190.
31. *Ibid.*, p. 145.
32. *Ibid.*, pp. 264 and 273.
33. Grindley, "Reading," p. 103. References to *Piers Plowman* C are to *Piers Plowman*, ed. Russell and Kane.
34. *Piers Plowman*, ed. Russell and Kane, p. 182.
35. Horobin, "Stephan Batman," pp. 361–65.
36. Kelen, *Langland's Early Modern Identities*, p. 34. On other annotations of prophecy in this copy see Johnson, *Reading*, pp. 149–53, and Griffiths, "Editorial Glossing," pp. 209–13.
37. King, *English Reformation Literature*, pp. 344 (first quotation) and 343–44 (second quotation).
38. "If bokes may be bolde / to blame and reproue" (STC 6088, iii^r), "Solomon the sage / in Sapience doeth saye" (xvii^v), "A flatterynge frende / is worse then a foe" (xxi^v), "Of late a Leasemongar / of London laye sycke" (xix^r), "If Marchauntes wold medle / wyth marchaundice onely" (xix^v), "Whan the Citye of Rome / was ruled aryght" (xxx^v), "The sonne of Sirache / of women doeth saye" (xxxi^r), "Of late as I laye / and lacked my reste" (xxxiv^r), and "An vnreasonable ryche man / dyd ryde by the way" (xxxiv^v).
39. On these two facets of the *Shepheardes Calender* see, respectively, Hamilton, "Spenser and Langland," and Dolven, "Spenser's Metrics," pp. 397–400, and (on both) Cornelius, *Reconstructing*, Epilogue.
40. Cornelius, "Accentual Paradigm."
41. Hardison, *Prosody and Purpose*, pp. 6–7, mentions the alliterative tradition, but incorrectly reports that "[n]o sixteenth-century English poet wrote alliterative verse pure and simple" (6). Duffell surveys the alliterative tradition in earlier chapters: *New History*, pp. 51–61 and 111.

Conclusion: Whose Tradition?

1. Both preceding quotations from Fenton, *Introduction*, p. 1. To the following discussion cp. Jones, "New Old English," pp. 1009–1011.
2. Fenton, *Introduction*, p. 2.
3. *Ibid.*, p. 1.
4. *Ibid.*, pp. 1 (second quotation) and 2 (first quotation).
5. Butterfield, *Familiar Enemy*, and Cannon, *Making*, esp. pp. 179–220.
6. Rigg, "Henry of Huntingdon," p. 69.
7. Pearsall, *Old English and Middle English*, p. 150.

8. Jones, *Strange Likeness*, "Anglo-Saxonism," "New Old English," and "Old English after 1066."
9. A preliminary contribution to the third research area is Weiskott, "Alliterative Meter and English Literary History."
10. *Letters*, ed. Colleer, pp. 156 and 163.

Appendix A

1. For lack of metrical resolution of *iu-* in 1b *iugoðe* (and probably also *da-* in 1a *dagum*), cp. *Durham* 16b.
2. MS *fesedon* probably represents a disyllabic form *fysdon* < *fysan*, as the meter would seem to require. See *DOE* Online, 'fēsan, fēsian,' and 'fȳsan, fȳsian,' 3, and Pons-Sanz, "OE *fēs(i)an*."
3. The poem was first noticed by Bredehoft, "OE *yðhengest*."
4. Neuter declension of *oðer* in MS E shows grammatical reanalysis according to natural gender (armies are things). Alternately, early loss of *-e* in *hawede*, for Type 1 with *operne* from MS C.
5. Lack of resolution of *-cweden-*.
6. The interpolation *cing* leaves the final line wanting a verse but creates no metrical problems: *Edmund cing* (Type A assuming disyllabic *cing* <OE *cyning*, lack of resolution of *cing*) | *Irensid was geclypod* (Type 3 with lack of resolution of *-clypod*)/ *for his snellscipe* (Type 5).
7. In 1a *wyrcean*, 1b *swencean*, and 8b *blendian* the scribe adds an unhistorical medial vowel to the inf. This vowel does not count in the meter.
8. Two long dips. Perhaps *mycelan* is demoted, for Type 5 with compound stress on *unrihte*.
9. I assume loss of the medial vowel of *folgian* (cp. ME *folwen*).
10. The *-e-* of *agenes* <OE *agnes* is not historically justified and does not count in the meter.
11. Orchard, "Word Made Flesh," p. 309, translates, 'Listen, I [have heard?] very many ancient tales,' as if emending to *eald[g]esæge[na]*. This is a defensible emendation in view of *Beowulf* 869 *se ðe ealfela* | *ealdgesegena*, but it renders the Harley 208 line a grammatical fragment. A more conservative solution would be to read *ealde[s]*, translating 'Lo, I tell very many old [things]' (*DOE* Online, 'fela,' A.2.a). The Northern form *sæge* is attested elsewhere, and the Harley scribble was likely written at York: Ker, *Catalogue*, item 229.
12. In *nadderes* <OE *nædre* (pl. *nædran*), *-e-*[1] is not historically justified and does not count in the meter.
13. Alternately, loss of dat. *-e* in *watere*, as in ME, and/or loss of inf. *-i-* in *wunien* (cp. ME *wonen*).
14. I assume monosyllabic *bute* (cp. ME *but*).

Appendix B

1. I count the unwritten -*es* of gen. sg. *hefdes* (cp. texts e, h, and i).
2. In 2b, *þer* is an evident error for nom. sg. *þe*. The -*e*- of weak nom. sg. *halewe* (<OE *halga*) is not historically justified and does not count in the meter. (For a different interpretation that makes 2b *halewe* gen. pl. see Pickering, "Early Middle English," p. 412.) Likewise the -*e*- of 3b *halewe* (<OE *halgena*), a form that shows assimilation of gen. pl. -*ena* to the more common –*a*.
3. The poem dates before *c.* 1200, the date of the MS, but after the second quarter of the twelfth century, when Ívarr and Hubba were first described as sons of Ragnar Lodbrok: McTurk, *Studies*, pp. 105–6.
4. James, *Descriptive Catalogue: Lambeth*, p. 153, has *al*, in evident error. Cp. *ac* in *Bracton*, ed. Woodbine, vol. 1, p. 83, where the transcription of the English proverb is attributed to Rev. Claude Jenkins, whose work underlies James, *Descriptive Catalogue: Lambeth*.
5. = *Proverbs*, ed. Arngart, ll. 4.9–10. Arngart does not provide lineation; I discount as extrametrical the speech tag "Þus cwað Alfred," numbering the next printed line 4.1.

Appendix C

1. Rigg, "Henry of Huntingdon," p. 65. Translation mine.
2. Alternately, suppression of *muros* as -*weal* would be suppressed in *bordweal* in an EME b-verse – a sort of poetic compound in Latin (*scutórum-muros*), for Type 1.
3. Long final dip. Syncope of -*quéntib*- for Type 1, or three-lift with compound stress on *frequéntibús* (cp. 9a)?
4. Synaeresis of -*iae* or, perhaps, *muta cum liquida* before -*tr*- and English-style resolution of *patri*-.
5. Synaeresis of -*io*, or, perhaps, English *Akzentverschiebung* on *cóncilio* for Type 1.

Bibliography

Primary Sources

Allen, Hope Emily, ed. *English Writings of Richard Rolle, Hermit of Hampole.* Oxford: Clarendon Press, 1931.

Andrew, Malcolm, and Ronald Waldron, eds. *The Poems of the Pearl Manuscript: "Pearl," "Cleanness," "Patience," "Sir Gawain and the Green Knight"* (5th edn.). University of Exeter Press, 2007, repr. 2010.

Arngart, O[lof], ed. *The Proverbs of Alfred: An Emended Text.* Lund: Gleerup, 1978.

Barr, Helen, ed. *The Piers Plowman Tradition.* London: J. M. Dent, 1993.

Bawcutt, Priscilla, ed. *The Poems of William Dunbar* (2 vols.). Glasgow: Association for Scottish Literary Studies, 1998.

Benson, Larry D., ed. *The Riverside Chaucer* (3rd edn.). Boston: Houghton Mifflin, 1987.

Brock, Edmund, ed. *Morte Arthure, or The Death of Arthur.* EETS OS 8, 1871.

Brook, G. L., and R. F. Leslie, eds. *Laȝamon: "Brut"* (2 vols.). EETS OS 250 and 277, 1963 and 1978.

Brown, Carleton, ed. *English Lyrics of the XIIIth Century.* Oxford: Clarendon Press, 1932.

Cigman, Gloria, ed. *Lollard Sermons.* EETS OS 294, 1989.

Coxe, H. O., ed. *Chronica, siue Flores Historiarum* (4 vols.). English Historical Society 8, 1841–44.

D'Evelyn, Charlotte, and Anna J. Mill, eds. *The South English Legendary: Corpus Christi College Cambridge MS. 145 and British Museum MS. Harley 2277, with Variants from Bodley MSS. Ashmole 43 and British Museum MS. Cotton Julius D.ix.* EETS OS 235, 236, and 244, 1956–59.

Dickins, Bruce, ed. *The Conflict of Wit and Will: Fragments of a Middle English Alliterative Poem.* Kendal: Titus Wilson, 1937.

Duggan, Hoyt N., and Thorlac Turville-Petre, eds. *The Wars of Alexander.* EETS SS 10, 1989.

Dumville, David, and Simon Keynes, gen. eds. *The Anglo-Saxon Chronicle: A Collaborative Edition* (23 vols.). Cambridge: D. S. Brewer, 1983–.

Field, P. J. C., ed. *Sir Thomas Malory: Le Morte Darthur* (2 vols.). Cambridge: D. S. Brewer, 2013.

Fulk, R. D., Robert E. Bjork, and John D. Niles, eds. *Klaeber's Beowulf* (4th edn.). University of Toronto Press, 2008.

Gollancz, Israel, ed. *St. Erkenwald.* London: Oxford University Press, 1922.

Hall, Joseph, ed. *Selections from Early Middle English, 1130–1250* (2 vols.). Oxford: Clarendon Press, 1920.

Hanna, Ralph III, ed. *The Awntyrs off Arthure at the Terne Wathelyn.* Manchester University Press, 1974.

Hathaway, E. J., P. T. Ricketts, C. A. Robson, and A. D. Wilshere, eds. *Fouke le Fitz Waryn.* Oxford: Blackwell, 1975.

Holt, Robert, ed. *The Ormulum,* with nn. and gloss. by R. M. White (2 vols.). Oxford: Clarendon Press, 1878.

Horstmann, Carl, ed. *The Early South-English Legendary; or, Lives of Saints.* EETS OS 87, 1887.

Kane, George, and E. Talbot Donaldson, eds. *Piers Plowman: The B Version.* London: Athlone, 1975.

Kennedy, Ruth, ed. *Three Alliterative Saints' Hymns: Late Middle English Stanzaic Poems.* EETS OS 321, 2003.

Krapp, George Philip, and Elliott Van Kirk Dobbie, eds. *The Anglo-Saxon Poetic Records* (6 vols.). New York: Columbia University Press, 1931–53.

Langlois, Ernest, ed. *Le Roman de la Rose par Guillaume de Lorris et Jean de Meun* (5 vols.). Paris: Didot/Champion, 1914–24.

Love, Rosalind C., ed. and tr. *Three Eleventh-Century Anglo-Latin Saints' Lives: "Vita S. Birini," "Vita et miracula S. Kenelmi" and "Vita S. Rumwoldi."* Oxford University Press, 1996.

Luard, H. R., ed. *Mattæi Parisiensis Monachi S. Albani Chronica Maiora* (7 vols.). Rolls Series 57, 1872–83.

Lumby, J. R., ed. *Polychronicon Ranulphi Higden Monachi Cestrensis* (9 vols.). Rolls Series 41, 1865–86.

Miller, Thomas, ed. and tr. *The Old English Version of Bede's Ecclesiastical History of the English People* (4 vols.). EETS OS 95, 96, 110, and 111, 1890–98.

Moffat, Douglas, ed. *The Soul's Address to the Body: The Worcester Fragments.* East Lansing, MI: Colleagues Press, 1987.

Morse, Ruth, ed. *St. Erkenwald.* Cambridge: D. S. Brewer, 1975.

Oakden, J. P., ed. *Scotish Ffeilde.* Manchester: Chetham Society, 1935.

Panton, George A., and David Donaldson, eds. *The "Gest Hystoriale" of the Destruction of Troy: An Alliterative Romance* (2 vols.). EETS OS 39 and 53, 1869 and 1874.

Rhodes, Neil, Jennifer Richards, and Joseph Marshall, eds. *King James VI and I: Selected Writings.* Aldershot: Ashgate, 2003.

Riley, H. T., ed. *Gesta Abbatum Monasterii Sancti Albani* (3 vols.). Rolls Series 28, 1867–69.

Russell, George, and George Kane, eds. *Piers Plowman: The C Version.* London: Athlone, 1997.

Rychner, Jean, ed. *Les lais de Marie de France.* Paris: Champion, 1983.

Savage, Henry L., ed. *St. Erkenwald: A Middle English Poem*. New Haven: Yale University Press, 1926.
Skeat, W. W., ed. *The Romance of William of Palerne*. EETS ES 1, 1867.
Trigg, Stephanie, ed. *Wynnere and Wastoure*. EETS OS 297, 1990.
Vaughan, R., ed. *The Chronicle Attributed to John of Wallingford*. Camden Society Third Series 90, 1958.
Weiss, Judith, ed. and tr. *Wace's Roman de Brut: A History of the British* (2nd edn.). University of Exeter Press, 2002.
Wirtjes, Hanneke, ed. *The Middle English "Physiologus"*. EETS OS 299, 1991.
Woodbine, George E., ed. *Bracton: De legibus et consuetudinibus Angliæ* (4 vols.). New Haven, CT: Yale University Press, 1915–42.
Wright, Thomas, ed. *The History of Fulk Fitz Warine, an Outlawed Baron in the Reign of King John*. London: Warton Club, 1804.

Secondary Sources

Abram, Christopher. "The Errors in *The Rhyming Poem*." *RES* 58 (2007): 1–9.
Allen, David G., and Robert A. White, eds. *The Work of Dissimilitude: Essays from the Sixth Citadel Conference on Medieval and Renaissance Literature*. Newark: University of Delaware Press, 1992.
Allen, Rosamund. "Date and Provenance of *King Horn*: Some Interim Reassessments." In *Medieval English*, ed. Kennedy, Waldron, and Wittig, pp. 99–126.
"'Nv seið mid loft-songe': A Reappraisal of Lawman's Verse Form." In *Laȝamon*, ed. Allen, Perry, and Roberts, pp. 251–82.
Allen, Rosamund, Lucy Perry, and Jane Roberts, eds. *Laȝamon: Contexts, Language, and Interpretation*. London: Centre for Late Antique and Medieval Studies, 2002.
Allen, Rosamund, Jane Roberts, and Carole Weinberg, eds. *Reading Laȝamon's "Brut": Approaches and Explorations*. Amsterdam and New York: Rodopi, 2013.
Amos, Ashley Crandell. *Linguistic Means of Determining the Dates of Old English Literary Texts*. Cambridge, MA: Medieval Academy of America, 1980.
Aurell, Martin, ed. *Culture politique des Plantagenêt (1154–1224)*. Poitiers: Centre d'Études Supérieures de Civilisation Médiévale, 2003.
Baker, Peter S., ed. *The Beowulf Reader*. New York: Garland, 1995.
Bald, Wolf-Dietrich, and Horst Weinstock, eds. *Medieval Studies Conference Aachen 1983: Language and Literature*. Frankfurt: Peter Lang, 1984.
Barney, Stephen A. "Langland's Prosody: The State of Study." In *Endless Knot*, ed. Tavormina and Yeager, pp. 65–85.
"A Revised Edition of the C Text" [Review of *Piers Plowman*, ed. Derek Pearsall]. *YLS* 23 (2009): 265–88.
Barr, Helen. *Signes and Sothe: Language in the "Piers Plowman" Tradition*. Cambridge: D. S. Brewer, 1994.

Barron, W. R. J. "Alliterative Romance and the French Tradition." In *Middle English Alliterative Poetry*, ed. Lawton, pp. 70–87.

Bately, Janet M. "Linguistic Evidence as a Guide to the Authorship of Old English Verse: A Reappraisal, with Special Reference to *Beowulf*." In *Learning and Literature*, ed. Lapidge and Gneuss, pp. 409–31.

Battles, Paul. "Toward a Theory of Old English Poetic Genres: Epic, Elegy, Wisdom Poetry, and the 'Traditional Opening.'" *SIP* 111 (2014): 1–33.

Baugh, Albert C. "The Chronology of French Loan-Words in English." *Modern Language Notes* 50 (1935): 90–93.

Bawcutt, Priscilla. *Dunbar the Makar*. Oxford: Clarendon Press, 1992.

Bennett, J. A. W. "Survival and Revivals of Alliterative Modes." *LSE* 14 (1983): 26–43.

Benskin, Michael, and M. L. Samuels, eds. *So meny people longages and tonges: Philological Essays in Scots and Mediæval English Presented to Angus McIntosh*. Edinburgh, 1981.

Benson, C. David, and Lynne Blanchfield. *The Manuscripts of "Piers Plowman": The B Version*. Woodbridge, Suffolk: Boydell & Brewer, 1997.

Benson, Larry D. "The Authorship of *St. Erkenwald*." *JEGP* 64 (1965): 393–405.

Benson, Larry D., and Siegfried Wenzel, eds. *The Wisdom of Poetry: Essays in Early English Literature in Honor of Morton Bloomfield*. Kalamazoo, MI: Medieval Institute, 1982.

Bergman, Madeleine M. "Supplement to *A Concordance to 'The Anglo-Saxon Poetic Records'.*" *Mediaevalia* 8 (1982): 9–52.

Bjork, Robert E., ed. *Cynewulf: Basic Readings*. New York and London: Garland, 1996.

Blake, Norman F. "The Dating of Old English Poetry." In *English Miscellany*, ed. Lee, pp. 14–27.

"Middle English Alliterative Revivals" [Review of Turville-Petre, *Alliterative Revival*]. *Review* 1 (1979): 205–14.

"Rhythmical Alliteration." *MP* 67 (1969): 118–24.

Blanton, Virginia, and Helene Scheck, eds. *Intertexts: Studies in Anglo-Saxon Culture Presented to Paul E. Szarmach*. Tempe: Arizona Center for Medieval and Renaissance Studies, 2008.

Bliss, Alan J. "Some Unnoticed Lines of Old English Verse." *N&Q* 18 (1971): 404.

Blurton, Heather, and Jocelyn Wogan-Browne, eds. *Rethinking the "South English Legendaries"*. Manchester University Press, 2011.

Boffey, Julia, and A. S. G. Edwards. *A New Index of Middle English Verse*. London: British Library, 2005.

Borroff, Marie. "Narrative Artistry in St. *Erkenwald* and the *Gawain*-Group: The Case for Common Authorship Reconsidered." *Studies in the Age of Chaucer* 28 (2006): 41–76.

"Sir Gawain and the Green Knight": A Stylistic and Metrical Study. New Haven: Yale University Press, 1962.

Bredehoft, Thomas A. "Ælfric and Late Old English Verse." *ASE* 33 (2004): 77–107.

Authors, Audiences, and Old English Verse. University of Toronto Press, 2009.

"The Date of Composition of *Beowulf* and the Evidence of Metrical Evolution."
In *Dating*, ed. Neidorf, pp. 97–111.

Early English Metre. University of Toronto Press, 2005.

"OE *yðhengest* and an Unrecognized Passage of Old English Verse." *N&Q* 54
(2007): 120–22.

Breeze, Andrew. "New Texts of *Index of Middle English Verse* 3513." *MÆ* 61 (1992):
284–87.

Brehe, S. K. "Rhyme and the Alliterative Standard in Laȝamon's *Brut*." *Parergon*
18 (2000): 11–25.

"'Rhythmical Alliteration': Ælfric's Prose and the Origins of Laȝamon's Metre."
In *Text and Tradition*, ed. Le Saux, pp. 65–87.

Bryan, Elizabeth J. "Laȝamon's *Brut* and the Vernacular Text: Widening the
Context." In *Reading*, ed. Allen, Roberts, and Weinberg, pp. 661–89.

"The Two Manuscripts of Laȝamon's *Brut*: Some Readers in the Margins."
In *Text and Tradition*, ed. Le Saux, pp. 89–102.

Burrow, J. A. "The Endings of Lines in 'Piers Plowman' B." *N&Q* 59 (2012):
316–20.

"*Saint Erkenwald* Line 1: 'At London in Englond.'" *N&Q* 40 (1993): 22–23.

"Winning and Wasting in *Wynnere and Wastoure* and *Piers Plowman*."
In *Makers and Users*, ed. Meale and Pearsall, pp. 1–12.

Burrow, John A., and Hoyt N. Duggan, eds. *Medieval Alliterative Poetry: Essays in
Honour of Thorlac Turville-Petre*. Dublin: Four Courts, 2010.

Busse, Wilhelm. *Altenglische Literatur und ihre Geschichte: Zur Kritik des
gegenwärtigen Deutungssystems*. Düsseldorf: Droste, 1987.

Busse, Wilhelm, and R. Holtei. "*Beowulf* and the Tenth Century." *Bulletin of the
John Rylands University Library* 63 (1981): 285–329.

Butterfield, Ardis. *The Familiar Enemy: Chaucer, Language, and Nation in the
Hundred Years' War*. Oxford University Press, 2009.

Cable, Thomas. *The English Alliterative Tradition*. Philadelphia: University of
Pennsylvania Press, 1991.

"Foreign Influence, Native Continuation, and Metrical Typology in Alliterative
Lyrics." In *Approaches*, ed. Jefferson and Putter, pp. 219–34.

"Metrical Style as Evidence for the Date of *Beowulf*." In *Dating*, ed. Chase,
pp. 77–82.

"Progress in Middle English Alliterative Metrics" [Review of Putter, Jefferson,
and Stokes, *Studies*, and Yakovlev, "Development"]. *YLS* 23 (2009): 243–64.

Cameron, Angus F. "Middle English in Old English Manuscripts." In *Chaucer
and Middle English*, ed. Rowland, pp. 218–29.

Camp, Cynthia Turner. "Spatial Memory, Historiographic Fantasy, and the
Touch of the Past in *St. Erkenwald*." *New Literary History* 44 (2013):
471–91.

Campbell, Alistair. *Old English Grammar*. Oxford: Clarendon Press, 1959.

Cannon, Christopher. *The Grounds of English Literature*. Oxford University Press,
2004.

The Making of Chaucer's English: A Study of Words. Cambridge University Press, 1998.

"The Style and Authorship of the Otho Revision of Layamon's *Brut.*" *MÆ* 62 (1993): 187–209.

Carney, Clíodhna, and Frances McCormack, eds. *Chaucer's Poetry: Words, Authority and Ethics.* Dublin: Four Courts, 2013.

Cartlidge, Neil. "The Date of *The Owl and the Nightingale.*" *MÆ* 65 (1996): 230–47.

Chambers, R. W. *On the Continuity of English Prose from Alfred to More and His School.* EETS OS 191A, 1932.

Chase, Colin, ed. *The Dating of "Beowulf".* University of Toronto Press, 1981, repr. with an afterword, 1997.

Chism, Christine. *Alliterative Revivals.* Philadelphia: University of Pennsylvania Press, 2002.

Clifton, Nicole. "The Romance Convention of the Disguised Duel and the Climax of *Piers Plowman.*" *YLS* 7 (1993): 123–28.

Cole, Kristin Lynn. "Chaucer's Metrical Landscape." In *Chaucer's Poetry*, ed. Carney and McCormack, pp. 92–106.

"*The Destruction of Troy*'s Different Rules: The Alliterative Revival and the Alliterative Tradition." *JEGP* 109 (2010): 162–76.

"Rum, Ram, Ruf, and Rym: Middle English Alliterative Meters." Diss., University of Texas at Austin, 2007.

Colleer, Claude, ed. *The Letters of Gerard Manley Hopkins to Robert Bridges* (2nd edn.). Oxford University Press, 1955.

Conner, Patrick W. "On Dating Cynewulf." In *Cynewulf*, ed. Bjork, pp. 23–53.

"The Ruthwell Monument Runic Poem in a Tenth-Century Context." *RES* 59 (2008): 25–51.

"The Structure of the Exeter Book Codex (Exeter, Cathedral Library, MS. 3501)." *Scriptorium* 40 (1986): 233–42.

Cooper, Helen. "Langland's and Chaucer's Prologues." *YLS* 1 (1987): 71–81.

Cornelius, Ian. "The Accentual Paradigm in Early English Metrics." *JEGP* 114 (2015): 459–81.

"Alliterative Revival: Retrospect and Prospect" [Review of Schiff, *Revivalist*]. *YLS* 26 (2012): 261–76.

Reconstructing Alliterative Verse: The Pursuit of a Medieval Meter. Cambridge University Press, in press.

Cronan, Dennis. "Poetic Words, Conservatism, and the Dating of Old English Poetry." *ASE* 33 (2004): 23–50.

Curzan, Anne, and Kimberly Emmons, eds. *Studies in the History of the English Language II: Unfolding Conversations.* Berlin: Mouton de Gruyter, 2004.

Dance, Richard, and Laura Wright, eds. *The Use and Development of Middle English.* Frankfurt: Peter Lang, 2013.

Davis, Bryan P. "The Prophecies of *Piers Plowman* in Cambridge University Library MS Gg.4.31." *Journal of the Early Book Society* 5 (2002): 15–36.

Doane, A. N., and Kirsten Wolf, eds. *Beatus vir: Studies in Early English and Norse Manuscripts in Memory of Phillip Pulsiano*. Tempe: Arizona Centre for Medieval and Renaissance Studies, 2006.

Dolven, Jeff. "Spenser's Metrics." In *Oxford Handbook*, ed. McCabe, pp. 385–402.

Donoghue, Daniel. "Laȝamon's Ambivalence." *Speculum* 65 (1990): 537–63.

Doyle, A. I. "The Manuscripts." In *Middle English Alliterative Poetry*, ed. Lawton, pp. 88–100.

Duffell, Martin J. *A New History of English Metre*. London: Modern Humanities Research Association, 2008.

Duggan, Hoyt N. "The End of the Line." In *Medieval Alliterative Poetry*, ed. Burrow and Duggan, pp. 67–79.

"Extended A-Verses in Middle English Alliterative Poetry." *Parergon* 18 (2000): 53–76.

"Notes toward a Theory of Langland's Meter." *YLS* 1 (1987): 41–70.

"Stress Assignment in Middle English Alliterative Poetry." *JEGP* 89 (1990): 309–29.

Edwards, A. S. G. "The Blage Manuscript and Alliterative Verse in the Sixteenth Century." In *Medieval Alliterative Poetry*, ed. Burrow and Duggan, pp. 80–84.

"Editing and Manuscript Form: Middle English Verse Written as Prose." *English Studies in Canada* 27 (2001): 15–28.

Evans, Ruth. "An Afterword on the Prologue." In *Idea*, ed. Wogan-Browne et al., pp. 371–78.

Everett, Dorothy. *Essays on Middle English Literature*, ed. Patricia Kean. Oxford: Clarendon Press, 1955.

Faulkner, Mark. "Rewriting English Literary History, 1042–1215." *LC* 9 (2012): 275–99.

Feilitzen, Olof von. *The Pre-Conquest Personal Names of the Domesday Book*. Uppsala: Almqvist & Wiksell, 1937.

Fein, Susanna. "Form and Continuity in the Alliterative Tradition: Cruciform Design and Double Birth in Two Stanzaic Poems." *MLQ* 53 (1992): 100–125.

Fein, Susanna, and Michael Johnston, eds. *Robert Thornton and his Books: Essays on the Lincoln and London Thornton Manuscripts*. York Medieval Press, 2014.

Fenton, James. *An Introduction to English Poetry*. London: Penguin, 2002.

Field, P. J. C. "Malory's Sir Phelot and the Problems of Minor Sources." *Bulletin Bibliographique de la Société Internationale Arthurienne* 54 (2002): 345–61.

Field, Rosalind. "The Anglo-Norman Background to Alliterative Romance." In *Middle English Alliterative Poetry*, ed. Lawton, pp. 54–69.

Fletcher, Alan J. "The Genesis of *The Owl and the Nightingale*: A New Hypothesis." *CR* 34 (1999): 1–17.

Frank, Roberta. "The *Beowulf* Poet's Sense of History." In *Wisdom of Poetry*, ed. Benson and Wenzel, pp. 53–65.

"A Scandal in Toronto: *The Dating of 'Beowulf'* a Quarter Century On." *Speculum* 82 (2007): 843–64.

"Sharing Words with *Beowulf*." In *Intertexts*, ed. Blanton and Scheck, pp. 3–15.

"Three 'Cups' and a Funeral in *Beowulf*." In *Latin Learning*, ed. O'Brien O'Keeffe and Orchard, vol. 2, pp. 407–20.

Frantzen, Allen J. "The Form and Function of the Preface in the Poetry and Prose of Alfred's Reign." In *Alfred the Great*, ed. Reuter, pp. 121–36.

Friedlander, Carolynn VanDyke. "Early Middle English Accentual Verse." *MP* 76 (1979): 219–30.

Fulk, R. D. "*Beowulf* and Language History." In *Dating*, ed. Neidorf, pp. 19–36.

A History of Old English Meter. Philadelphia: University of Pennsylvania Press, 1992.

"Old English Meter and Oral Tradition: Three Issues Bearing on Poetic Chronology." *JEGP* 106 (2007): 304–24.

Fulk, R. D., and Christopher M. Cain. *A History of Old English Literature* (2nd edn.). Oxford: Blackwell, 2013.

Furrow, Melissa. "Radial Categories and the Central Romance." *Florilegium* 22 (2005): 121–40.

Galloway, Andrew. "Laȝamon's Gift." *PMLA* 121 (2006): 717–34.

"Middle English Prologues." In *Readings*, ed. Treharne and Johnson, pp. 288–305.

The Penn Commentary on "Piers Plowman": Volume 1. Philadelphia: University of Pennsylvania Press, 2006.

Georgianna, Linda. "Periodization and Politics: The Case of the Missing Twelfth Century in English Literary History." *MLQ* 64 (2003): 153–68.

Gerritsen, Johan. "Leiden Revisited: Further Thoughts on the Text of the Leiden Riddle." In *Medieval Studies*, ed. Bald and Weinstock, pp. 51–59.

Glaser, Ben. [Review of Martin, *Rise and Fall*]. *MLQ* 74 (2013): 422–25.

Godden, Malcolm. "Prologues and Epilogues in the Old English *Pastoral Care*, and their Carolingian Models." *JEGP* 110 (2011): 441–73.

Godden, Malcolm, and Michael Lapidge, eds. *The Cambridge Companion to Old English Literature* (2nd edn.). Cambridge University Press, 2013.

Goffart, Walter. "The Name 'Merovingian' and the Dating of *Beowulf*." *ASE* 36 (2007): 93–101.

Gollancz, Israel. "The Middle Ages in the Lineage of English Poetry." In *Mediæval Contributions*, ed. Hearnshaw, pp. 174–89.

Grady, Frank. "*Piers Plowman, St. Erkenwald*, and the Rule of Exceptional Salvations." *YLS* 6 (1992): 63–86.

Grady, Frank, and Andrew Galloway, eds. *Answerable Style: The Idea of the Literary in Medieval England*. Columbus: Ohio State University Press, 2013.

Gretsch, Mechthild. *The Intellectual Foundations of the English Benedictine Reform*. Cambridge University Press, 1999.

Griffiths, Jane. "Editorial Glossing and Reader Resistance in a Copy of Robert Crowley's *Piers Plowman*." In *Makers and Users*, ed. Meale and Pearsall, pp. 202–13.

Grindley, Carl James. "Reading *Piers Plowman* C-Text Annotations: Notes toward the Classification of Printed and Written Marginalia in Texts from the British Isles 1300–1641." In *Medieval Professional*, ed. Kerby-Fulton and Hilmo, pp. 73–141.

Hales, John W., and Frederick J. Furnivall, eds. *Bishop Percy's Folio Manuscript* (3 vols.). London: Trübner, 1867–68.

Hamilton, A. C. "Spenser and Langland." *SIP* 55 (1958): 533–48.

Hanford, James H., and John M. Steadman, Jr. *"Death and Liffe*: An Alliterative Poem." *SIP* 15 (1918): 221–94.

Hanna, Ralph. [Review of Cannon, *Grounds*]. *Studies in the Age of Chaucer* 28 (2006): 281–84.

"Alliterative Poetry." In *Cambridge History*, ed. Wallace, pp. 488–512.

"Defining Middle English Alliterative Poetry." In *Endless Knot*, ed. Tavormina and Yeager, pp. 43–64.

Hanna, Ralph, and Thorlac Turville-Petre. "The Text of the Alliterative *Morte Arthure*: A Prolegomenon for a Future Edition." In *Robert Thornton*, ed. Fein and Johnston, pp. 131–55.

Hardison, O. B., Jr. "Crosscurrents in English Sixteenth-Century Prosody." In *Work of Dissimilitude*, ed. Allen and White, pp. 116–30.

Prosody and Purpose in the English Renaissance. Baltimore: Johns Hopkins University Press, 1989.

Hartman, Megan E. "The Limits of Conservative Composition in Old English Poetry." In *Dating*, ed. Neidorf, pp. 79–96.

Hearnshaw, F. J. C., ed. *Mediæval Contributions to Modern Civilisation: A Series of Lectures Delivered at King's College University of London*. London: Harrap & Co., 1921.

Hickey, Raymond, and Stanisław Puppel, eds. *Language History and Linguistic Modelling: A Festschrift for Jack Fisiak on his 60th Birthday* (2 vols.). Berlin: Mouton de Gruyter, 1997.

Hill, Thomas D. "*Beowulf* and Conversion History." In *Dating*, ed. Neidorf, pp. 191–201.

Hines, John. "The *Benedicite* Canticle in Old English Verse: An Early Runic Witness from Southern Lincolnshire." *Anglia* 133 (2015): 257–77.

Hoffman, Donald L. "'Renischsche Renkes' and 'Runisch Sauez.'" *N&Q* 17 (1970): 447–49.

Hogg, Richard. "Old English Palatalization." *Transactions of the Philological Society* 77 (1979): 89–113.

Horobin, Simon. "Stephan Batman and his Manuscripts of *Piers Plowman*." *RES* 62 (2011): 358–72.

Houwen, L. A. J. R., and A. A. MacDonald, eds. *Loyal Letters: Studies on Mediaeval Alliterative Poetry and Prose*. Groningen: Egbert Forsten, 1994.

Howe, Nicholas. *Migration and Mythmaking in Anglo-Saxon England*. New Haven: Yale University Press, 1989.

Writing the Map of Anglo-Saxon England: Essays in Cultural Geography. New Haven: Yale University Press, 2007.

Hunt, R. W. "The Introductions to the 'Artes' in the Twelfth Century." In *Studia Mediaevalia*, ed. students of Raymundi Josephi Martin, pp. 85–112.

James, Montague Rhodes. *A Descriptive Catalogue of the Manuscripts in the Library of Lambeth Palace: The Mediaeval Manuscripts.* Cambridge University Press, 1932.

A Descriptive Catalogue of the Manuscripts in the Library of Peterhouse. Cambridge University Press, 1899.

Jansen, Sharon L. "Politics, Protest, and a New *Piers Plowman* Fragment: The Voice of the Past in Tudor England." *RES* 40 (1989): 93–99.

Jarvis, Simon. "For a Poetics of Verse." *PMLA* 125 (2010): 931–35.

"What Is Historical Poetics?" In *Theory Aside*, ed. Potts and Stout, pp. 97–116.

Jefferson, Judith, and Ad Putter. "Alliterative Metre and Editorial Practice: The Case of Death and Liffe." In *Approaches*, ed. Jefferson and Putter, pp. 269–92.

Jefferson, Judith, and Ad Putter, eds. *Approaches to the Metres of Alliterative Verse.* Leeds: Leeds Studies in English, 2009.

Johnson, Barbara A. *Reading "Piers Plowman" and "The Pilgrim's Progress": Reception and the Protestant Reader.* Carbondale and Edwardsville: Southern Illinois University Press, 1992.

Jones, Chris. "Anglo-Saxonism in Nineteenth-Century Poetry." *LC* 7 (2010): 358–69.

"New Old English: The Place of Old English in Twentieth- and Twenty-First-Century Poetry." *LC* 7 (2010): 1009–19.

"Old English after 1066." In *Cambridge Companion*, ed. Godden and Lapidge, pp. 313–30.

Strange Likeness: The Use of Old English in Twentieth-Century Poetry. Oxford University Press, 2006.

Kane, George. *Chaucer and Langland: Historical and Textual Approaches.* Berkeley and Los Angeles: University of California Press, 1989.

Karkov, Catherine E., and Helen Damico, eds. *Aedificia Nova: Studies in Honor of Rosemary Cramp.* Kalamazoo, MI: Medieval Institute, 2008.

Keefer, Sarah Larrat, Karen Louise Jolly, and Catherine E. Karkov, eds. *Cross and Cruciform in the Anglo-Saxon World: Studies to Honor the Memory of Timothy Reuter.* Morgantown: West Virginia University Press, 2010.

Kelen, Sarah A. *Langland's Early Modern Identities.* New York: Palgrave, 2007.

Kelly, Stephen, and John J. Thompson, eds. *Imagining the Book.* Turnhout: Brepols, 2005.

Kendall, Calvin B. *The Metrical Grammar of "Beowulf".* Cambridge University Press, 1991.

Kennedy, Edward Donald, Ronald Waldron, and Joseph S. Wittig, eds. *Medieval English Studies Presented to George Kane.* Suffolk, England: St. Edmundsburg Press, 1988.

Ker, N. R. *A Catalogue of Manuscripts Containing Anglo-Saxon.* Oxford University Press, 1957.

Kerby-Fulton, Kathryn, and Maide Hilmo, eds. *The Medieval Professional Reader at Work: Evidence from Manuscripts of Chaucer, Langland, Kempe, and Gower.* Victoria: ELS, 2001.

King, John N. *English Reformation Literature: The Tudor Origins of the Protestant Tradition*. Princeton University Press, 1982.

Kleist, Aaron J., ed. *The Old English Homily: Precedent, Practice, and Appropriation*. Turnhout: Brepols, 2007.

Kooper, Erik. "Laȝamon and the Development of Early Middle English Alliterative Poetry." In *Loyal Letters*, ed. Houwen and MacDonald, pp. 113–29.

"Laȝamon's Prosody: Caligula and Otho – Metres Apart." In *Reading*, ed. Allen, Roberts, and Weinberg, pp. 419–41.

Lapidge, Michael, and Helmut Gneuss, eds. *Learning and Literature in Anglo-Saxon England: Studies Presented to Peter Clemoes on the Occasion of his Sixty-Fifth Birthday*. Cambridge University Press, 1985.

Lavezzo, Kathy, ed. *Imagining a Medieval English Nation*. Minneapolis: University of Minnesota Press, 2004.

Lawton, David. [Review of Cannon, *Grounds*]. *Speculum* 81 (2006): 820–21.

"The Diversity of Middle English Alliterative Poetry." *LSE* 20 (1989): 143–72.

"Larger Patterns of Syntax in Middle English Unrhymed Alliterative Verse." *Neophilologus* 64 (1980): 604–18.

"Literary History and Scholarly Fancy: The Date of Two Middle English Alliterative Poems." *Parergon* 18 (1977): 17–25.

"The Unity of Middle English Alliterative Poetry." *Speculum* 58 (1983): 72–94.

Lawton, David, ed. *Middle English Alliterative Poetry and its Literary Background: Seven Essays*. Cambridge: D. S. Brewer, 1982.

Lee, Brian S., ed. *An English Miscellany Presented to W. S. Mackie*. Oxford University Press, 1977.

Le Saux, Françoise. *Layamon's "Brut": The Poem and its Sources*. Cambridge: D. S. Brewer, 1989.

Le Saux, Françoise, ed. *The Text and Tradition of Layamon's "Brut"*. Cambridge: D. S. Brewer, 1994.

Levy, Bernard S., and Paul E. Szarmach, eds. *The Alliterative Tradition in the Fourteenth Century*. Kent State University Press, 1981.

Lockett, Leslie. "An Integrated Re-examination of the Dating of Oxford, Bodleian Library, Junius 11." *ASE* 31 (2002): 141–73.

Liu, Yin. "Middle English Romance as Prototype Genre." *CR* 40 (2006): 335–53.

Liuzza, Roy M. "The Old English *Christ* and *Guthlac* Texts, Manuscripts, and Critics." *RES* 41 (1990): 1–11.

"On the Dating of *Beowulf*." In *Beowulf Reader*, ed. Baker, pp. 281–302.

MacDonald, A. A. "Alliterative Poetry and its Context: The Case of William Dunbar." In *Loyal Letters*, ed. Houwen and MacDonald, pp. 261–79.

Mancho, Guzmán. "Is *Orrmulum's* Introduction an Instance of an Aristotelian Prologue?" *Neophilologus* 88 (2004): 477–92.

Martin, Meredith. *The Rise and Fall of Meter: Poetry and English National Culture, 1860–1930*. Princeton University Press, 2012.

Martin, R. J., students of, eds. *Studia Mediaevalia in Honorem admodum Reverendi Patris Raymundi Josephi Martin*. Bruges: De Tempel, 1948.

Matonis, A. T. E. "Middle English Alliterative Poetry." In *So meny people*, ed. Benskin and Samuels, pp. 341–54.

McCabe, Richard A., ed. *The Oxford Handbook of Edmund Spenser*. Oxford University Press, 2010.

McCulloh, John M. "Did Cynewulf Use a Martyrology? Reconsidering the Sources of *The Fates of the Apostles.*" *ASE* 29 (2000): 67–83.

McIntosh, Angus. "Early Middle English Alliterative Verse." In *Middle English Alliterative Poetry*, ed. Lawton, pp. 20–33.

McMullen, A. Joseph. "*Forr þeȝȝre sawle need*: The *Ormulum*, Vernacular Theology and a Tradition of Translation in Early England." *ES* 95 (2014): 256–77.

McTurk, Rory. *Studies in "Ragnars saga loðbrókar" and its Major Scandinavian Analogues*. Oxford: Society for the Study of Medieval Languages and Literature, 1991.

Meale, Carol M., and Derek Pearsall, eds. *Makers and Users of Medieval Books: Essays in Honour of A. S. G. Edwards*. Cambridge: D. S. Brewer, 2014.

Meyvaert, Paul. "An Apocalypse Panel on the Ruthwell Cross." In *Medieval and Renaissance Studies*, ed. Tirro, pp. 3–32.

"Necessity Mother of Invention: A Fresh Look at the Rune Verses on the Ruthwell Cross." *ASE* 41 (2012): 407–16.

Middleton, Anne. "The Audience and Public of 'Piers Plowman'." In *Middle English Alliterative Poetry*, ed. Lawton, pp. 101–23.

Minkova, Donka. "Velars and Palatals in Old English Alliteration." In *Historical Linguistics*, ed. Schmid, Austin, and Stein, pp. 269–91.

Minkova, Donka, and Robert P. Stockwell, eds. *Studies in the History of the English Language: A Millennial Perspective*. Berlin: Mouton de Gruyter, 2002.

Minnis, A. J. "The Influence of Academic Prologues on the Prologues and Literary Attitudes of Late Medieval English Writers." *Mediaeval Studies* 43 (1981): 342–83.

Medieval Theory of Authorship: Scholastic Literary Attitudes in the Later Middle Ages. London: Scolar Press, 1984.

Momma, Haruko. *The Composition of Old English Poetry*. Cambridge University Press, 1997.

Moorman, Charles. "The Origins of the Alliterative Revival." *Southern Quarterly* 7 (1969): 345–71.

Morgan, Chloe. "'Lite bokes' and 'grete relikes': Texts and their Transmission in the *South English Legendary*." In *Rethinking*, ed. Blurton and Wogan-Browne, pp. 149–67.

Morrison, Stephen. "Vernacular Literary Activity in Twelfth-Century England: Redressing the Balance." In *Culture politique*, ed. Aurell, pp. 253–67.

Mossé, Ferdinand. "On the Chronology of French Loan-Words in English." *ES* 25 (1943): 1–6, 33–40.

Mueller, Alex. *Translating Troy: Provincial Politics in Alliterative Romance*. Columbus: Ohio State University Press, 2013.

Myklebust, Nicholas. "Misreading English Meter: 1400–1514." Diss., University of Texas at Austin, 2012.

Neidorf, Leonard. "*VII Æthelred* and the Genesis of the *Beowulf* Manuscript." *Philological Quarterly* 89 (2010): 119–39.

"Cain, Cam, Jutes, Giants, and the Textual Criticism of *Beowulf*." *SIP* 112 (2015): 599–632.

"The Dating of *Widsið* and the Study of Germanic Antiquity." *Neophilologus* 97 (2013): 165–83.

"Lexical Evidence for the Relative Chronology of Old English Poetry." *SELIM* 20 (2013): 7–48.

"Scribal Errors of Proper Names in the *Beowulf* Manuscript." *ASE* 42 (2013): 249–69.

Neidorf, Leonard, ed. *The Dating of "Beowulf": A Reassessment.* Cambridge: D. S. Brewer, 2014.

Niles, John D. *"Beowulf": The Poem and its Tradition.* Cambridge, MA: Harvard University Press, 1983.

Niles, John D., ed. *Old English Literature in Context: Ten Essays.* Cambridge: D. S. Brewer, 1980.

Norris, Ralph. *Malory's Library: The Sources of the "Morte Darthur".* Cambridge: D. S. Brewer, 2008.

Oakden, J. P. *Alliterative Poetry in Middle English: The Dialectal and Metrical Survey* (2nd edn.). Hamden, CT: Archon, 1968.

O'Brien O'Keeffe, Katherine, and Andy Orchard, eds. *Latin Learning and English Lore: Studies in Anglo-Saxon Literature for Michael Lapidge* (2 vols.). University of Toronto Press, 2005.

Ó Carragáin, Éamonn. "Sources or Analogues? Using Liturgical Evidence to Date *The Dream of the Rood*." In *Cross and Cruciform*, ed. Keefer, Jolly, and Karkov, pp. 135–65.

"Who Then Read the Ruthwell Poem in the Eighth Century?" In *Aedificia Nova*, ed. Karkov and Damico, pp. 43–75.

O'Donnell, Daniel Paul. "Manuscript Variation in Multiple-Recension Old English Poetic Texts: The Technical Problem and Poetical Art." Diss., Yale University, 1996.

O'Donnell, Thomas. "The Old English *Durham*, the *Historia de sancto Cuthberto*, and the Unreformed in Late Anglo-Saxon Literature." *JEGP* 113 (2014): 131–55.

Okasha, Elisabeth. *Hand-list of Anglo-Saxon Non-runic Inscriptions.* Cambridge University Press, 1971.

Orchard, Andy. "Old English and Latin Poetic Traditions." In *Blackwell Companion*, ed. Saunders, pp. 65–82.

"The Word Made Flesh: Christianity and Oral Culture in Anglo-Saxon Verse." *Oral Tradition* 24 (2009): 293–318.

Orton, Peter. "Deixis and the Untransferable Text: Anglo-Saxon Colophons, Verse-Prefaces and Inscriptions." In *Imagining*, ed. Kelly and Thompson, pp. 195–207.

Osberg, Richard H. "A Hand-List of Short Alliterating Metrical Poems in Middle English." *JEGP* 80 (1981): 313–26.

Otter, Monika. "'New Werke': *St. Erkenwald*, St. Albans, and the Medieval Sense of the Past." *Journal of Medieval and Renaissance Studies* 24 (1994): 387–414.

Page, Christopher. "A Catalogue and Bibliography of English Song from its Beginnings to *c*1300." *RMA Research Chronicle* 13 (1976): 67–83.

Page, R. I. *An Introduction to English Runes.* London: Methuen, 1973.

Parkes, M. B. "The Manuscript of the Leiden Riddle." *ASE* 1 (1972): 207–17.

Parks, Ward. "The Traditional Narrator and the 'I Heard' Formulas in Old English Poetry." *ASE* 16 (1987): 45–66.

Pearsall, Derek. "The Alliterative Revival: Origins and Social Backgrounds." In *Middle English Alliterative Poetry*, ed. Lawton, pp. 34–53.

Old English and Middle English Poetry. London: Routledge & Kegan Paul, 1977.

"The Origins of the Alliterative Revival." In *Alliterative Tradition*, ed. Levy and Szarmach, pp. 1–24.

Pearsall, Derek, ed. *Piers Plowman: A New Annotated Edition of the C-Text.* University of Exeter Press, 2008.

Perkins, Nicholas, ed. *Medieval Romance and Material Culture.* Cambridge: D. S. Brewer, 2015.

Perry, Lucy. "Origins and Originality: Reading Lawman's *Brut* and the Rejection of British Library MS Cotton Otho C.xiii." *Arthuriana* 10 (2000): 66–84.

Pickering, Oliver S. "An Early Middle English Verse Inscription from Shrewsbury." *Anglia* 106 (1988): 411–14.

Pollock, Sheldon. *The Language of the Gods in the World of Men: Sanskrit, Culture, and Power in Premodern India.* Berkeley: University of California Press, 2006.

Pons-Sanz, S. M. "OE *fēs(i)an* / ME *fēsen* Revisited." *Neophilologus* 90 (2006): 119–34.

Potts, Jason, and Daniel Stout, eds. *Theory Aside.* Durham, NC: Duke University Press, 2014.

Prins, Yopie. "Historical Poetics, Dysprosody, and *The Science of English Verse*." *PMLA* 123 (2008): 229–34.

Pulsiano, Phillip. "The Prefatory Matter of London, British Library, Cotton Vitellius E. xviii." In *Anglo-Saxon Manuscripts*, ed. Pulsiano and Treharne, pp. 85–116.

Pulsiano, Phillip, and Elaine Treharne, eds. *Anglo-Saxon Manuscripts and their Heritage.* Brookfield: Ashgate, 1998.

Putter, Ad. "Adventures in the Bob-and-Wheel Tradition: Narratives and Manuscripts." In *Medieval Romance*, ed. Perkins, pp. 147–63.

Putter, Ad, Judith Jefferson, and Myra Stokes. *Studies in the Metre of Alliterative Verse.* Oxford: Society for the Study of Medieval Languages and Literature, 2007.

Reaney, P. H. "Notes on the Survival of Old English Personal Names in Middle English." *Studier i Modern Språkvetenskap* 18 (1953): 84–112.

Reaney, P. H., and R. M. Wilson. *A Dictionary of English Surnames* (3rd edn.). London: Routledge, 1991.

Reuter, Timothy, ed. *Alfred the Great: Papers from the Eleventh-Century Centenary Conferences.* Aldershot: Ashgate, 2003.

Rhodes, Jim. *Poetry Does Theology: Chaucer, Grosseteste, and the "Pearl"-Poet.* University of Notre Dame Press, 2001.

Richards, Mary P. "Old Wine in a New Bottle: Recycled Instructional Materials in *Seasons for Fasting.*" In *Old English Homily,* ed. Kleist, pp. 345–64.

Rigg, A. G. "Henry of Huntingdon's Metrical Experiments." *Journal of Medieval Latin* 1 (1991): 60–72.

Robinson, Fred C. "Old English Literature in its Most Immediate Context." In *Old English Literature,* ed. Niles, pp. 11–29.

Rosier, James L. "'Instructions for Christians': A Poem in Old English." *Anglia* 82 (1964): 4–22.

Rowland, Beryl, ed. *Chaucer and Middle English Studies in Honour of Rossell Hope Robbins.* London: Allen & Unwin, 1974.

Russom, Geoffrey. "Constraints on Resolution in *Beowulf.*" In *Prosody and Poetics,* ed. Toswell, pp. 147–63.

"Dating Criteria for Old English Poems." In *Studies,* ed. Minkova and Stockwell, pp. 245–66.

"The Evolution of Middle English Alliterative Meter." In *Studies,* ed. Curzan and Emmons, pp. 279–304.

"Some Unnoticed Constraints on the A-Verse in *Sir Gawain and the Green Knight.*" In *Approaches,* ed. Jefferson and Putter, pp. 41–57.

Salter, Elizabeth. *English and International: Studies in the Literature, Art, and Patronage of Medieval England.* Cambridge University Press, 1988.

Sandison, Helen Estabrook. *The "Chanson D'Aventure" in Middle English.* Bryn Mawr College, 1913.

Sauer, Hans. "Knowledge of Old English in the Middle English Period?" In *Language History,* ed. Hickey and Puppel, vol. 1, pp. 791–814.

Saunders, Corinne, ed. *A Blackwell Companion to Medieval Poetry.* Oxford: Blackwell, 2010.

Scase, Wendy. "*Dauy Dycars Dreame* and Robert Crowley's Prints of *Piers Plowman.* " *YLS* 21 (2007): 171–98.

"Latin Composition Lessons, *Piers Plowman,* and the *Piers Plowman* Tradition." In *Answerable Style,* ed. Grady and Galloway, pp. 34–53.

Scattergood, John. *The Lost Tradition: Essays on Middle English Alliterative Poetry.* Dublin: Four Courts, 2000.

Schiff, Randy P. *Revivalist Fantasy: Alliterative Verse and Nationalist Literary History.* Columbus: Ohio State University Press, 2011.

Schmid, Monka, Jennifer Austin, and Dieter Stein, eds. *Historical Linguistics 1997.* Amsterdam: Johns Benjamin, 1998.

Schröer, Arnold. "The Grave." *Anglia* 5 (1882): 289–90.

Schustereder, Stefan. "Coming to Terms with a Pagan Past: The Story of *St Erkenwald.*" *Studia Anglica Posnaniensia* 48 (2013): 71–92.

Shippey, Tom. "The Merov(ich)ingian Again: *damnatio memoriae* and the *usus scholarum.*" In *Latin Learning*, ed. O'Brien O'Keeffe and Orchard, vol. 1, pp. 389–406.

"Names in *Beowulf* and Anglo-Saxon England." In *Dating*, ed. Neidorf, pp. 58–78.

Sievers, Eduard. *Altgermanische Metrik*. Halle: Niemeyer, 1893.

Simpson, James. [Review of Scattergood, *Lost Tradition*]. *RES* 53 (2002): 109–11.

Singh, Catherine. "The Alliterative Ancestry of Dunbar's 'The Tretis of the Tua Mariit Wemen and the Wedo.'" *LSE* 7 (1974): 22–54.

Sisam, Kenneth. *Studies in the History of Old English Literature*. Oxford: Clarendon Press, 1953.

Sisk, Jennifer L. "The Uneasy Orthodoxy of St. Erkenwald. " *ELH* 74 (2007): 89–115.

Skeat, W. W. "An Essay on Alliterative Poetry." In *Bishop Percy's Folio*, ed. Hales and Furnivall, vol. 3, pp. xi–xxxix.

Stanley, Eric Gerald. *A Collection of Papers with Emphasis on Old English*. Toronto: Pontifical Institute of Mediaeval Studies, 1987.

"The Date of Laʒamon's *Brut*. " *N&Q* 213 (1968): 85–8.

"Laʒamon's Antiquarian Sentiments." *MÆ* 38 (1969): 23–37.

"Laʒamon's Un-Anglo-Saxon Syntax." In *Text and Tradition*, ed. Le Saux, pp. 47–56.

"The Scansion of Laʒamon's *Brut*: A Historical Sketch." *N&Q* 56 (2009): 175–86.

Stinson, Timothy. "The Rise of English Printing and Decline of Alliterative Verse." *YLS* 22 (2008): 165–97.

Suzuki, Seiichi. *The Metrical Organization of "Beowulf": Prototype and Isomorphism*. Berlin: Mouton de Gruyter, 1996.

Swan, Mary, and Elaine Treharne, eds. *Rewriting Old English in the Twelfth Century*. Cambridge University Press, 2000.

Tavormina, M. Teresa, and R. F. Yeager, eds. *The Endless Knot: Essays on Old and Middle English in Honor of Marie Borroff*. Cambridge: D. S. Brewer, 1995.

Thornbury, Emily V. *Becoming a Poet in Anglo-Saxon England*. Cambridge University Press, 2014.

Tiller, Kenneth. "Anglo-Norman Historiography and Henry of Huntingdon's Translation of *The Battle of Brunanburh*. " *SIP* 109 (2012): 173–91.

"Romancing History: Masculine Identity and Historical Authority in Laʒamon's Prologue (Cotton MS Caligula A. ix ll. 1–35)." In *Laʒamon*, ed. Allen, Perry, and Roberts, pp. 371–83.

Tirro, Frank, ed. *Medieval and Renaissance Studies 9: Proceedings of the Southeastern Institute of Medieval and Renaissance Studies, Summer, 1978*. Durham, NC: Duke University Press, 1982.

Tolkien, J. R. R. "*Beowulf*: The Monsters and the Critics." *Proceedings of the British Academy* 22 (1936): 245–95.

Toswell, M. J., ed. *Prosody and Poetics in the Early Middle Ages: Essays in Honour of C. B. Hieatt*. University of Toronto Press, 1995.

Treharne, Elaine. "Categorization, Periodization: The Silence of (the) English in the Twelfth Century." *New Medieval Literatures* 8 (2006): 247–73.

Living through Conquest: The Politics of Early English, 1020–1220. Oxford University Press, 2012.

"Reading from the Margins: The Uses of Old English Homiletic Manuscripts in the Post-Conquest Period." In *Beatus vir*, ed. Doane and Wolf, pp. 329–58.

Treharne, Elaine, and David Johnson, eds. *Readings in Medieval Texts: Interpreting Old and Middle English Literature.* Oxford University Press, 2005.

Trilling, Renée R. *The Aesthetics of Nostalgia: Historical Representation in Old English Verse.* University of Toronto Press, 2009.

Turville-Petre, Thorlac. "Afterword: The Brutus Prologue to *Sir Gawain and the Green Knight*." In *Imagining*, ed. Lavezzo, pp. 340–46.

The Alliterative Revival. Cambridge: D. S. Brewer, 1977.

"The Prologue of *Wynnere and Wastoure*." *LSE* 18 (1987): 19–29.

"'Summer Sunday', 'De Tribus Regibus Mortuis', and 'The Awntyrs off Arthure': Three Poems in the Thirteen-Line Stanza." *RES* 25 (1974): 1–14.

"*Wynnere and Wastoure*: When and Where?" In *Loyal Letters*, ed. Houwen and MacDonald, pp. 155–66.

Tyler, Elizabeth M. *Old English Poetics: The Aesthetics of the Familiar in Anglo-Saxon England.* York Medieval Press, 2006.

Waldron, Ronald. "Trevisa's Original Prefaces on Translation: A Critical Edition." In *Medieval English*, ed. Kennedy, Waldron, and Wittig, pp. 285–99.

Wallace, David, ed. *The Cambridge History of Medieval English Literature.* Cambridge University Press, 1999.

Warner, Lawrence. *The Myth of "Piers Plowman": Constructing a Medieval Literary Archive.* Cambridge University Press, 2014.

Warren, Michelle R. *History on the Edge: Excalibur and the Borders of Britain, 1100–1300.* Minneapolis: University of Minnesota Press, 2000.

Watson, Jonathan. "The Minim-istic Imagination: Scribal Invention and the Word in the Early English Alliterative Tradition." *Oral Tradition* 17 (2002): 290–309.

Watson, Nicholas. "The Politics of Middle English Writing." In *Idea*, ed. Wogan-Browne et al., pp. 331–52.

Weiskott, Eric. "Alliterative Meter after 1450: *The Vision of William Banastre*." In *Early English Poetic Culture and Metre: The Influence of G. R. Russom*, ed. Lindy Brady and M. J. Toswell. Kalamazoo, MI: Medieval Institute, in press.

"Alliterative Meter and English Literary History, 1700–2000." *ELH*, in press.

"Before Prosody: Early English Poetics in Practice and Theory." *MLQ*, in press.

"*The Ireland Prophecy*: Text and Metrical Context." *SIP*, in press.

"The Meter of *Widsith* and the Distant Past." *Neophilologus* 99 (2015): 143–50.

"Phantom Syllables in the English Alliterative Tradition." *MP* 110 (2013): 441–58.

"*Piers Plowman* and the Durable Alliterative Tradition." *YLS*, in press.

"Prophetic *Piers Plowman*: New Sixteenth-Century Excerpts." *RES* 67 (2016): 21–41.

"A Semantic Replacement for Kaluza's Law in *Beowulf.*" *ES* 93 (2012): 891–96.

"Three *Beowulf* Cruces: *healgamen, fremu, Sigemunde.*" *N&Q* 58 (2011): 3–7.

"Three-Position Verses in *Beowulf.*" *N&Q* 60 (2013): 483–85.

Weldon, James F. G. "The Structure of Dream Visions in *Piers Plowman*." *Mediaeval Studies* 49 (1987): 254–81.

Whitelock, D[orothy]. "Anglo-Saxon Poetry and the Historian." *Transactions of the Royal Historical Society* 31 (1949): 75–94.

The Audience of "Beowulf". Oxford: Clarendon Press, 1951.

Wilson, R. M. *The Lost Literature of Medieval England*. London: Methuen, 1952, repr. 1970.

Wogan-Browne, Jocelyn. "Locating Saints' Lives and their Communities." In *Rethinking*, ed. Blurton and Wogan-Browne, pp. 251–70.

Wogan-Browne, Jocelyn, Nicholas Watson, Andrew Taylor, and Ruth Evans, eds. *The Idea of the Vernacular: An Anthology of Middle English Literary Theory, 1280–1520*. University Park: Pennsylvania State University Press, 1999.

Wormald, Patrick. *The Times of Bede: Studies in Early English Christian Society and its Historian*, ed. Stephen Baxter. Oxford: Blackwell, 2006.

Wrenn, C. L. "On the Continuity of English Poetry." *Anglia* 76 (1958): 41–59.

Wymer, Kathryn. "A Poetic Fragment on the Soul's Address to the Body in the *Trinity Homilies.*" *N&Q* 55 (2008): 399–400.

Yakovlev, Nicolay. "The Development of Alliterative Metre from Old to Middle English." Diss., University of Oxford, 2008.

"Metre and Punctuation in the Caligula Manuscript of Laȝamon's *Brut*." In *Use and Development*, ed. Dance and Wright, pp. 261–79.

Yeager, Stephen. *From Lawmen to Plowmen: Anglo-Saxon Legal Traditions and the School of Langland*. University of Toronto Press, 2014.

Zeeman, Nicolette. "Tales of Piers and Perceval: *Piers Plowman* and the Grail Romances." *YLS* 22 (2008): 199–236.

Index

CAMBRIDGE STUDIES IN MEDIEVAL LITERATURE

Made in the USA
Coppell, TX
24 May 2020

26371787R00144